Russian
Economic History

The Nineteenth Century

Arcadius Kahan

Edited by

Roger Weiss

The University of Chicago Press
Chicago and London

ARCADIUS KAHAN taught at the University of
Chicago from 1958 until his death in 1982. His
many publications include *The Plow, the
Hammer, and the Knout,* published by the
University of Chicago Press.

ROGER W. WEISS is professor of social sciences
at the University of Chicago.

The University of Chicago Press, Chicago 60637
The University of Chicago Press, Ltd., London

© 1989 by The University of Chicago
All rights reserved. Published 1989
Printed in the United States of America
98 97 96 95 94 93 92 91 90 89 5 4 3 2 1

Library of Congress Cataloging-in-Publication Data

Kahan, Arcadius
  Russian economic history : the nineteenth century / Arcadius Kahan;
edited by Roger Weiss

     p. cm.
  Includes bibliographies and index.
  ISBN: 0-226-42242-9   0-226-42243-7 (pbk)
  1. Soviet Union—Economic conditions—1861–1917. 2. Soviet Union—
Social conditions—1801–1917. 3. Soviet Union—Economic
conditions—to 1861. 4. Soviet Union—Social conditions—to 1801.
I. Weiss, Roger, 1930–   . II. Title.
HC334.5.K34 1989   88-26093
330.947—dc19   CIP

Contents

Preface

In this third collection of Arcadius Kahan's social and economic historical writings, as in *The Plow, the Hammer, and the Knout* (1985) and *Essays in Jewish Social and Economic History* (1986), the editor's work has been encouraged and greatly simplified by the dedicated efforts of Pearl Kahan in collecting and organizing her late husband's papers. Acknowledgment and thanks are due the publishers of the essays listed below who have given permission for their inclusion in this volume.

1. The Russian Economy, 1860–1913, *Ost- und Südosteuropa, 1850–1914*, Stuttgart: Verlagsgemeinshaft Ernst Klett-J. G. Cotta, 1980.
2. Government Policies and the Industrialization of Russia, *Journal of Economic History*, December 1967.
3. The Tsar "Hunger" in the Land of the Tsars, Social Science History Association, University of Pennsylvania, 1976, unpublished.

    Natural Calamities and Their Effect on the Food Supply in Russia, *Jahrbuch für Geschichte Osteuropas*, Neue Folge, Band 16, Wiesbaden: Otto Harrassowitz, 1968.
4. Notes on Serfdom in Western and Eastern Europe, *Journal of Economic History*, March 1973.
5. Forms of Social Protest by the Agrarian Population in Russia, unpublished.
6. Social Structure, Public Policy, and the Development of Education, in C. Arnold Anderson and Mary Jean Bowman, eds, *Education and Economic Development*, Chicago: Aldine Publishing Company, 1965.
7. The "Hereditary Workers" Hypothesis and the Development of a Factory Labor Force in Eighteenth- and Nineteenth-Century Russia, in Anderson and Bowman, eds., *Education and Economic Development*.
8. Determinants of the Incidence of Literacy in Rural Nineteenth Century

Russia, in Anderson and Bowman, eds., *Education and Economic Development*.

9. Russian Scholars and Statesmen on Education as an Investment, in Anderson and Bowman, eds., *Education and Economic Development*.
10. Data for the Study of Russian History, in Val R. Lorwin and Jacob M. Price, eds., *The Dimensions of the Past: Materials, Problems, and Opportunities for Quantitative Work in History,* New Haven: Yale University Press, 1972.

The texts that Kahan left, both published and unpublished, have received editorial revisions, partly to remove redundancies among the parts of the collection, partly to make the transliterations and citations more consistent, and partly to "improve" the author's style. I have borne in mind the dangers of changing the characteristic voice of the author and the almost arbitrary standard of what is good academic prose, and usually have erred on the side of my own taste. Still, here and there Kahan's labors with English exposition will be still unmistakable and welcomed by his colleagues. Richard Hellie's generous efforts to provide a consistent and acceptable form of transliteration are not to be judged by the lapses that remain; he is to be absolved from all responsibility, particularly for my rendering of the Russian citations in Chapter 10 and in the tables. I have not checked the data against the sources, and some transcription errors may be hidden that would have been corrected if the author and not I had brought the material to publication.

Introduction

While his colleagues knew him primarily as a leading scholar of the Soviet period, particularly for his work on soviet agriculture, Arcadius Kahan for many years published articles and taught courses on the Russian economy in the eighteenth and nineteenth centuries. At the same time he was publishing his research on the economic and social history of Jews in eastern Europe in the nineteenth and early twentieth centuries. The University of Chicago Press has now published three volumes of this important work.

The comprehensive and definitive volume on the eighteenth century, *The Plow, the Hammer, and the Knout,* was completed before his death and edited for publication by Kahan's distinguished student and colleague, Richard Hellie. Its scope and interpretations had been mapped out in a series of articles published over many years before the book was undertaken. Following the same plan of research and publication, had he lived he would undoubtedly have proceeded to rework the published material on the nineteenth century into a book of the same scope and comprehensiveness. Although there is no indication of when he would have written the book from these materials and from the massive collection of statistics he gathered, I have no doubt that a volume would have been produced with the same exhaustive care as the eighteenth century volume. And just as he referred to the chapters of *The Plow, the Hammer, and the Knout* as "provisional essays," and never stopped adding new tables to the completed chapters, the volume on the nineteenth century would have been long in completion, perhaps appearing only after his friends and the publisher would forcibly pull it from him, not unlike Peter the Great's dentistry performed on unwitting friends.

The chapters collected here are therefore a provisional statement of Kahan's work on the nineteenth century, but, like the eighteenth-century work, were put to the professional trial of colleagues at conferences and in professional journals during Kahan's lifetime.

The editor's task was to order them, eliminate some material that was repetitious, and smooth out the English. There is a risk in this work of arbitrarily changing the author's voice, and the editor has tried to restrict his intrusions to places where clarity was gained. But the reader will miss the true modesty of the author's frequent use of "perhaps" and the "on the one hand . . . and on the other hand" that I have often removed from the texts; the reader may also miss some of Kahan's frequent complaints about the absence or poor quality of the data.

As in all his work, Kahan's narrative has a strong point of view; he is participating in a debate with other writers, often unnamed. We see him discretely differ with Gerschenkron and Von Laue, to name only two, and he tries to balance the view that saw the state, or its leading statesmen, as the guiding force, the tutor of the development of the economy. Kahan's reading of the history often saw the state leading in the wrong direction or standing in the way of development. Industrialization and agricultural development largely grew out of the forces of the market and the initiatives of entrepreneurs whose success was opposed and delayed by restrictions of the often clumsy "tutor." It is perhaps a paradox that Kahan, raised and active in his early years as a socialist, had come to see the forces of the market so powerfully responding to opportunities of investment, of labor mobility, of returns to education, and of innovation of new techniques, when given a free hand by the government. It would be too simple to attribute this to his work in the milieu of the Chicago School. But he told us in *The Plow, the Hammer, and the Knout,* "I have a bias in favor of recognizing market forces in the Russian economy and reject the myth that the Russian state successfully put the entire economy into a Procrustean bed of state controls and that things happened only because of exclusive state initiative" (p. 274).

He catalogued the opposition of the bureaucratic autocracy to fundamental change and its steady work to perpetuate the social and economic primacy of the landed aristocracy. The settlement of the emancipation of the serfs in 1861 failed to free the peasantry to modernize agriculture by consolidating plots and enlarging the scale of production. Urban settlement was discouraged out of fear of political instability and at the cost of retarding the formation of an industrial labor force. Railroads were heavily subsidized by the government, but often to serve the exigencies of the military rather than the growth of the economy. The slow growth of commercial and investment banking, the strong anti-inflationary bias, and the excessive investment of resources in the gold standard reflect policies that delayed or retarded growth. The fiscal system placed too heavy a burden on the peasantry and repressed consumer demand for the products of industry. In pointing to the consequences of government policy in these areas, Kahan effectively answered those who saw the government as tutor to a lazy and incompetent body of students.

But one might ask how we are to judge the alternatives. Could the limited savings of a poor, uneducated agrarian population have been more effectively marshalled for better growth? If we are rightly skeptical of the steady and evenhanded judgment of the tsarist bureaucrats, what were the possibilities of better policy making? If we economists were making policy, how much more effective would a grain reserve have been under the conditions of the time? The tsar "hunger" was always shadowed by the fear of rebellion. If we see that the conservative bureaucrats acted under the constraint of safeguarding the existing social system, is it always obvious what else they might have done viewing the risks as they saw them? And if economic goals were sacrificed to the political priorities of the ruling class, ought we not to see the risks as the bureaucrats did, ex ante?

Although we may be aware that "for over a century the Russian political system bred pygmies not giants" to staff its bureaucracy, whose efforts perhaps well served the "perpetuation of an archaic political regime," we may still seek a better administration and still look to the government for leadership in modernization. Kahan was as free from illusions about the enlightenment of the administration as anyone could be. But is there not an occasional and implicit finding that government ought to have provided this or that—an educational system that responded sooner to the new needs for engineering and industrial skills; a better way of dealing with famines. The forces of the private sector, of individual initiatives, in the long run carried the economy to its goals. But the government was inextricably involved—as monopsony buyer of military goods, as monopolist in the output of alcohol and other products vital to its fiscal interests, and as provider of the "infra structure"—the roads, navigable waterways, and railroads. The primacy of the government's role in the economy was determined by the fiscal importance of the state as buyer and seller.

Kahan struggled to detach himself from the received wisdom about modernization with its heroic image of statecraft in much of the histories of tsarist and soviet policy. But even the classical follower of Adam Smith, Jeremy Bentham, believed that what was *sponte acta* in Britain, with its rich provision of private capital and entrepreneurial ability, was *agenda* for the government of Peter the Great in an economy that lacked all these resources. Is there a clear judgment of the proper limits of the role of government in the economy, whether its administration was in the hands of pygmies or giants?

With the publication of this third volume of Kahan's work, we can see the broad scope of his scholarly vision; his learning comprehended three centuries of Russian economic and political institutions. His deep sympathies and his excitement in his subject are manifest in the eloquent and moving first pages of this volume and in the chapters on agriculture and the political system in the eighteenth-century volume, not to speak of his analysis of the position of the Jewish population in the last hundred years. Kahan's work combined a profound sympathy for human values, perhaps filtered through his personal experience with the autocracy, with a scholar's perspective of the long span of history and his careful scientific canon of work with statistical sources.

The editor, having completed his work of gathering the chapters together, and with an exaggerated conceit of knowing the author's intentions perfectly, has no doubt that this volume would have been lovingly dedicated to the four Kahan grandchildren—Audrey, Adam, Noah, and Joshua. They who carry his noble inheritance will continue his good works for the generations to come.

ONE

The Russian Economy, 1860–1913

Introduction

The social and political history of Russia during the period 1861–1913 is one of the more dramatic chapters in the history of Europe. Emancipation of the serfs, the Balkan War, the Russo-Japanese War, the revolution of 1905–6, social unrest, terror, pogroms, assassinations, and strikes of factory workers and students are some of the birth pangs of a new social order, of the decline of the age-old rule of the landed aristocracy and the absolutist bureaucratic state. The turbulent social and political history of Russia found its expression in the writings of the giants of Russian literature such as Tolstoy, Dostoevsky, Chekhov, and others who made the period one of the great chapters in European intellectual history, introducing the socio-ideological concept of an intelligentsia.

The economic history of Russia had its dramatic moments. Whether the image of oxen and horse caravans dragging modern railroad equipment over the dusty, roadless expanse of the southern steppes, or the construction by bearded peasants of a railroad through the forests and swamps of Siberia, or the oil pipeline through the precipices of the Caucasus mountains is less vivid than the images of political strife is not the issue. One could argue that a modern piece of agricultural machinery or a sewing machine in a peasant hut might have had a more revolutionizing effect upon the minds and behavior of the masses of the Russians than all the pamphlets, broadsides, and leaflets calling for the overthrow of the government; or that the opening up of new lands for peasant colonization in Asiatic Russia created a migration that affected the lives of millions more than all the writings of the brilliant authors of prose and poetry.

However, it is not the spectacular and dramatic in economic activity to which the following essay addresses itself. It is an attempt to perceive the economic activities of individuals, groups, and institutions as a phase in a historical process. In trying to describe the process—the essence of which was the growth of the market economy, an industrial sector, and a more efficient use of the physical and human resources—the acts of individuals, whether statesmen, entrepreneurs, or investors, are less important than the piecemeal accretion of capital and skills and the process of migration of the factors of production. It is customary in the field of Russian economic history to present the Russian government as the "big brother" or the "great tutor" of Russian society along the road of economic development toward the goal of modernization of Russian life. To this writer, who does not believe in the infallibility of "big brothers" or "great tutors," the problem of how Russian society, in the economic sphere at least, was trying to emancipate itself from the "great tutor" at a time when the interests of the "tutor" did not necessarily coincide with the interests of the majority of its "pupils" is much more interesting.

I am thoroughly aware that the attempt to "evolutionize" a period which was marked by turbulence and discontinuities robs the narrative of the dramatic and does not provide clear-cut answers to some complicated questions. However, it appears to this writer at least, that this method of analysis and presentation provides a closer approximation to the economic and social reality of the period—a period of search, of forward movement, interrupted by setbacks; by no means a straight line conceived in the mind of a master planner, but a vector of movements and thrusts in different directions operating under constraints of past history, cultural attitudes, scarcity of resources, and conflicting interests. That the analysis concentrates on the examination of the motives for rational actions of the performers in the economic and social arena is not to deny the existence of the irrational in social behavior: it is simply the admission that the tools for dealing with such situations are not to be found in the economic historian's toolbox.

Population

One of the most remarkable features of Russia's development during its period of modernity, which we assume to have started with the abolition of serfdom in 1861, was population growth. The population of the Russian Empire (excluding the Grand Duchy of Finland and the emirates of Bukhara and Khiva) increased from 73.6 million in January 1861 to 165.1 million in January 1914.[1] A part of this increase came from territorial expansion of the Empire, particularly in Central Asia, where Russia absorbed about 3.25 million of the indigenous population by 1880, but most of the population growth came from the population increase in European Russia.

The net increase of population can be traced to a number of factors, among which the diminished impact of wars, famines, and epidemics was very significant.[2] The mechanism of the increase in the size of population during this period was the decline of the mortality rate (especially infant mortality), followed by a substantial lag in the decline of the birth rate.

The data in table 1.1 indicate the relationship between the mortality and birth rates for selected periods.

The fact that in percentage terms the highest rates of population growth were achieved by the regions on the fringes of the Empire—the southern districts of European Russia, Siberia, and the kingdom of Poland—links the process of population growth to the process of expansion of the crop-land areas, to the industrial development in particular regions, and to the interregional population migration. Agricultural land in Siberia and the southeast and industrial employment in the southern districts and in Poland were the main attractions for the settlement of migrants. Obviously, when one focuses on the process of internal migration, particularly of the rural population, one is conscious of the fact that this constitutes a part of the process of spatial mobility of the population. Although it is difficult to link the rate of population growth rigorously to the degree of population mobility, the latter is important not only for its purely demographic aspect but also for both economic and cultural aspects of the population problem.

The data in table 1.2 indicate, for the second half of the nineteenth century, some aspects of the changes in population mobility, be it for seasonal migration or as an indicator of future rural-urban migration.

When considering migration, a distinction ought to be drawn between seasonal migration of laborers from areas of excessive labor supply to areas of seasonal labor deficits and the migration of whole families to areas of permanent settlement. The latter was represented by migration from the core and the adjacent areas of the central agricultural region and from some areas of the Ukraine to the Asiatic part of the empire (Siberia and

Table 1.1 Deaths and Births per 1,000 Population in European Russia, 1861–1913

Years	Deaths	Births	Excess of Births over Deaths
1861–70	38.7	51.9	13.2
1871–80	35.5	49.1	13.6
1881–90	34.2	48.7	14.5
1891–1900	32.8	48.7	15.9
1901–5	31.0	47.7	16.7
1906–10	29.2	45.3	16.1
1911–13	27.7	44.1	16.9

Table 1.2   Sale of Tickets and Passports of Different Time-Duration, 1861–1900
(in 1,000s)

Years	1–3 Months	6 Months	Yearly	Over 1 Year	Total
1861–70	1,869.6	5,661.1	5,332.9	59.2	12,913
1871–80	17,258.5	10,169.8	9,414.0	87.1	36,929
1881–90	24,366.7	13,118.9	11,889.4	91.2	49,466
1891–1900	20,539.8	11,101.6	37,880.1	1,844.7	71,366

Kazakhstan). The migration to the southeastern provinces of European Russia and to Asiatic Russia developed on a larger scale during the 1880s and 1890s, and diminished during 1901–5. The migration to Asiatic Russia was given a new stimulus after 1906 (as a part of attempts to deal with the peasant problem), reaching its peak of a net migration of 626,895 persons in 1908 and 537,033 in 1909, and declining afterwards. Nevertheless, a net migration of over 4 million people to Asiatic Russia alone and an internal migration toward Southeastern European Russia, where land was still relatively abundant, were helpful in maintaining a high birth rate in the areas of new settlement as well as in somewhat relieving the pressure on land in the areas of old settlement. The location of much of Russian industry outside the large cities, in areas within reach by the rural population, was also a significant factor, since it contributed less to the breaking up of existing families and counteracted the impact of urban culture, one of the characteristics of which was the sharp decline of the birth rate.

Another aspect of the internal migration related to population growth was the migration to urban areas. Although the data on the urban population suffer from a number of shortcomings, it is nevertheless possible to get a definite impression of the pattern of population growth in the cities. Since migration from rural to urban areas played the decisive role in the population growth of urban areas, the data on population growth can be used as a proxy for migration data.

In the period from 1860 to the 1890s, the population of cities of various sizes was increasing, especially of cities that were centers of communication, trade, and industry, as distinguished from those that were primarily administrative centers.[3]

After the industrial boom of the 1890s, the growth of urban population took place primarily in the large cities such as the capitals, St. Petersburg and Moscow, followed by the large industrial centers such as Kiev, Ekaterinoslav, Riga, Warsaw, and Baku, and in major commercial centers such as Odessa and Tiflis.

The process of migration to large urban centers from rural areas was very often made either directly to the large cities or in two stages, the first to smaller cities. The process of skill acquisition and acculturation to the urban environment played an important role in the more complex migration pattern that developed during and after the 1890s.

Thus, while the urban population in Russia increased from 5.68 million in 1856 and 8.46 million in 1867 to 16.86 million as registered by the population census in 1897, it reached 26.30 million by 1914. But even these periods of relatively rapid urbanization left Russia with only 16 per cent of its total population in cities. Although this percentage seems small by comparison with other countries, the degree of concentration of the urban population in relatively free locations had a particular effect upon the subsequent economic and political development of Russia.

Agriculture

One of the most direct effects of population growth on the agricultural sector of the economy was the expansion of the planted area. In order to follow this process of expansion and to understand its significance both as a response to population increase as well as one of the causes of the growth of agricultural production in Russia, one must first turn to the conditions of agricultural production itself and to the impact that the emancipation of the serfs in Russia had on the agrarian sector of the economy.

Only privately owned serfs were emancipated in 1861; the state-owned serfs had been emancipated in a series of reforms starting in the 1840s. While land tenure did not present much of a problem for state-owned serfs (they were allowed to till the land they occupied prior to emancipation), land tenure for privately owned serfs was much more complicated. One has to keep in mind the fact that emancipation of the private serfs was opposed by many serfowners.

Thus the terms of emancipation—the compensation for lost ownership rights over human beings as well as the distribution of the privately owned land between the serfowners and the peasants—reflected a compromise among the interests of the peasants, of the government, and of the serf-owners. Since the government's point of view of emancipating the serfs with land prevailed, the price of land was fixed at a level that would satisfy the former serfowners by including an implicit compensation payment for the former serfs themselves. The bargaining over the amount of land to be distributed and its price, which was derived not from the market prices for land but by computing a capitalized value of the existing payments of the serfs to their masters, resulted in some reduction of the amount of land transferred to the emancipated serfs, by comparison with their previous holdings, and raised the landowners' valuation of the land to be transferred. The price of land was raised to the former serfs to compensate for the loss of their labor on the estates of their former lords.

The reduction of the plowland at the disposal of the peasants after emancipation by comparison with their previous land tenure was in fact minimal, but what perhaps really mattered was the extinction of their traditional right to use the pastures, meadows, and forests for which they were, from the time of emancipation, forced to negotiate with the landlords, who became the sole owners of much of those lands.

The government, concerned about the future viability of the private landed estates, particularly with their ability to recruit a hired labor force, stipulated as a condition of emancipation a period of rendering by the peasants of labor services on the estates at least until the settlement of the conditions of land division and payment for their land allotments. But on top of this, the land was not transferred to the peasants in individual ownership but in communal ownership. The stipulation of communal financial and fiscal responsibility and communal autonomy forced the commune to act on behalf of the collective, thus curbing the freedom of decisions, movement, and actions by the individuals as they saw fit in their individual interests. As a result, after emancipation, the system of agriculture in the Russian villages resembled the pre-enclosure period in Western European agriculture. The land in the villages, within basically a three-field system, had to be cultivated according to the crop rotation generally accepted by the village. What remained of the former commons provided the pasture for the villagers on a basis of communal ownership. Land parcels of many households, often separated in numerous strips throughout the fields, were subject to land redistributions that proportioned each household's share as much as possible according to its relative size, production possibilities, and sometimes consumption needs.

The layout of Russian villages after emancipation remained very much the same as before: two rows of residential dwellings lining the main village road, backed by farm buildings and extending into vegetable gardens or potato patches, but separated from the fields located in various parts of the village lands. Much has been written about this pattern of village settlement, one that differed fundamentally from the farmstead familiar in other parts of the world. Whether one can attribute this pattern to the need for mutual protection against outsiders, or to the relative scarcity of water in arid areas, or to the greater facility of control over the village either by the lords or by the government, or to other considerations is still a debatable issue. There is, however, no doubt that this particular form of village settlement had a great deal to offer the peasants socially, both while working in the fields and in times of leisure forced upon them by the severe climate. It is also clear that while the Russian peasants were quite easily persuaded to concentrate their strips in a continuous bloc, a special incentive would have been needed to change the pattern of village settlement in compensation for the lessening of social contacts in a change to farmsteads.

It would be a mistake to consider the institutional factors affecting Russian agriculture as the primary determinants of agricultural development over a long period of time. It is true that the serf-lord relation that existed for more than two centuries continued to affect later developments. But climate also exercised a powerful influence on the pattern and structure of Russian agriculture. It is customary to distinguish two major regions in European Russia: the nonblacksoil region of the northern part of the East European plain, and the blacksoil region of the southern, mainly steppe, part of Russia. The nonblacksoil region of Russia was settled earlier and had a higher population density. The Russians started the colonization of the southern and eastern regions from the nonblacksoil region.

The different soil structures favor different crops; growing the same crops would produce very different yields in the two regions. The nonblacksoil zone is less fertile, has a shorter growing season, but has higher and often excessive rainfall. The blacksoil zone is more fertile, has a long growing season, but has deficient rainfall. The yields in the nonblacksoil zone are usually lower per unit of land, but when the land is properly drained and lime and fertilizer are applied, the yields tend to be much more stable than in the blacksoil zone. Thus the combination of poor soil, a short growing season, and excess precipitation in one major region and fertile soil, a long growing season, but frequent lack of sufficient precipitation in the other has constrained the development of Russian agriculture up to the present time. During the period of concern to us, the two regions exchanged agricultural products; the nonblacksoil area imported grain from the blacksoil area in exchange for industrial crops, and in some cases, livestock products. The commercialization of agriculture, with its increasing specialization, was supported by the expanding railway network in creating a truly national market, as distinguished from fractionated regional markets, for agricultural products.

Although detailed data on the planted area in Russia were collected for the whole empire only in the twentieth century, and most probably underestimate the planted area, circumstantial evidence (e.g., deforestation data) support the general picture of expansion.

The main sources of the increase in the planted area were: 1) bringing virgin land under cultivation; 2) deforestation; 3) ploughing up of pastures; and 4) reduction in fallow land. Although it is not possible to estimate with a high degree of confidence the shares of the particular sources, we do know that the expansion of the planted area in Siberia came from the cultivation of virgin soil, the expansion in the nonblacksoil zone came from deforestation, the expansion in the Northern Caucasus came from plowing up pasture, and the expansion in the central blacksoil zone came from fallow land.

The expansion of the planted area was related to the problem of land ownership and farm management. Given the conditions of land ownership after the reform of 1861, we would expect that bringing virgin land under cultivation would require a transfer of ownership from the state to the peasants, while the other sources of expansion would involve either an increase of the arable land within both the peasant farms and the landed estates or a transfer of ownership of estate land to the peasants. The available evidence appears to support this hypothesis, especially if one considers the peculiarities of the land market that arose out of the conditions of emancipation. The allotments of land received by the private serfs at the time of emancipation and those of the state land turned over to the former state serfs were taken off the land market; they could neither be bought nor sold because they became communal property given in perpetuity to the village communes.

Thus the land market became more rather than less restricted. Neither the peasant allotments nor most of the state lands entered the land market; transactions in land were confined to privately owned land. The demand for land, rising as a result of population pressure, and the imperfections of such a restricted market led to steep price rises and violent price fluctuations in various districts of European Russia. The demand for land included not only additional plowland but also pastures to sustain the livestock and workstock of the peasants. In addition, there was a demand for land on the part of institutional landowners, such as railroads, and on the part of the nonagricultural population for whom land was an object of investment.

The operation of the land market led to a significant shift in the ownership of privately held land; landholdings of the nobility decreased from about 85 million desiatinas (one desiatina is 1.0925 hectares) in 47 of the 50 provinces of European Russia after the reform of 1861 to about 39 million prior to World War I, and the holdings of the state and imperial family from about 160 million desiatinas to about 144 million. The holdings of peasants and other nongentry rural inhabitants increased from about 112 million desiatinas at the time of the emancipation to about 170 million desiatinas at the outbreak of World War I. Even more significant was the fact that the peasantry purchased over 34 million desiatinas of land in private rather than communal ownership.

Private ownership of peasant land has a significance beyond the question of land titles; it affected individual decision making and allocation of resources by agricultural producers. Ownership becomes significant primarily to the extent that either communal ownership or conditions of land leasing caused irrational decision making and inefficient resource allocation. Thus, the development of agriculture and its commercialization, the land-labor ratio in some regions, the production possibilities, and consumption needs of the agricultural population were at variance with the existing decision-making pattern of communal ownership and with the conditions of land lease as dictated by the nobility, the chief holders of privately owned plowland (about 95 per cent of the state-owned land was either forest or wasteland not suitable for agricultural production). Thus, the shift in land ownership was one of the means by which more efficient decisions by the agricultural producers, chiefly peasants, could be made; the other would have been to break up the communes and transfer ownership to individual households.

The so-called reform of Stolypin, started in 1906, had this latter solution as its main goal. In the period 1907–14 about 14.5 million desiatinas of land previously belonging to the communes were added to land held under private ownership titles. As a result, prior to World War I, in the territory of European Russia, at least 51 million desiatinas of peasant land were privately owned. This figure indicates not only the progress of commercial agriculture within the peasant sector, a development that required a large measure of private decision making and control over farm operations, but also the progress of social and economic differentiation and stratification within the peasant milieu. Thus, if the original system of communal ownership, postulated by the terms of emancipation, envisaged the existence of a nondifferentiated peasant population, this expectation did not materialize. Probably this aspect never entered the minds of the emancipators, certainly not as much as safeguarding the interests of the landowners and those of the state's fiscal and political control over the peasant population.

The differentiation of the peasantry was helpful in increasing both the total and the marketable output of agriculture, creating a strata of market-oriented producers who sold grain and other products not at the expense of their own consumption, but because of their expectation of profits. One ought not, however, overlook the fact of immiseration of a substantial part of the peasantry whose landholdings diminished, and who for all practical

9

purposes became agricultural laborers whose wage earnings supplemented their diminished incomes from farming activities. Neither the expansion of the cropland area nor the absorption capacity of the cities was sufficient to prevent the decline of income of this group. Although this source of abundant, relatively cheap agricultural labor made Russian agricultural products more competitive in the world market, its impact upon the growth of the internal market was certainly detrimental.

While population increase provided an expanding labor force and the growth of the planted area provided additional land inputs, the growth of capital was slow and made an insignificant contribution to agricultural production. Although the capital stock in agriculture was increasing, its composition didn't change much over the period. The growth in farm population stimulated the growth of capital in farm dwellings, and the increase in the number of farms required construction of farm buildings. Together all farm structures constituted about 45 per cent of the total capital stock in agriculture, excluding land. The livestock herd, after an initial growth following the emancipation and lasting until the beginning of the 1890s, experienced a serious setback during the famine of 1891 and recovered slowly, while the numbers of workstock increased sluggishly. The only component of capital that exhibited a relatively rapid rate of growth was farm equipment, but its share in the total agricultural capital, excluding farm dwellings, was about 8 per cent. The stock of capital in irrigation and drainage facilities was small indeed for a country that suffered simultaneously from excessive and deficient precipitation. Facilities to foster agricultural research, improvement of breeding stock, or varieties of crops were either in their infancy or grossly inadequate; the use of mineral fertilizers was minimal, so the modern agricultural revolution largely bypassed Russia at a time when other countries were already benefiting from it. The large landed estates had alternative ways to increase their revenue (such as leasing land to neighboring peasants or selling timber from their forest lands), and heavy capital investment was not considered the optimal solution of their problems; the majority of the peasants were too poor and the credit system too weak to enable them to engage in a major effort to introduce new farming methods. Even the richer peasants often lacked the necessary skills or information on how to acquire the skills for changing the structure of agricultural production. The state, except in the last few years prior to World War I, viewed the agricultural sector as a source of revenue and tried to transfer resources out of agriculture into the area of overhead capital.

Therefore, relatively little was achieved to change the structure of Russian agriculture or the composition of agricultural production. The share of grains remained predominant, although under the impact of relative prices the share of wheat and barley increased at the expense of rye and oats. It should be acknowledged that there was for the country as a whole a significant increase in the average level of grain yields per unit of land. The rise in yields was not continuous; it was still interrupted by years of famine and severe droughts; it took place both as a result of the expansion of the planted area into regions suitable for grain production and as a result of some improvements in the methods of cultivation (e.g., the planting of grasses to restore the fertility of the soil). Thus Russia's grain output was rising to meet the increasing demand, both domestic and foreign. The only available continuous series of grain production data includes the fifty districts of European Russia, excluding the Polish provinces (see table 1.3). The series understates the growth of the entire empire because it omits the new lands settled and cultivated in the provinces of Asiatic Russia and the Northern Caucasus. Nevertheless, the growth of the new areas resembles that in European Russia.

Among the industrial crops, flax and hemp were still the most important, although a major expansion took place in the production of sugar beets and cotton. The livestock sector of agriculture was increasing very slowly, but the commercial output of butter and eggs grew rapidly; the two commodities were second to grain in the export market. It would probably not be incorrect to estimate that during the period 1860–1913 the share of the marketed product in agricultural output increased from one fifth to over one third, while the total grew at a rate of about 1.5 per cent yearly.

It is very difficult, indeed, to find a consistent pattern of government agricultural policies. The government responded to economic necessities and political pressures, but it exhibited less initiative in farm policies than one would have expected in a state in which agriculture was still the largest sector of the economy and peasants were the largest population group.

The one policy followed consistently throughout the period was that

Table 1.3 Yearly Average of Grain Production in Fifty Districts of European Russia (in 1,000s of Metric Tons), 1861–1913

Years	Average Grain Production	Years	Average Grain Production
1861–65	26,926	1891–95	40,606
1866–70	27,977	1896–1900	44,427
1871–75	30,128	1901–5	52,259
1876–80	31,237	1906–10	52,308
1881–85	34,639	1910–13	59,563
1886–90	37,138		

agriculture (the agrarian population and its economic activity) ought to carry the chief burden, not only of maintaining the political strength of the state, but also of subsidizing the modernization of the Russian economy — the creation and expansion of its overhead capital as well as the process of industrialization. Whether it was to be achieved by increasing the fiscal burden of direct taxation of the rural population, or by charging higher prices for protected consumption goods, or by fostering an export policy of influencing agricultural prices with the help of preferential railroad tariffs to the ports, or by imposing revenue tariffs on imported farm machinery and implements, or by imposing indirect taxes and state monopolies on items high on the preference scale of rural consumption, it did not really matter as long as resources were being transferred out of agriculture. When the pace of Russian agricultural development was still greatly influenced by weather conditions, when the agricultural output and welfare of the rural population moved with the rhythm of droughts or bumper crops, the state was willing to provide relief for the victims of famine, but it was unwilling to help to restructure agriculture. Thus, until the revolution of 1905–6, the government policies of aiding agriculture consisted of half-hearted measures designed to help particular groups within the rural population (e.g., providing loans to the nobility through a special government-supported land bank, helping peasants to acquire land through a government-sponsored peasant bank, protecting European grain producers against the competition of Siberian grain, etc.), but none was designed for dealing with fundamental problems of the agricultural sector. It was only after the revolution of 1905–6 that the government developed policies which in the long run were expected to have an impact upon the shape of Russian agriculture. Starting with the cancellation of the peasants' debts on account of their redemption payments and allowing them to leave the communes, intensifying the colonization of Siberia by making state land available for settlement, and allowing the rural population greater mobility, government policies became more supportive of private or local government activities to foster irrigation, drainage, and land improvement. The government also embarked upon training programs to increase the number of agronomists and veterinarians to popularize results of agricultural research, and to support through the banking system the construction of grain elevators as well as other storage and marketing facilities. In other words, government policies after 1906 perhaps did not revolutionize Russian agriculture, but they certainly introduced an element of dynamism that with greater momentum would have helped to modernize the agricultural sector. That these policies were insufficient and at variance with the continuation of long-standing fiscal and trade policies is indicated by the slow pace of progress in agriculture. In any event, the outbreak of World

War I prevented the policies from being tested in terms of their long-run impact.

Industry

If we understand industrialization to mean the introduction of steam power in mining and manufacturing as the major source of energy, with the spread of labor-saving machinery both in manufacturing and in agriculture, and the growth in the share of industry in total output, and for a broader market of consumers, coupled with attitudes of unabashed profit maximization and an increased sensitivity for market conditions, then we can date the beginning of Russia's "industrial revolution" in the 1840–50s. That the industrial revolution in Russia took a longer time, relative to other countries, to affect Russian economic and social life was due to a number of factors, including serfdom and the conditions of their emancipation. Among the other factors that account for the relatively slow pace of industrialization, the relative scarcity of domestic capital that was available for industrial investment and the scarcity of modern entrepreneurial and managerial skills ought to be mentioned. Thus, the early period of industrialization, from the 1860s to the late 1880s, was anything but a period of "Sturm und Drang." With the notable exception of overhead capital (primarily railroads), neither the government nor the society as a whole gave industrialization a high priority. The protection and encouragement extended to industrial development by the government was often tied to other government objectives and concerns, like military production, the balance of trade or payments, or state revenue, rather than to a preoccupation with the development of industry itself. It was, however, the development of parts of the infra-structure, such as the railroad network and the slow growth of a domestic market, that created more favorable conditions for industrial development by the increasing demand for industrial goods and the decrease of transportation costs. When combined with a more explicit set of government policies supporting the industrial sector, an influx of foreign investment, and a transfer of resources from the agricultural to the industrial sector, the growth of the infra-structure created the conditions for the rapid rise in industrial capital and production during the 1890s, repeated later during the "second boom" of Russian industrial activity in 1909–13.

A simple compilation of output data, capital data, or labor data for all manufacturing and mining industries obscures more than it enlightens. It appears, therefore, more advisable to concentrate on two major industries in the hope that such a procedure might provide better insight into the problems of the entire manufacturing sector.

Textiles

Throughout the nineteenth century, the textile industry was the most important in terms of employment and output. To discuss this industry it is convenient to use the following framework: 1) The supply of raw materials; 2) the changes in technology and organization; 3) the conditions of demand; 4) the growth of the labor force and production; 5) the contribution to the national economy; and 6) government policies.

The textile industry of Russia, like that of many other countries, consisted of a number of branches (woolen, cotton, linen, silk, etc.) which could be considered either as complementary or as substitutes. The most rapidly growing branch of the textile industry during the period under consideration was cotton. During the first half of the period the Russian cotton mills depended almost exclusively on the import of ginned cotton or cotton yarn from abroad (largely American, some Persian, etc.), while the domestic supply from the Caucasus was insignificant. After the completion of the Transcaspian Railroad, a link between the cotton textile centers of Central Russia and Poland and the potential cotton-producing region of Central Asia, the domestic raw material base for the Russian cotton industry could be expanded. Within about five years the local, low-yielding varieties of Central Asian cotton were replaced by higher-yielding American varieties, the planted area under cotton expanded rapidly, and both short as well as long-staple cotton suitable for large-scale industrial processing were made available in increasing volume to the Russian cotton mills. A protective tariff made Central Asian and Caucasian cotton both profitable to its producers and competitive in the protected domestic market. The period from the 1880s to 1913 was one of uninterrupted increase in supply of domestic cotton and of substantial decrease in the relative share of cotton imports in total cotton consumption. Thus, during the last few years of the tsarist regime the domestic supply grew to over one-half the total cotton consumption of the Russian cotton-spinning industry.

The consumption of cotton and its distribution between imports and domestic supply can be traced by using some of the available data and estimates shown in table 1.4.

The substitution of domestically grown cotton for cotton imports had its counterpart in a drastic decline of the imports of cotton yarn, starting at the beginning of the 1880s as a result of the increased production capacity of the Russian cotton-spinning mills.

The amount and quality of machinery grew as a substitute for manual labor and primitive equipment; the plant size and employment in the mills and factories increased, in part at the expense of the declining cottage industry. In the cotton industry the two phenomena operated parallel and

Table 1.4   Consumption of Cotton (in 1,000s of Tons)

Years	Imports	Domestic Supply	Total Consumption
1861–65[a]	18,280	—	—
1866–70	42,211	—	—
1871–75	66,257	—	—
1876–80	82,408	—	—
1881–85	116,855	—	—
1888	130,139	19,836	149,975
1890	140,180	52,056	192,236
1895	134,332	52,547	186,879
1900	168,534	95,676	264,209
1905	171,548	100,858	272,416
1908	238,493	169,386	407,878
1913	197,166	259,836	457,002

Source: K. A. Pazhitnov, *Ocherki istorii tekstilnoi promyshlennosti dorevolutsionnoi Rossii.* (Moscow: Akademia Nauk SSSR, 1958), pp. 100, 101, 145.

[a]Yearly average. The low level of cotton imports during this period was due primarily to the American Civil War. In fact, the average yearly imports for 1856–60 were 39,656 tons or only somewhat lower than the imports of the 1866–70 period.

simultaneously. The rate of decline of the cottage industry depended on the demand in the various centers of the industry. Since cotton spinning and weaving were widely practiced by the rural population of the non-blacksoil zone of Russia and constituted an important income supplement for rural households, the interests of the craftsmen often coincided with the interests of the industrial entrepreneurs. At times of imbalance between the spinning and weaving capacities of their enterprises, industrial entre-preneurs employed under contract, in the form of a putting-out system, thousands of rural craftsmen in the production of either yarn or cloth. Thus, although basically the cottage industries and factory industries were in a competitive relation to one another, the symbiosis of the two helped the cottage industry to survive during most of the century, and the sharp decline of the cottage industry became apparent only during the 1890s,[4] when it began to release much labor to the factories.

Simultaneously with the increase in cotton textile employment, the rate of technological change quickened, as can be judged from table 1.5 indi-cating the growth of the basic equipment of the cotton industry. This growth was accompanied by further shifts in the geographic distribution of the industry. Of the three major centers, the relative size of the ones located in the central industrial region (Moscow, Vladimir, Kostroma, Yaroslavl') and the Polish region continued to grow, while the share of the northwestern region (St. Petersburg and Estland) tended to decline.[5]

The growth of production of the cotton spinning and weaving industry can be illustrated by a number of indicators in physical and value terms.

15

Table 1.5   Growth of Basic Equipment in the Cotton Textile Industry

Year	Spindles (Total)	Old Type Spindles	Self-Actor Spindles	Power Looms
1879	3,018,000	—	—	81,000
1890	3,457,116	2,454,552	1,002,564	87,190
1900	6,645,559	3,754,854	2,890,705	151,306
1910	8,306,372	3,746,665	4,559,707	213,179
1913	8,950,000	—	—	—

Table 1.6   Growth of Cotton Yarn and Cloth Production, 1879–1913

Year	Production of Yarn		Production of Raw Cotton Cloth	
	(in tons)	(1,000s of rubles)	(in tons)	(1,000s of rubles)
1879	104,700	—	100,600	—
1890	121,120	119,603	109,273	146,762
1900	239,236	233,680	240,830	259,807
1910	331,143	464,968	279,311	494,508
1913	371,826	—	320,868	—

The data in table 1.6 are indicative of the changes in a few selected measures of production growth.

As far as the organization of the industry is concerned, at least two features are worth mentioning. One was the increase in the average size of plant or perhaps the degree of concentration of production in large-scale firms. In cotton spinning, concentration and the growth of average plant size were completed by around 1900; the subsequent growth of the number of spinning mills (from 117 to 159) was equal to the growth rate of the labor force, while the number of spindles per plant declined slightly from 56,800 to 52,200, a decline attributed to the substitution of more advanced equipment for less advanced. In cotton weaving, however, the period of 1900–1910 was one of the entry of 174 new firms, a 94 per cent increase, while the labor force increased by only 51 per cent.

The other feature was the conversion of family-owned, private enterprises into joint-stock companies, slower in the textile industry than in most others. The ability to raise capital in the Moscow money market, the policy of plowing back substantial profits, and the ability of gradually adding capacity helped the textile entrepreneurs to maintain the family-owned character of their firms. However, competition from new firms in the industry, often organized as joint-stock companies, and the growth in demand forced many of the private firms to reorganize. Thus, toward the end of the period the factories owned by joint-stock companies employed

16

a larger labor force and had a larger capital and higher output than the family-owned enterprises in the cotton textile industry.

The relatively rapid growth of the cotton textile industry was facilitated by its ability to increase its labor force. Recruitment of an industrial labor force in Russia, even after emancipation of the serfs, was not an easy matter. The conditions of emancipation limited the mobility of the peasants, and the urban population was too small to provide the necessary supply of labor for the growing industrial sector. It was, therefore, not an historical accident that the textile industry was originally located and remained largely concentrated in a region where the peasants had to supplement their income by nonagricultural pursuits, in crafts of various types, cottage industry employment, or seasonal migration to other areas. Available evidence indicates that a high proportion of the factory labor force in the cotton textile industry was recruited from among those employed in the cotton putting-out cottage industry. Women and children accounted for an increasing proportion of recruits to the textile industry labor force in the early period. Whether the subsequent decline of child labor was due to increased mechanization, closer supervision by government factory inspectors, an increase in schooling among children, or the competition of female labor is difficult to determine—all these factors probably played a role. However, the participation of women in the cotton textile labor force tended to increase over the whole period. Married women in the cotton industry constituted the largest share of female employment in the industrial sector.

Training of the cotton factory labor force, in addition to recruitment, was a serious problem. In the major cotton textile regions, the growth of the number of hereditary factory workers and urban dwellers within the labor force was slow and the level of skill rose slowly—less visible at times of rapid growth of the labor force, more visible during periods of relative stability.

As a result of the slow increase of skills, whenever a significant change in technology occurred, foreign specialists were used not only at the management level but also at the level of factory foremen. The use of foreigners not only in the western districts of Russia but also in the central industrial region, the heartland of the Russian textile industry, indicates the existence of skill acquisition problems and the lack of highly trained personnel throughout the period.

The cotton textile industry represented the largest single industry in prerevolutionary Russia in terms of employment (except for the railroads) and in terms of the value of gross output. Its growth depended to a large extent upon the demand of the population for its goods, a demand that was rising with population growth and the secular increase in the purchasing power of the population, but also as a result of the substitution of cotton goods for woolens and linen. In terms of quality, most of the output was of the cheaper varieties used by the peasants and lower classes of the urban population; in other words, it was produced for mass consumption. Although small relative to other countries, the per capita consumption of cotton goods increased during the period of 1890–1910 by 65 per cent.

Government policy with respect to industry and industrial development in Russia was neither uniform nor consistent throughout the post-emancipation period. During the first two decades after emancipation, although admitting in principle the advantage of domestic manufacturing, the government was visibly uneasy about the prospect of a growing industrial labor force, since an urban proletariat awoke fears of social and political unrest in the minds of the policymakers. Thus, during the 1860s and part of the 1870s government policy tried to combine a moderate degree of tariff protection with some direct support to industry in the form of government contracts. This provided a comfortable profit margin and eliminated foreign competition for selected industries considered vital to the political independence and economic development of Russia (e.g., rails and railway equipment). Toward the end of the 1870s, perhaps as a consequence of the Balkan War, the government increased tariff protection for both fiscal and general economic reasons. The policy that emerged was one of protectionist attitudes and attempts to stabilize the ruble on the foreign exchanges by expanding exports. The subsequent period, closely identified with the policies of the Finance Minister Count Witte, although falling short of a "master plan" to develop Russian industry, at least represented as closely related a set of coordinated policies to stimulate industrial development as Tsarist Russia ever produced. The government's intention was to develop the necessary overhead capital, to attract both foreign and domestic investments, and to stimulate the growth of supply of domestically produced manufactured goods alongside the growth of supply of primary products for export.

During the period of industrial expansion of the 1890s the government exhibited little direct interference in the industrial sector (except railroads), and the amount of direct subsidies was modest indeed, although the government did not exclude the possibility that in times of slumps in industrial activity direct support of particular industries considered to be "in the national interest" would be forthcoming. As long as this was considered a countercyclical measure, it was not disputed. However, the slump that began in 1900 extended for much longer than was expected, and the government decided that Witte's expansionist policies outstripped the level of demand and that the government ought to avoid a repetition of such policies in the future. Thus, during the industrial boom of 1909–13,

18

government policies to support industrial development were limited almost exclusively to tariff protection. Given the increase in demand for industrial goods during this second boom of industrial activity and the increase in the supply of both domestic and foreign capital, the government assumed a noninterventionist policy and even withstood the clamor for direct support coming from various industries, especially from some of the monopolistic or cartelized industrial associations.

Iron

The stimulus for the growth of the iron industry after emancipation was exogenous to the previous development pattern of this industry in Russia, but it was similar to that in a number of other countries on the European continent during the nineteenth century. The stimulus was provided by the massive investment in railroad construction that required iron products for the rails and rolling stock. But the Russian iron industry, concentrated in the Urals and using an old technology, was totally unprepared to meet the rather sudden upsurge in demand for its output. After an initial period of railroad construction drawing almost entirely on foreign imports, the modernization of the domestic iron industry became imperative.

The main problem was the ability or willingness to invest in new plant and equipment and, given the conditions of both the capital market and the expected returns on such investment, the response was less than the government expected. Some investments were made, mostly by foreign firms in the area of the Dombrowa coal basin (on the territory of the Polish districts adjacent to Germany), but this could hardly solve the problem, and the government felt forced both to revise its tariff policies to provide protection for the iron industry[6] and to invite and encourage foreign capital to develop the iron industry in the south of European Russia where coal and iron ore resources were found in relatively close proximity. The new center of the iron industry was located there in the 1870s and began to meet the demand for the new type of iron products.

The development of this industry illustrates the degree of technical advancement that most Russian industries had to experience in their attempts to survive competition with the more highly developed countries of Western Europe. The case of Russia is also interesting because within Russia itself the competition between the old establishments and the new exemplified the process of differential growth, which assumed the form of competition of "the South against the Urals." In many respects the difference between the two regions was striking. The Ural region represented the old Russian ferrous metallurgy (established there in the first half of the eighteenth century) based on rich ore deposits and vast wood resources, using charcoal as its basic fuel. It represented the old skills of generations of factory serfs and dependent labor as well as a class of entrepreneurs that had merged into the Russian aristocracy and thus was protected by the state and the bureaucracy. In other words, a region dominated by tradition and not in any hurry to modernize, at least as long as the costs of fuel and labor remained relatively low. The "new South" represented the merging of the Donets coal basin with the iron mines of Urivor-Rog; it represented a newer technology, largely imported from abroad and applied to a considerable extent by joint-stock companies, many of them using foreign technical specialists and hired labor that had to be trained from the start. The south represented larger scale enterprises and a much more aggressive approach to marketing, product differentiation, and price policy.

It was due to the dynamism of Russia's southern center of iron production that the total output of the basic product, pig iron, began to rise rapidly. If it initially took about 28 years (1860–88) for output to double, it took only another 6 years to double again, and another 5 years to double the output of 1894.

To a large extent this growth can be attributed to the acceleration of investment of private capital in ferrous metallurgy, which increased from a yearly average of 3.34 million rubles in 1875–80, to 20.2 million in 1880–95, to 26 million in 1895–1900. But it was not only the sheer size of the capital investment that was crucial; it was accompanied by a steady growth of generating power capacity (mostly steam power, but after 1900, also electrical power) and power per worker; by the introduction of elements of Western technology that saved raw materials per unit of output; by the processes of new product development; and by the acquisition of those new skills on the part of the labor force.[7]

While during the last decades of the nineteenth century the productivity of pig iron output was still increasing (primarily as a result of the rapidly growing share in output of the southern blast furnaces, substituting for the Ural production which grew only moderately), the early years of the twentieth century did not witness any further growth in this industry. Iron, steel, and rolling stock, areas that were still growing both in output and productivity, made technical advances as well as enjoyed rising demand from other metal industries (e.g., machine building); see table 1.7. Table 1.8 shows the growth in the output of the basic products of ferrous metallurgy.

The contribution of the ferrous metallurgy industry to Russian industrialization is intimately related to the growth in demand for overhead capital and the output of the capital goods industries. The case of railroads has already been discussed for its contribution to the reconstruction of ferrous metallurgy and the location of production in the southern region. There is no doubt that the railroad boom of the 1890s and railroad con-

Table 1.7   Yearly Output per Worker in Tons of Steel

Year	South	Ural	Poland
1890	78.5	41.1	71.0
1895	100.7	73.2	78.1
1900	193.4	69.5	92.5
1905	214.1	105.0	85.7
1910	361.5	126.2	111.1

Source: S. G. Strumilin, Istoriia chernoi metallurgii v SSSR, 2d ed. (Moscow, 1967), p. 389.

Table 1.8   Output of Major Products of Ferrous Metallurgy in Russia (in 1,000s of tons)

Year	Coal	Pig Iron	Steel	Rolled Iron	Ferrous Metals Total Output (in mill. of rubles)
1860	298	336	212	—	—
1870	695	369	257	—	—
1875	1,709	428	317	—	—
1880	3,276	449	289	292	—
1885	4,269	527	183	362	—
1890	6,015	927	857	678	88
1895	9,099	1,453	1,389	1,080	125
1900	16,155	2,934	2,711	2,191	249
1905	18,668	2,732	2,750	2,356	187
1910	25,000	3,045	3,017	3,017	215
1913	36,038	4,635	4,918	4,039	322

Source: S. G. Strumilin, Istoriia chernoi metallurgii v SSSR, 2d ed. (Moscow, 1967), p. 383.

struction prior to World War I exercised an influence upon the growth rates of ferrous metallurgy.

While the increases in railroad construction activities on the part of the government and private companies created opportunities for guaranteed sales, often at stable prices, as well as allowing a comfortable profit margin, during years of decline in railroad construction the demand would slacken, production decline, and part of the productive capacity remained idle. Thus government and railroad industry contracts had a destabilizing effect on the ferrous metal industry, especially because the lack of demand for railway equipment was not necessarily compensated by a demand for, let us say, naval equipment (although substantial armament programs preceding wars had a stimulating effect on demand for metal).

Among the manufacturing industries that extensively used metals as raw material, the machine-building industry was the most important. It had a complex and changing structure in meeting the demand for machinery and equipment not only of a variety of industries but of other sectors of the economy (e.g., agriculture, transportation, and construction). In addition, the problems of the machine-building industry were compounded by foreign competition and by the scarcity of skilled labor for the production of highly specialized or complex modern machinery. In other words, it was an industry of high cost and less than top quality, one that clamored for protection and received it during the 1890s. (The high cost was a result of both the high costs of raw materials, which were protected by the tariff, and the relatively low level of labor productivity.) Under the umbrella of a highly protective tariff, its growth accelerated and it began to develop import substitutes for a whole range of products, starting with farm machinery and ship building and reaching into areas like food processing and textile machinery.

The protective tariff provided conditions favorable to the growth of some branches of industry and encouraged some foreign firms to establish factories within Russia to overcome the tariff barriers. However, it raised the cost of machinery to domestic users and thereby discouraged modernization of Russian industrial plants. Therefore the effects of the tariff were mixed; it certainly stimulated domestic machine building on the one hand, but it made capital goods more expensive.

A high rate of concentration of capital and labor in a few firms was as characteristic of the Russian cotton textile industry as of the iron industry. This high degree of concentration, by the standards of contemporary, developed, industrialized countries, is often explained by the need to spread scarce highly skilled labor and management over a large number of unskilled labor. It is possible that the pattern of capital formation, especially in areas of foreign capital and the government preference for large-scale enterprises, played a supporting role. The impact of business fluctuations on Russian industry also contributed to the survival of enterprises with a higher capital endowment.

Although the degree of concentration in Russian industry was high, it ought not to be equated with the prevalence of monopoly. The author did not find evidence to support the view that monopoly and cartel arrangements were effective and widespread. The requirement of initial high capital endowment was as effective a barrier to entry of new firms as monopolistic policies.

The Growth of Private Capital

There can be no doubt that the growth of the Russian economy from 1860 to 1913 was accompanied by a growth of "the stock of means, separable from human beings and legally disposable in economic transactions, intended for use in producing goods or income," as capital is defined by Professor Simon Kuznets. To the extent that Russia was primarily an agricultural economy, the main form of capital was land, and the expansion of agricultural land constituted an important part of capital formation. It is, therefore, unfortunate indeed that the existing data do not permit the calculation of the growth of capital in the form of the value of increments of the crop-producing area or in the form of land improvements. Other elements of capital in agriculture—dwellings, farm buildings, agricultural machinery, livestock and workstock—can be calculated with any degree of accuracy only after 1890.

Preliminary data for the private capital stock of the farm sector, expressed in 1913 constant prices, are given in table 1.9 for the terminal years of the period. The relatively low rate of growth clearly requires some explanation. The range of plausible explanations is unfortunately very wide and can be, generally speaking, divided into two categories: exogenous (factors that affected the volume of income of the agricultural population) and endogenous (factors affecting the distribution of income between consumption and savings and those determining the type of expenditures on increments of the capital stock or to its composition).

The exogenous factors include the movement of agricultural prices and the burden of taxation on agricultural producers, with low prices during the 1890s as well as a continuously high level of direct and indirect government taxation. The agricultural producers, who made up the bulk of the population, bore the burden of the national debt incurred for financing the Balkan War (1877–78), the Russo-Japanese War (1904–5), and the preparation for World War I, but also of the government-financed programs of creating a high overhead capital (railroads, etc.). In addition, the agricultural producers had to bear the consumption costs of the tariff policy that protected various branches of the developing Russian industry and provide, through taxes gathered by state monopolies on consumption goods, the means to maintain the apparatus of government control as well

Table 1.9 Private Capital Stock of the Farm Sector
(3-Year Averages, in Millions of Rubles, 1913 Prices)

	1891	1913
Farm dwellings	5,285.6	6,891.6
Farm buildings	2,618.0	3,414.4
Transportation equipment	1,078.2	1,417.1
Farm equipment & machinery	373.6	979.9
Workstock	2,488.5	2,816.8
Livestock	3,609.1	3,898.8
Total	15,453.0	19,418.6

as the subsidy payments to the social groups that held political power within the Russian state. Thus, a continuation of unfavorable prices in the world and internal markets and the burden of taxation, occasionally supplemented by natural calamities (e.g., droughts, famines, epidemics, livestock diseases), limited the total and disposable income of the agricultural population. Those constraints operated against the background of a high rate of population growth and a relatively small, although increasing, share of commercial output in total agricultural production. It therefore becomes understandable that, unless counterbalanced by other forces, the exogenous factors did not provide a direct stimulus to capital formation in Russian agriculture. The situation changed only at the point when both agricultural prices began to rise and the foreign as well as the domestic demand for agricultural products were increasing.

Among the endogenous factors that influenced the size of capital formation and its distribution among its components, of considerable importance was the structure of landholdings and the conditions of land ownership in Russian agriculture. Land purchases absorbed a sizeable part of the peasants' savings, leaving relatively little for other types of investment in agriculture, and these were coupled with the conditions of short-term leases in agriculture that were not particularly conducive to investment in the land or other forms of capital. The large estates, even market-oriented ones, were not capital intensive; even their proceeds from land sales to the peasants were not necessarily used for improvements on the remaining land. Communal land ownership by the peasants and the open-field organization of cultivation conditioned the behavior of the various types of agricultural producers and influenced the changes in the amount and distribution of capital in the agricultural sector. Thus, the increase in capital in farm dwellings and buildings was largely a response to the creation of new farm households to which livestock and workstock growth hardly kept pace. The only dynamic element in agricultural capital formation was in farm equipment and machinery, which constituted a very small share of the total.

A crude estimate of the rate of growth of the capital stock in the farm sector, excluding land, would be in the neighborhood of 1 per cent annually. Excluding residential construction, we get a growth rate of 1 per cent for the agricultural sector. The estimated growth rate in the planted area is 2 per cent. In terms of the size of the privately owned capital stock, excluding land, the largest component is accounted for by structures, especially residential structures (see table 1.10). The rate of growth of urban building exceeded that of rural building, both residential and nonresidential. Urban construction was prompted by population growth and the industrial booms, particularly in the 1890s.

**Table 1.10 Capital Stock in Structures
(in Millions of Rubles, 1913 Prices)**

Type of Structure	1890	1913
Total structures	12,166	18,159
Total residential	9,007	13,324
Residential urban	3,763	6,319
Residential rural	5,244	7,005
Farm buildings	2,594	3,481
Industrial structures	565	1,353

Table 1.11 Private Industrial Capital (in Millions of Rubles, 1913 Prices)

Year	Structures	Equipment	Inventories	Total
1890	565	598	545	1,708
1895	655	868	945	2,468
1900	898	1,090	1,188	3,177
1905	998	1,313	1,607	3,919
1910	1,071	1,384	1,992	4,411
1913	1,353	1,785	2,274	5,413

The third category of capital stock was industry.[8] During the period 1890–1913, it exhibited the highest growth rate among the broad categories under consideration. It is customary to classify industrial capital in three large components: structures, equipment, and inventories. Given the conditions of Russian production, transportation, and distribution, the share of inventories in the industrial capital stock was substantial and consistently grew. The next largest component was equipment, for which the periods of most rapid growth were the second half of the 1890s until 1902 and from 1908 until World War I, but by the end of the period it barely maintained its share in the total industrial capital stock. The share of structures decreased markedly during the period 1890–1913, displaying the lowest rate of growth among the three categories, a development that one would have expected during industrialization. Table 1.11 summarizes some of the features of private industrial capital for selected years. It would be wrong to interpret these figures as representing the total industrial capital, since the share owned by the state is excluded from the totals, and government-owned factories, ships, shipyards, etc., constituted a sizeable portion of industrial capital. But for the private sector of manufacturing industries the totals in table 1.11 appear to be reasonable approximations of the pattern of growth.

If we assemble the data for the private capital stock of the various categories considered, with the notable exceptions of land, transportation facilities, communications and most public utilities, we get the pattern illustrated in table 1.12. The negligible growth of the capital stock during 1890–95 can be attributed partly to the heavy losses suffered by the agricultural sector during the famine of 1891 and the epidemics of 1892. The growth from 1895–1900 coincided with the industrial boom of the late 1890s and is therefore in line with our expectations for the period. Much more puzzling, however, are the growth of the capital stock during 1900–1905 and the slow growth during 1910–13 when the Russian economy experienced another rapid rate of industrial and agricultural growth. In the case of the 1910–13 period, a rapid rise in prices accompanied the economic expansion, and therefore the price deflators affected the results, which are given in terms of stable prices. No such explanation applied in reverse to the 1900–1905 period, which witnessed a decline in prices, would be sufficient. It is possible that some of the capital stock of a longer gestation period was a result of earlier investment outlays; it is also possible that some substitution of capital for labor took place and perhaps even some capital replacement for stock that was depreciated and obsolete. Whatever the reasons, there is obviously a need for further research to explain in greater detail the capital estimates for 1900–1905.

To the extent that the growth of the capital stock, or the volume of investment in income-generating assets, is used by economists to explain the growth of production and income, our discussion would be incomplete without mentioning another form of investment which for the later part of the period under investigation was of utmost importance—the investment in the education and skills of the labor force. This is not the place to discuss in detail the rapid growth of literacy of both the workers and the peasants, the training of Russian engineers and technicians, etc. By the standards of Western Europe and the United States it was inferior, and in terms of what was needed to get Russia to move faster among the industrialized nations it was insufficient. However, the pace increased rapidly and provides evidence of a high economic return to education and technical training. Although the government subsidized education on various levels, it concentrated its effort on primary education. Thus, secondary and higher education, apart from the income forgone by the students, was

Table 1.12   Estimates of Private Capital
(in Millions of Rubles, 1913 Prices)

Year	Total	Year	Total
1890	21,242	1905	27,409
1895	21,971	1910	29,880
1900	24,460	1913	31,593

to a very large extent privately supported. It was estimated that the yearly cost per student of secondary school education was approximately equal to the per capita GNP in 1913, and the costs of higher education approximately 2.4 times the per capita GNP.

The data for 1890 in table 1.13 would indicate not only a smaller percentage of the total students to the total population, but also a smaller percentage of secondary school attendants to the number of primary school attendants than in 1913. While secondary and higher education still remained a monopoly of the higher-income groups of the population, evidence indicates that social advancement through education by the end of the period became more available to the members of the urban middle classes and to the more affluent stratum within the peasantry.

To the extent that formal schooling facilitated the acquisition of modern industrial and business skills, the contribution of education to the formation of what is termed "human capital" was of first-rate significance for the industrialization of Russia and complemented in an important manner the growth of physical capital.

Transportation

The sheer size of Russia's territory and the degree of geographical dispersion of its population suggest the importance of a transportation network for the economic as well as the political and cultural aspects of social life in Russia. Without an efficient transportation network the relative isolation of the various regions and the fragmentation of the market could hardly be overcome.

Steam power as applied to transportation provided the facilities that both the economy and polity of Russia needed. Without steam power any upstream movement of goods on the Russian rivers (when they were not frozen) required enormous inputs of horsepower and human labor and made the transportation of goods very expensive, even with the relative cheapness of Russian unskilled labor. Under such circumstances the volume of goods transported upstream could hardly be increased. Overland transportation with the use of horses was both time consuming and expen-

Table 1.13   School Enrollment in Russia (in 1,000s)

Level	1890	1913
Primary	2,283	7,570
Secondary	130	536
Higher	n.a.	130

sive even when the roads were passable, and the improvement of the road network would not have solved the long-run problem of increasing the volume, given the use of human and horsepower. Thus, the new industry, consisting of steam-powered railroads and steamships on the waterways, staked out its claim for the investment resources of a Russian society still under serfdom, with a weak and fragmented market structure, and with government policies primarily interested in the military and political aspects of a transportation network. It therefore took a few decades of observation of foreign experience and realization of the true economic potential of this new industry before Russia became one of the countries that tied its future economic development to the revolutionizing impact of steam power in transportation.

Roads and Rivers

The most widely used means of transportation during the pre-emancipation period were overland (mostly by the use of horses) and river transportation. The major shortcomings of both forms, stemming in part from the climatic conditions, were the difficulties of moving freight and passengers during spring and autumn by overland transportation and of maintaining navigation on the rivers during the extended winter season. Additional shortcomings of the transportation system were the dearth of improved riverbeds or canals connecting the separate river basins and the virtual absence of paved roads. Apart from a few roads maintained for postal service, government couriers, and perhaps military movements, a road maintenance system was nonexistent (except for corvée service of the rural population). The "roads" were passable primarily during the dry summer season and in the winter by the use of horse-drawn sleighs.

Railways

The railway network in Russia, developed chiefly during the post emancipation period, ought to be considered, at least from the viewpoint of transportation facilities operating in all seasons, as a net addition rather than a substitute for available transportation for the seasons when no substitutes existed. This does not preclude the possibility that, for particular regions of Russia, resources expended in the construction of better roads and in the improvement of rivers would have constituted a more profitable or economically advantageous investment than the same investment in the development of railroads. But on the whole, from the point of view of both the economic and political objectives of the state, railroads were considered the preferable alternative.

One of the characteristics of the development of the Russian railway network was its dual purpose—political (including military) and economic. These two roles were not necessarily congruent in the choices of the routes developed or the timing of their construction. It is, therefore, little wonder that during much of the period under consideration many railway lines were built with strategic objectives in mind and could hardly pass the test of profitability or economic efficiency.

After the disastrous results of the Crimean War, railroad construction was put high on the government's agenda for the development of the country's overhead capital. But in its quest for resources, the railroad had to compete with other claims upon the domestic capital market and the government budget, neither of which was in a position to provide the massive outlays that a vigorous program of railway construction required. The solution was found in the solicitation and importation of foreign capital, which had already built railroads in Russia during the pre-emancipation period. Foreign investors responded massively in two ways: first, by participating in the formation of private companies and subscribing to the bond offerings of private companies involved in railroad construction, and second, by purchasing Russian government bonds earmarked for railroad construction. However, the basic prerequisite for floating Russian railroad bonds on the Western European exchanges was a guarantee by the Russian government that the stipulated payments of bond interest (by both governmental and private railroad companies) be paid in foreign currency, regardless of the profitability of the railroad companies. One would suspect that this guarantee was promoted less because of the relative credit rating of the Russian government vis-à-vis the Russian capitalists, than as a security against the government's arbitrary policies that could affect the profit rates of the railroad companies and thus their ability to pay the stipulated bond interest, as well as a security against sudden changes in Russian monetary policies and the fluctuating values of the Russian inconvertible paper currency. In other words, the Russian government guarantees of the railroad bonds tended to diminish risks and raise the effective yield.

Foreign capital for the Russian railways was important not only as a source of financing but also as a means of acquiring foreign-made railway equipment and specialized knowledge in railroad construction. At least at the beginning, both equipment and skills had to be obtained abroad until, under both the pressure and incentives provided by the government, Russian industry developed the capacity to supply domestically produced railway equipment and a domestically educated and trained labor force for the construction as well as for the operation of a rapidly growing railroad network.

From the 1850s and throughout most of the period, competition among foreign investors for financing railway construction and for supply contracts of equipment facilitated the task of railroad development. Obviously, the preference given to one of the competing parties (whether the French, the Germans, or the British) depended to a considerable extent on the constellation of political alliances in Europe and on general patterns of economic relations (e.g., trade tariffs), but at least until the middle of the 1890s Russia benefited from international competition in attracting foreign capital into railroads on terms most advantageous for itself. The subsequent turn in Russian foreign economic policies, particularly the conditions of Russian-French cooperation, provided the French with a better bargaining position. Although the flow of foreign investment from Paris met the demands for Russian railway construction, the degree of political interference of both the French and the Russian governments in railroad policy increased and did not necessarily result in making the operation of the railway network more efficient.

The growth of the railway network in Russia is illustrated by the data in table 1.14. It is apparent that the periods of the greatest expansion in railroad construction were 1865–80 and the decade of the 1890s. The growth of freight carried by the railroads was somewhat greater than the growth of mileage for the whole period, and (while keeping in mind the presence of predominantly strategic railroads) for the railroads primarily serving economic purposes (freight and passenger traffic) the growth of freight carried was even larger, thus indicating improvement in efficiency of operations over time.

Thus the growth of freight carried by railroads could be explained not only by the fact that on a per kilometer basis the costs and price of railroad transportation were less than that of overland horse transportation, for

Table 1.14   The Growth of the Russian Railway Network, 1860–1916

Year	Length (in km.)	Volume of Freight (million ton-km.)	No. Passengers (million passenger-km.)	Total Employees (yearly average in 1,000s)
1860	1,626	—	—	—
1865	3,842	571	—	—
1870	10,731	2,404	—	—
1875	19,029	5,146	—	—
1880	22,865	8,000	—	—
1885	26,024	11,238	3,929	213
1890	30,596	14,925	5,013	248
1895	37,058	22,615	7,581	344
1900	53,234	38,869	13,003	554
1905	61,085	45,109	19,467	751
1910	66,581	60,594	23,229	772
1913	70,156	69,731	29,312	815
1916	80,139			

which it became a major substitute, but also by the growth of the volume of goods that were produced and moved to the various markets. The contribution of the railroads, as a cheaper and more efficient mode of transporting goods and people, to the development of the Russian economy was considerable. There is no doubt that without railroads the commercialization of Russian agriculture would have proceeded more slowly, the location of various industries and the pattern of interregional and international trade would have been different, and the GNP would have risen more slowly than it actually did.

But the railroads also had a number of direct effects on industry, the output of which was used as inputs in the construction and operation of the railroads, and on the acquisition of skills by the labor force they employed.

The Russian railroad network created a market for rails and rolling stock and thereby stimulated the development of the Russian ferrous metal and machine-building industries. It used sleepers (railroad ties) and thereby stimulated this branch of forestry and woodworking. It built stations, railway depots, and other structures using the resources made available by the construction industry. It used large quantities of coal and oil, thus becoming one of the major customers of the mining industry.

The growing labor force of the traffic service, rolling stock service, construction, repair, and administration of the railroads was provided with incentives and avenues for the acquisition and utilization of higher skills, and, what is also important, they then disseminated these skills in the various areas of Russia as the railway network expanded.

Waterways

It would be presumptuous in discussing the development of transportation facilities in Russia to concentrate exclusively on the railroads. Although the railroads were the most rapidly growing modern means of transportation and were given high priority in terms of investment allocation, the freight-carrying capacity of the internal waterways also increased. It is true that, even to a greater extent than the railroads, the internal waterways were developed without any general blueprint in mind. Nevertheless, the demand of the market and the growing opportunities of connecting certain centers of production with major terminals of the developing railroad network provided direct stimuli for the expansion of the internal waterways and their freight-carrying facilities.

Since the greatest cost savings of using water transportation were achieved in bulk shipments of low cost per unit of weight, the services of internal waterway transportation were widely used for grains, oil, and forestry products. The floating of unprocessed logs was another significant, although traditional, means of using the waterways, especially since the basins of the Volga and Dnepr rivers provided an excellent opportunity to haul the forest products from the more densely wooded areas of the center of European Russia downstream southward to the sparsely wooded steppes. The rivers flowing westward and northward also provided outlets for wood exports.

The actual length of the waterways used for commercial transportation was much smaller than the length of the Russian rivers, a fraction of which were actually navigable. The standard classification would list: 1) the length of the waterways suitable for the floating of logs; 2) the length of the waterways used for downstream transportation; and 3) the actual length of the waterways, natural and improved, including canals used for both upstream and downstream transportation. Table 1.15 provides the approximate relationship of the various categories for 1907.

The distribution of waterways that were used for the transportation of goods (except logs) and passengers was as uneven over the territory of Russia as that of railways. The western and northwestern areas of Russia accounted for almost all of the canals and improved waterways, with the exception of the largest natural basin of the Volga River that connected the central provinces with the foothills of the Ural Mountains and the Caspian Sea. But even the Volga basin and part of its large freight movements and most of the other waterways were directed toward the Baltic Sea, the main outlet for Russian foreign trade during the pre-emancipation period. The growing importance of the Black Sea as an outlet for Russian goods, such as grain and oil, was not fully reflected in the improvement of waterway facilities, the most obvious example being the lack of continuous waterway transportation on the second largest Russian river, the Dnepr. Except for many plans of development of the waterways discussed during the immediate pre-World War I period, most of which remained on the drawing board (such as the Volga-Don canal, improvement of the Dnepr, etc.), the actual investments appear to be ad hoc and only partial responses rather

Table 1.15   Navigable Length of Rivers, Lakes, and Canals, in 1907
(in Kilometers)

Total length of rivers and navigable lakes	221,573
Total length for log-floating only	61,021
Total length for floats only	49,895
Total length for ships up and downstream	41,610
Total length for steamships	29,471
Total length for heavily loaded ships	15,752
Total length of canals and rivers with locks	1,859

than components of a pattern to correct the imbalances in the distribution of the available facilities.

However, in spite of its shortcomings, whether in performance vis-à-vis its potential or in policy, internal waterway transportation constituted an important addition, and in some cases an alternative, to the railroad transportation network of Russia as can be surmised from the general indicators of its performance shown in table 1.16. Although the waterways with a total of 50.9 million tons of total freight, 1.3 billion rubles worth of goods, and about 8 million passengers remained a distant second behind the railways, nevertheless the great increase of their use, especially in view of the limited resources supporting new investment in the waterways, was quite impressive.

Their growth can be explained in part by the large-scale introduction of steamboats for freight traffic, which made the upstream transportation of goods much cheaper. Although we lack reliable data for the early period, we know that the value of freight carried by steamships increased from 1893 to 1913 from 40.5 million rubles to 405.1 million rubles, the highest growth rate for any form of waterway transportation. Thus, technological improvement certainly cheapened the costs of transportation of freight on the Russian waterways and contributed to the growth of traffic.

Communications

Closely connected with the development of a transportation system is the expansion of a communication network. Improved information accompanies market expansion and the movement of people and goods. The construction of railways in all countries was used for at least two forms of

Table 1.16   Volume and Value of Freight Carried on the Inland Waterways of European Russia (Volume in 1,000s of Tons, Value in Millions of Rubles)

Year	Total		By Ships		By Floats	
	Volume	Value	Volume	Value	Volume	Value
1878	13,759	—	7,436	—	6,323	—
1883	13,808	210	7,764	200	6,044	10
1888	17,222	216	9,265	203	7,957	13
1893	19,353	257	11,598	238	7,756	18
1898	29,468	468	17,732	425	11,736	43
1903	36,490	779	23,836	717	12,654	61
1908	36,119	897	21,493	824	14,626	72
1913	50,887	1,299	29,842	1,167	21,045	131

improved communications: the telegraph and mail service. The third, the construction of a telephone network, was less tied to the railways.

Whether for purposes of improving communications for government administration or for the needs of the population, or both, the telegraph network of Russia grew steadily. In terms of institutional affiliation, one ought to distinguish between the state-owned and administered telegraph lines and the telegraph lines within the railroad network that provided services not exclusively for its own needs but made its facilities available for established fees. The data in table 1.17 provide the general order of magnitude for the development of the telegraph network. A most vigorous construction of telegraph stations and telegraph lines was conducted during the 1860s and 1870s, when most of the international lines connecting Russia with its neighbors in the West, South, and East were being built and which also coincided with the early railway boom in Russia. In terms of ownership and service, most of the line mileage was owned by the state, while the rest was owned by the private railroads and some private telegraph companies. As far as the telegraph stations were concerned, the share of those located at the railroad offices and operated by the railroads indicates the mutual interdependence of the telegraph services, the postal services, and the railroads.

Although the yearly data for the number of telegrams sent are not available for some consecutive years, by 1913 the total telegrams sent approached 50 million, an impressive number by comparison with the size of the urban population or the size of the industrial and commercial sectors of the economy.

Another indicator of the development of communications is the use of the mail for either personal or business purposes. The intensification of

Table 1.17   Development of the Telegraph Network

Year	Total Telegraph Stations	Railroad Telegraph Stations	Total Length of Line (km)	State Telegraph Lines (km)	Railroad Telegraph Lines (km)
1880	2,623	1,466	94,632	—	—
1885	3,206	1,646	112,597	—	—
1890	4,035	2,067	122,503	115,821	—
1895	4,623	2,377	135,891	126,166	—
1900	5,789	2,991	164,697	146,693	13,342
1905	—	—	—	165,330	13,361
1910	—	—	—	184,277	14,542
1913	—	—	—	212,178	16,979

communication through the mail accompanies both the growth of the market and the rise in the cultural level of the population.

The figures of the sale of postage stamps and postcards in table 1.18 illustrate the development of this particular type of communication. The growth in volume is almost as great as in value because the rates charged for postal services during this period increased only slightly.

Since the railway network became the main carrier of mail, this form of intensified communication ought to be considered, in part at least, a social benefit of the railway development. Thus the growth in the operation of the postal system, based largely on the carrying function of the railroads, reflected the growth of the social infrastructure of Russia.

Domestic Commerce

Domestic commerce, defined as the total trade turnover of mercantile enterprises, grew more slowly during the post-emancipation period than foreign trade or the industrial sector of the economy. The relatively slow growth of domestic trade was a result of the slow rise in disposable incomes of the rural population, the slow growth of commercial production, the low rate of urbanization, and the expansion of Russia into areas with a relatively primitive economy.

The forms and institutions of trade prevailing prior to the emancipation survived and new, more efficient institutions developed only gradually. Domestic trade, unlike foreign trade, did not benefit from encouragement by the government; instead it was subjected to special taxation and was in some cases replaced by government monopolies (as in the case of alcohol and other products). Administrative measures hampered commercial enterprises. Not only were the commercial enterprises classified, licensed, and taxed according to differential rates, but the old system of merchant gilds was preserved with some of its discriminatory features. Discrimination was also applied by excluding some population groups either from

Table 1.18 Sale of Postage-Stamps and Postcards (in 1,000s of Rubles)

Year	Sales	Year	Sales
1860	1,451	1890	10,415
1865	1,704	1895	14,052
1870	2,907	1900	20,788
1875	4,855	1905	40,066
1880	6,025	1910	59,449
1885	8,166	1913	72,736

Note: For the sources of these figures see Glavnoe upravlenie pocht i telegrafov, *Pochtovo-telegrafnaia statistika za 1913 god* (Petrograd, 1917).

some branches of trade or from particular locations. One of the traditional forms of pre-emancipation trade—the local, regional, and central trade fairs—survived throughout the period. These trade fairs played an important role in domestic trade either by their specialization in particular commodities (furs, cattle, leather, wool, fish, flax, etc.) or by their role as a substitute for both localized wholesale trade and for mercantile exchanges. In particular, the local fairs provided opportunities to exchange agricultural products for manufactured consumer goods or for farm implements and equipment.

The most famous central fair of Russia was the Nizhnii-Novgorod fair, during which 150–200 million rubles of merchandise were sold, some of it for export abroad. The Irbit fair, with sales of 25–40 million rubles, was the center of the fur trade. Although the share of the fairs in total trade declined somewhat over the period, data for European Russia in table 1.19 give an approximate order of magnitude of the number of fairs and the sales for selected years. In spite of the growth of permanent mercantile establishments, the growing separation of wholesale trade from retail trade, and the growth of the number of mercantile exchanges, the trade during fairs did not decline. Even if we allow for increasingly better statistical coverage of the number of fairs and for changes in the purchasing power of money, we would still find some growth in the number and sales of the fairs.

While there was without any doubt growth in specialization of trade, whether along the lines of size and destination of trade (wholesale vs. retail) or along the lines of commodity groups, the basic distribution of trade among the size classes remained almost unchanged. Up to 15 per cent of the total was accounted for by larger stores employing hired labor, about 50 per cent was accounted for by small stores, typically family enterprises employing only family members, while about 30 per cent was accounted for by market stalls with very little inventory and perhaps geared to trade during market days.

Table 1.19   Fairs in European Russia

Year	No. of Fairs	Total Sales (in million rubles)
1868	6,496	305
1894	14,033	447
1904	15,497	955

Sources: P. A. Khromov, *Ekonomicheskoe razvitie Rossii v XIX-XX vekakh* (Moscow, 1950), appendix table 18. G. A. Dikhtiar, *Vnutrenniaia torgovlia v dorevolutsionnoi Rossii* (Moscow, 1960), p. 143.

The figures in table 1.20 give an incomplete but nevertheless character-istic pattern of the development of the trade establishments in Russia for some selected years, by size and type of operation. Although these data indicate an almost unchanged distribution of the various groups of mercan-tile establishments, with only a slightly higher growth of the small-scale ones, evidence about the volume of sales of the various categories indi-cates a higher rate of growth of sales by the larger stores and a relative decline of sales by the smaller ones. Thus, there was some concentration of sales in the larger-sized establishments and an increased competition among the smaller-sized enterprises.

Russian internal trade suffered from a relative shortage of capital and credit, and much of the development of trade during the second half of the nineteenth century was marked by the attempts on the part of the mer-chants to obtain credit from commercial banks that started to operate in Russia only during the post-emancipation period. Short-term bank loans were clearly preferable to private credit because of lower interest rates. Bank credit was available either to wholesalers or to owners of large stores, but not directly to the great mass of petty traders who continued to use private credit. Out of this plight of the petty merchants arose the ini-tiative to establish mutual credit societies in which the members could deposit their savings or short-term cash receipts and borrow in the form of short-term loans. Such mutual credit societies became very popular with the merchants and provided a model for mutual credit societies of crafts-men, workers, and peasants. It is worthwhile mentioning that the idea of mutual assistance led to the establishment of consumer cooperative soci-eties, which toward the end of the period (by January 1, 1914) numbered 10,080 associations with about 1,400,000 members. The turnover of the cooperative stores accounted for about 250–300 million rubles, and the cooperatives established themselves as a potentially important element in trade.[9]

Table 1.20   Distribution of Trade Establishments in Russia (in 1,000s)

Year	Large Stores	Small Stores	Market Stalls	Delivery Trade	Total
1885	—	—	—	—	575
1900	144	430	240	29	846
1904	139	458	257	27	883
1908	139	498	283	20	941
1912	173	608	349	25	1,156

Source: G. A. Dikhtiar, *Vnutrenniaia torgovlia v dorevolutsionnoi Rossii* (Moscow, 1960), p. 87.

Data on wholesale and retail trade are readily available for the period 1885–1913, while for the earlier period the available estimates are both too ill-founded and contradictory to be of real use. The more or less reliable data on the growth of sales by trading establishments are presented in table 1.21.

Foreign Trade

Agricultural exports occupied a central and dominant position in Russian exports, but while during the eighteenth century and the first quarter of the nineteenth century the center of the stage was held by industrial crops—fiber exports such as flax and hemp—during the period under consideration the primacy of grains was already firmly established. A few developments contributed to the growth of grain exports. The growth of the nonagricultural population of Western Europe boosted the requirements for food grains, supplemented later by the demand for feed grains to support the growing livestock herd in Western Europe. That the demand for Russian grain was not by any means smooth or continuous can be surmised from the competition that Russia faced, particularly beginning with the 1880s when the world grain market was flooded by the grains coming from the prairie areas of North and South America and the price of grain took a long dive. It was not until the beginning of the twentieth century that prices started to rise again, and both the price rise as well as the increase in the volume benefited Russian export trade. On the supply side the construction of railroad lines extending into the expanding grain-producing areas of southern and eastern Russia both reinforced this expansion and opened an outlet for the grains to the ports of the Black Sea. Therefore, there is small wonder that the volume of grain exports from the southern ports surpassed the volume handled by the Baltic ports. Odessa

Table 1.21 Sales in the Wholesale and Retail Trade Network,
1885–1913 (in Millions of Rubles)

Year	Sales
1885	3,503
1890	4,033
1895	5,207
1900	7,036
1905	7,833
1910	9,245
1913	11,538

Sources: P. A. Khromov, *Ekonomicheskoe razvitie Rossii v XIX–XX vekakh* (Moscow, 1950), p. 248. G. A. Dikhtiar, *Vnutrenniaia torgovlia v dorevolutsionnoi Rossii* (Moscow, 1960), pp. 79, 101.

and Nikolaev became two of the main outlets for Russian grains abroad at the time when wheat and barley replaced the older staples of Russian grain exports, such as rye and oats. The pattern of change in Russian grain exports can therefore be summarized as follows: the 1870s witnessed a major growth in exports rising constantly until the middle of 1880s, when the growth was arrested and fluctuated around a stable average level until about 1903, when the volume increased to be stabilized between 1905 and 1908, and rose significantly from 1909 until the outbreak of World War I.

The share of fibers in total agricultural exports, together with a decline of oilseed, most often a by-product of the fiber supply, was mentioned above; the one industrial crop which exhibited growth in export was sugar beets, encouraged by various means, including export subsidies and quotas for home consumption.

The place of fibers in the composition of export trade was taken by livestock products, particularly eggs and butter. This rise is somewhat surprising in view of the extreme backwardness of the livestock sector and its virtual stagnation over a long period of time. It was due in part to the growth of the livestock herd in Siberia, with its relatively abundant supply of meadows and pastures, but more specifically to the growth of the foreign demand for livestock products and to the use of refrigeration on the railroads, that enabled the long-haul transportation of perishables of a high value per unit of weight.

One more observation concerning agricultural exports might be in order: there was a slight shift from nonprocessed agricultural commodities to processed ones. Thus, the slight increase in the volume of grain flour, some substitution of vegetable oil for oil seeds, of meat for animals, and last but not least, the export of sugar exemplify the emergence or direction of a new pattern.

The export of forestry products, both of timber and of processed lumber, increased under the impact of an increasing foreign demand. This provided a stimulus for the government and private individuals not only to take stock of the immense resources available but also to begin a more rational policy of both production and conservation of this resource.

Alongside the growth in exports of forestry products, the growth of exports of raw materials from the mining sector was also significant. Oil headed the list of such products in terms of both value and volume, followed by manganese ore. The exports of oil, very successful during the last decades of the nineteenth century, later encountered fierce competition from other sources, primarily the United States, and faced problems of increasing production costs when output in the Baku oil fields began to decrease. In the attempt to maintain Russia's role as oil exporter and to decrease transportation costs, in addition to a railroad, a pipeline from Baku (on the Caspian Sea) to Batumi (on the Black Sea) was laid through the mountainous terrain of the Caucasus.

While agricultural goods and other raw materials or semi-manufactured goods made up the bulk of Russian exports, it is necessary to point out that the share of industrial goods in the export trade was on the increase. While it was difficult for Russia to compete in the European market of industrial products, certain advantages were derived from markets in Asia, such as Iran and China, where Russia gained a foothold primarily through its exports of textiles.

Simultaneously with the increase in exports, Russian imports also increased. The most important items in Russian import trade were cotton, fine wool, and machinery. Thus, raw materials for Russian industry and industrial goods (primarily capital equipment) headed the list of imports, followed by a large variety of manufactured consumer goods. The determinants of the size of imports can be categorized into three groups: first, the demand of industry for foreign raw materials based on the expectations of Russian entrepreneurs about changes in the volume of production in the short run; second, the demand for capital goods both for replacement and for new equipment for existing or new enterprises; third, the demand for manufactured consumer goods based on changes in income—itself related to changes in the value of exports. Thus, the value of imports could have been estimated, or even predicted with a greater degree of accuracy than the value of Russian exports. In fact, the value of imports exhibited a much more stable pattern of growth than the widely fluctuating values of exports that had suffered both from changing world market prices and from variations in the supply of agricultural goods dependant on changing weather conditions. Thus, the net balance of Russian foreign trade was subject to violent fluctuations underscored by the differential behavior of exports and imports.

During most of the period, the balance of commodity trade was in surplus, although perhaps somewhat less than the official Russian trade statistics would have us believe. This does not mean that the balance of payments was in surplus. Although we lack the necessary systematic data on Russia's "invisible" imports and payments for various types of services (freight, insurance, etc.), there is available a great deal of evidence that the balance of payments on current account was in deficit. The fact that Russia was also a major borrower of foreign capital—imported either for the construction of Russia's overhead capital (primarily railroads) and the development of its mining and manufacturing industries, or for meeting the budgetary obligations of the state and maintaining a gold reserve for its currency—indicates that the interest and dividend payments for the foreign debt had a tendency to grow, thus offsetting surpluses in the trade balance.

The above situation explains, at least in part, the preoccupation with the trade balance by high-ranking Russian policymakers. Perhaps an additional reason for fostering exports could be traced to the notion on the part of the policymakers that the demand for domestically produced goods was limited and thus income which could be earned from exports would not accrue if the goods were offered in the domestic market. This notion of the limited purchasing power and lagging domestic demand, regardless whether it accurately reflected the existing situation, or, as some critics of the Russian government claimed was in fact a result of the state's economic policies, played some role in the tendency for exports to increase. If one added Russia's comparative advantage in producing agricultural products (which also might have been a myth) and the vision of Russia's industrialization, the policy of export expansion becomes at least understandable if not necessarily optimal. Therefore, the Russian government tried to encourage exports by the use of most of the weapons in its arsenal: 1) outright export subsidies; 2) assignments of export quotas; 3) lower freight rates to the ports; 4) low interest loans to exporters; and 5) bargaining about lowering tariffs on Russian exports before signing commercial treaties.

The government pursued a policy on imports that was consistent with its encouragement of exports. In general, the Russian government, after a short flirtation with liberal policies became committed to a protectionist policy which persisted during most of the period beginning with the middle of the 1870s.

Perhaps the best summary of the Russian imperial tariff policy was provided by the outstanding authority in the field, M. N. Sobolev,[10] who noted that out of the three main objectives in its tariff policy, the government was consistently successful in one, the fiscal objective of raising revenue. As far as protection for the young Russian industries, the tariff was moderately effective; with respect to the objective of discouraging imports of foreign consumer goods, the Russian population assumed the consumption costs of the tariff, similar to the consumption costs of the tariff-protected domestic industry. Thus, Sobolev found very little of redeeming value in Russian tariff policies. The main objectives could perhaps have been achieved by the use of other means that would have had less of a distorting effect on the allocation of resources in the Russian economy.

The Stock of Money and Monetary Policy

Government policy pertaining to the stock of money was conservative, characterized by attempts to keep it as stable as possible. The fact that the stock of money did not necessarily behave as the policymakers would wish was due either to such exogenous variables as wars, financing deficits, and famine relief, on the one hand, and to the behavior of the commercial banks that contributed their share to the stock of money, on the other.

Economists, depending on the objectives of their study, define the stock of money in a number of conventional measures with various degrees of inclusiveness. Given the availability of data for the stock of money in Russia, one can define it either as the amount of currency in circulation, or as the amount of currency plus demand and time deposits in commercial banks, or as the sum of the two aforementioned plus the current accounts in commercial banks, which by their nature were not dissimilar to bank deposits.

Table 1.22 presents data on the various definitions of the stock of money that are available from secondary sources. The following discussion, however, will be limited to the pattern that emerges from the definition of the stock of money as the sum of currency in circulation, and bank deposits and current accounts in the private commercial banks for the period 1875–1914. For the earlier period the data are not complete, and the inclusion of the liabilities of the State Bank might introduce double counting that is difficult to assess without access to the yearly reports of the State Bank.

The growth of the stock of money is presented in table 1.23 which shows the distribution of growth within particular time periods. The significance of the overall growth of the stock of money cannot be assessed in the absence of other important indicators, such as the velocity of money in circulation or the relation of the stock of money to the GNP of Russia. It is, however, possible to indicate the growth of the stock of money on a per capita basis, although one ought to beware of reaching sweeping conclusions in the absence of data on the income distribution of the population or even on the occupational structure of the population during this period. Therefore, table 1.24 is of limited analytical value, although it might provide some comparative perspectives for both Russia and other countries. The table reveals that on a per capita basis the stock of money hardly increased until 1900, and it was only subsequently that it began to increase appreciably. It also indicates rather vividly the effect of the deflationary policies of the 1880s and underscores the growth of the 1890s, which although not spectacular, nevertheless indicated a reversal of the trend prevailing during the 1880s.

Currency made up a very substantial component of the stock of money.

In spite of the overall growth and the growth pattern which differed between the periods, there was a relative stability of the share of currency for most of the period, with the notable exception of 1908–14 (see table 1.25). It is also interesting to note that this preponderance of a high share of currency in the stock of money existed during the periods of inflation, but also persisted during the period of deflationary policies of the 1880s. The distribution of the elements of the stock of money during the period 1900–1908 can probably be explained by the coincidence of a business contraction at the beginning of the period and an expansion of the supply of currency during and as a result of the Russo-Japanese War. In a certain sense the data would indicate that the coming of age of the Russian banking system, as far as its impact on the stock of money was concerned, began around 1908 and lasted a very short period. It is, therefore, necessary to concentrate on the supply of currency in order to understand the growth pattern and changes in the stock of money.

As the detailed table of the stock of money indicates (see table 1.22), during and in connection with major wars the supply of currency in Russia increased. During the 1850s, after the major bank reforms and abortive attempts to introduce a convertible currency, the amount of currency in circulation reached 664.1 million rubles. During the next decade, until 1876, the amount of currency in circulation increased by about 100 million rubles. (Although it was a decade of intensive railroad building and other investments in overhead capital, they were financed by foreign loans and domestic savings and not primarily by the printing press.) But the Balkan War raised the amount of currency to 1,153 million by 1879, the highest level of currency in circulation prior to the introduction of the gold standard in 1897. The decade of the 1880s marked a definite deflationary trend, characterized by attempts to reduce and curtail the amount of currency at about a level of 900 million rubles. Although this policy was not entirely successful for every single year, its failure was due to budget deficits rather than to a change of heart of the policymakers. The decade of the 1890s, one of rapid industrial growth, witnessed a rather modest growth of currency in circulation, from 928 million to 1,277 million rubles, or 37.6 per cent; the second half of the decade accounting for most of the growth. The next major rise in the amount of currency was related to the Russo-Japanese War, when it rose from 1,486 million rubles in 1904 to 2,179 million in 1906. The government subsequently tried to lower it by 10–15 per cent or to maintain it at the already achieved level until the 1906 level was surpassed in 1912. It would thus appear that the decisions originating in the Ministry of Finance with regard to the amount of currency in circulation were in most cases responses to such "exogenous" factors as budget deficits, war financing, or balance of payments problems;

43

Table 1.22A   Money Supply in Russia, 1861–1914 (Millions of Rubles)

	State Bank Currency in Circulation*	State Bank Private Deposits and Current Accounts	Joint Stock Commercial Banks Deposits and Current Accounts	Municipal Banks Deposits and Current Accounts	Mutual Credit Associations Deposits and Current Accounts	Exchange Banks Deposits and Current Accounts	Other	Total Private Banks, Deposits and Current Accounts	Total Private Banks and State Bank Deposits and Current Accounts
1861	713.0	32.0							
1862	713.6	112.9							
1863	691.1	151.2							
1864	636.5	157.9	1.4						
1865	664.1	164.3	3.3						
1866	661.6	170.8	4.4						
1867	697.2	164.0	6.5						
1868	674.9	154.5	23.4						
1869	702.8	181.9	77.7						
1870	694.4	198.8	99.4						
1871	694.1	171.2	170.2						
1872	752.0	174.1	234.8						
1873	748.3	193.4	274.5						
1874	774.0	206.0	299.7						
1875	763.9	224.7	277.7	115.1	110.6			525.1	749.8
1876	751.6	261.5	227.3	134.8	107.3			519.0	780.5
1877	766.9	229.6	274.6	140.0	104.1			471.1	700.7
1878	1014.4	265.6	254.3	149.1	120.9			544.8	810.4
1879	1132.5	258.0	197.0	163.1	90.2			501.5	759.5
1880	1129.9	224.8	206.9	171.7	84.5			447.8	672.6
1881	1085.1	223.4	227.0	206.2	112.8			525.9	749.3
1882	1028.1	229.1	210.5					525.9	749.3
1883	973.2	259.7	213.6						
1884	959.3	264.7	219.2						
1885	899.8	290.7	264.2						
1886	906.7	319.7							

1887	941.0	288.0	255.1						
1888	971.2	263.6	235.0						
1889	973.1	249.5	211.6						
1890	928.4	224.6	230.1						
1891	907.4	233.9	287.7						
1892	1054.8	231.8	319.5						
1893	1074.1	226.5	285.4	89.9	115.1	13.6		506.0	732.5
1894	1071.9	207.3	267.8	86.7	103.9	13.6		472.0	679.3
1895	1047.1	197.7	307.7	87.2	109.6	12.7		517.2	714.9
1896	1055.3	185.8	305.2	87.2	115.3	15.8		523.5	709.3
1897	1133.8	199.3	354.0	87.2	125.6	15.8		582.6	781.9
1898	1127.7	205.8	448.1	88.8	143.7	19.9		704.5	910.3
1899	1234.7	204.2	551.3	94.5	166.3	21.7		842.6	1046.8
1900	1277.8	195.6	547.9	97.0	168.1	21.3		849.7	1049.3
1901	1383.8	167.6	536.1	97.3	177.9	22.4	3.9	850.4	1019.0
1902	1376.9	183.9	544.9	98.0	179.8	25.2	8.8	872.1	1036.0
1903	1422.9	257.3	613.3	103.9	198.2	25.6	15.4	972.9	1230.4
1904	1485.4	231.0	722.1	106.6	213.6	25.5	16.7	1105.3	1396.1
1905	1660.3	255.1	775.6	108.7	214.6	24.4	24.2	1160.3	1415.1
1906	2178.7	263.8	671.4	108.4	190.0	24.2	31.9	1048.7	1312.5
1907	1956.3	249.2	760.9	108.8	202.8	27.7	37.3	1170.5	1419.7
1908	1896.7	231.1	818.1	111.4	228.9	26.0	37.3	1235.0	1466.9
1909	1758.7	309.7	976.8	115.8	270.1	30.4	34.7	1445.6	1759.9
1910	1867.2	273.7	1262.2	128.3	329.5	32.2	34.7	1851.3	2125.2
1911	1992.1	261.3	1675.1	146.1	405.7	34.9	70.3	2261.1	2522.4
1912	2099.9	258.3	1817.3	166.0	487.3	35.7	51.3	2506.3	2764.6
1913	2244.0	266.0	2293.3	183.5	545.0	35.6	52.5	3058.4	3324.4
1914	2231.6	244.9	2539.0	198.3	595.3	31.9	99.3	3364.3	3627.6

*Through 1896 only bank notes; from 1897 bank notes, gold, and silver.

Table 1.22B Money Supply in Russia, 1861–1914 (million rubles)

	Money Stock (1) Currency in Circulation	Total Deposits and Current Accounts of Private Banks	Total of (1) and (2)	Money Stock (2) State Bank Deposits and Current Accounts	Total of (3) and (4)	State Bank Savings and Institutions Deposits	Treasury Special Funds and Deposits	Treasury Current Accounts	Treasury Total [(7) + (8)]
1861	713.0			32.0			30.3		30.3
1862	713.6			112.9			33.1		33.1
1863	691.1			151.2		8.5	42.2		42.2
1864	636.3			157.9		3.5	62.4		62.4
1865	664.1			164.3		1.5	40.3		40.3
1866	661.6			170.8		1.1	40.4		40.4
1867	697.2			164.0		0.5	32.1		32.1
1868	674.9			154.5		0.5	48.7		48.7
1869	702.8			181.9		0.7	50.0		50.0
1870	694.4			198.8		0.4	42.5		42.5
1871	694.1			171.2		0.3	56.4		56.4
1872	752.0			174.1		0.2	32.4		32.4
1873	748.3			193.4		0.5	16.9		16.9
1874	774.0			206.0		0.2	17.3		17.3
1875	763.9	525.1	1289.0	224.7	1513.7	0.7	30.3		30.3
1876	751.6	519.0	1270.6	261.5	1532.1	1.0	48.2		48.2
1877	766.9	471.2	1238.0	229.6	1467.6	0.1	60.0		60.0
1878	1014.4	544.8	1559.2	263.6	1824.8	0.5	38.8		38.8
1879	1152.5	501.5	1654.0	238.0	1912.0	1.0	30.4		30.4
1880	1129.9	447.8	1577.7	224.8	1802.5	0.8	42.1		42.1
1881	1085.1	525.9	1611.0	223.4	1834.4	0.8	38.9		38.9
1882	1028.1			229.1		0.4	35.3	34.5	69.8
1883	973.7			259.7		0.2	39.2	19.2	58.4
1884	959.3			264.7		0.5	41.3	37.0	78.3
1885	899.8			290.7		0.4	41.2	24.3	65.5
1886	906.7			319.7		0.5	45.0	26.8	71.8

Year									
1887	941.0			288.0		1.4	91.9	25.9	117.8
1888	971.2			263.6		1.5	88.3	78.8	167.1
1889	973.1			249.5		1.5	86.0	79.0	165.0
1890	928.4			224.6		2.7	92.1	69.9	162.0
1891	907.4			233.9		3.7	139.9	59.7	199.6
1892	1054.8			231.8		17.9	175.3	28.8	204.1
1893	1074.1	306.0	1380.1	226.3	1806.6	52.4	108.6	39.1	147.7
1894	1071.9	472.0	1543.9	207.3	1751.2	74.3	110.7	61.3	172.0
1895	1047.7	517.2	1564.9	197.7	1762.6	50.7	154.6	176.4	331.0
1896	1055.5	523.3	1578.8	185.8	1764.6	46.7	171.9	151.7	323.6
1897	1133.8	582.6	1716.4	199.3	1915.7	27.9	89.6	242.8	332.4
1898	1127.7	704.5	1832.2	205.8	2038.0	73.0	130.4	288.7	419.1
1899	1234.7	842.6	2077.3	204.2	2281.5	8.3	141.4	330.2	471.6
1900	1277.8	849.7	2127.5	195.6	2322.1	23.0	144.6	449.4	594.0
1901	1383.8	850.4	2234.2	167.6	2401.8	23.9	146.2	333.6	479.8
1902	1376.9	872.1	2249.0	183.9	2431.9	84.4	136.9	347.4	484.3
1903	1422.9	972.4	2396.0	257.3	2653.3	114.5	167.1	186.9	354.0
1904	1485.4	1105.1	2590.5	231.0	2261.5	69.7	179.2	374.4	553.6
1905	1660.3	1140.0	2820.3	255.1	3075.4	43.7	177.0	174.2	351.2
1906	2178.7	1048.7	3227.4	263.8	3491.2	—	169.8	93.9	263.7
1907	1956.3	1170.5	3126.8	249.2	3375.0	36.4	202.8	98.3	301.1
1908	1876.7	1255.8	3132.5	231.1	3353.6	51.3	206.0	151.4	357.4
1909	1758.7	1445.6	3204.3	309.7	3514.0	52.0	211.5	221.0	432.5
1910	1867.2	1851.5	3718.7	273.7	3992.4	37.7	252.9	174.3	427.2
1911	1992.1	2261.1	4253.2	261.3	4514.5	24.0	275.3	375.9	651.2
1912	2099.9	2306.3	4406.2	258.3	4864.5	18.3	303.1	353.9	657.0
1913	2244.0	3058.4	5302.4	266.0	5568.4	15.1	344.6	528.3	872.9
1914	2281.6	3364.5	5646.1	263.1	5909.2	13.8	343.3	607.9	951.2

**Table 1.23   Growth of the Stock of Money in Russia
(in Millions of Rubles)**

Years	Growth during Period	% Increase during Period
(January 1)		
1875–81	322	25
1881–93	– 18	– 1
1893–1900	535	34
1900–1908	1,006	47
1908–14	2,396	76
1875–1914	4,241	329

Table 1.24   Per Capita Stock of Money (in Rubles)

Year	Stock of Money (in millions of rubles)	Population Estimate (in millions)	Per Capita Stock of Money (in rubles)
1875	1,289	90.2	14.29
1878	1,560	93.0	16.77
1881	1,611	100.1	16.09
1893	1,593	121.5	13.11
1900	2,128	131.7	16.16
1908	3,134	146.9	21.33
1914	5,530	165.1	33.49

Table 1.25   Percentage Distribution of the Components of the Money Stock

Year (at Jan. 1)	Currency	Demand Deposits Joint-Stock Banks	Demand Deposits Other Private Banks
1875	59.3	23.3	17.4
1878	65.1	17.6	17.3
1881	67.3	12.8	19.8
1893	67.4	17.9	14.6
1900	60.0	25.8	14.2
1908	60.5	26.1	13.4
1914	41.3	44.4	14.3

the Ministry was sufficiently strong to resist increasing the supply of currency out of a fear of inflation.

A much more complex problem is that of attitudes and actions on the part of the commercial banks with respect to their discretion, circumscribed as it was, in creating money or money substitutes.

The data on deposits and current accounts of the commercial banks for the period 1875–93, that span both the growth of the supply of currency of 1877–78 and the subsequent period of contraction of currency supply of the 1880s, indicate a virtually unchanged amount of commercial bank liabilities. This may reflect the banks' inability to attract deposits during the inflationary period as well as their reluctance or inability to expand during the period of deflationary pressures. However, during the period of industrial expansion, between 1893 and 1900, the growth of deposits and current accounts exceeded the expansion of the currency, and this factor indicates, at least in part, one of the underlying sources of industrial expansion. The period of relative economic stagnation that followed the industrial spurt of the 1890s, and lasted in Russia from 1900 to at least 1908, was marked not only by the expansion of the supply of currency as a result of war financing of 1904–5 but also by a further increase of the commercial bank resources that grew primarily through the expansion of current accorʷnts against the collateral of securities. This particular phenomenon can perhaps in part be attributed to the need for replenishing a part of the capital stock in industry and any additions to the capital stock that were made in view of rising wages as a result of the revolution of 1905. Obviously the above-mentioned reasons do not exhaust the range of explanations for the growth of bank deposits, and additional research might shed new light on this interesting problem.

The period of 1908–14, which I would surmise bears witness to the maturation of the Russian banking system, very much resembled the period of 1893–1900, but this time with an overwhelming role played by the commercial banks that were primarily responsible for providing the resources to sustain an unprecedented boom of the Russian economy, with both deposits and current accounts increasing at high rates.

One more comment is required with respect to the stock of money. Given the relative stability of the share of currency in circulation at least until 1908, would it not be reasonable to restrict the definition of the stock of money to currency in circulation and measure the growth of the money stock by the use of an index of currency alone? My choice would still be for a measure, uniform over time, that could cover the whole period, 1908–14 included. But it is necessary to add that a definition of the stock of money restricted to currency in circulation assumes implicitly that no payments were made by checks drawn against deposits or current accounts. It would be my contention that this cannot be assumed for twentieth-century Russia. It is in fact correct that our data on this matter are far from complete; however, evidence from the clearing offices set up by the State Bank and used by the major banking institutions indicate a high volume of transactions conducted by checks and drawings against current accounts (see table 1.26). The order of magnitude for the recent years of the period cannot be ignored in the consideration of a definition of the stock of money.

The discussion on the development pattern of the stock of money, in-

Table 1.26 Development of Clearings and Payments by Checks through the Clearinghouse of the State Bank (in Millions of Rubles)

Year	Claims	Cleared by Counterclaims	Paid by Checks and Accounts
1899	1,838.7	1,250.1	588.5
1901	2,974.7	2,026.2	948.5
1903	4,770.3	3,431.8	1,338.5
1905	6,336.9	4,528.1	1,808.8
1907	6,697.4	4,916.0	1,781.4
1909	9,884.7	7,003.3	2,881.4
1911	15,409.2	10,773.1	4,636.1
1913	21,431.3	15,426.4	6,004.9

Sources: I. N. Slansky, ed., *Gosudarstvennyi bank. Kratkii ocherk deiatel'nosti za 1860–1910 gody* (St. Peterburg, 1910), p. 20. Gosudarstvennyi Bank, *Otchet za 1913 g. (LIV)* (St. Petersburg, 1914), p. 38.

cluding its components, would be incomplete without a short review of the monetary policies followed by the Russian government that would elaborate in greater detail some of the remarks made about the currency. The Russian monetary system underwent considerable change during the period 1860–1913, of which the most pronounced was the official adoption of the gold standard in 1897. During the earlier part of the period, prior to 1897, the prevailing monetary unit, called the *credit ruble,* represented a nonconvertible paper currency, defined in terms of quantity of silver that it was supposed to represent. This particular unit, established during 1839–40, in turn replaced a paper currency, the *assignat ruble,* that dominated the Russian money market from the 1780s to 1840. The *credit ruble* very soon depreciated inside Russia and fluctuated widely below par on the foreign exchanges. The credit ruble was made convertible during a short period of the early 1860s, but as a result of the loss of foreign exchange and precious metals the attempt was aborted. Thus, the credit ruble was not supported by a fixed amount of a reserve of precious metals; its exchange rate abroad fluctuated; and all foreign indebtedness was cleared by transfers of precious metals or foreign currencies. While the credit ruble circulated in Russia either as a Treasury note or as a note of the State Bank, both the unit of account and the medium of settling foreign debts remained the so-called metallic ruble, or the original standard of the credit ruble as a multiple of silver coins. The Russian government was not indifferent, however, to the exchange rate and engaged quite often and extensively in operations designed to manipulate it, especially on the Berlin exchange where there was a lively trade in Russian currency and Treasury notes.

At the same time, public opinion was divided on the problem of governmental monetary policy. Although this is not the place for a detailed analysis of the views and attitudes of the various social and political groups on this subject, the general impression of the intensive discussions in the Russian press and journals can be summarized. Those who considered themselves "liberals" favored convertibility of the ruble and a conservative anti-inflationist policy until convertibility; whereas the "conservatives" by-and-large favored a free hand for the government in increasing the amount of currency in circulation. Faced with such divergent views, it is no wonder that the policy often appeared inconsistent; the generally anti-inflationary bias of the government policies would nevertheless indicate a measure of independence from public opinion.

The government decision to adopt the gold standard during the 1890s was, to a large extent, motivated by the need to facilitate foreign trade, to provide greater certainty and protection to foreign lenders of capital, as well as to simplify government operations in the area of the national debt held by foreigners. The decision in favor of gold rather than in favor of a bimetallic standard was in part influenced by the recent experience of other European countries which adopted the gold standard, and in part by the movements of the relative price ratios of silver and gold.

The adoption of the gold standard in Russia had two features worth mentioning. First, it was preceded by a long process of building up a substantial gold reserve, primarily through a favorable balance of foreign trade and by huge foreign loans provided in convertible currencies. Second, the value of the ruble in terms of gold was fixed at the prevailing exchange rate of the credit ruble, which for all practical purposes meant an official devaluation of the ruble to two-thirds of its previous nominal value in terms of precious metals. In addition, very conservative and strict provisions were adopted with respect to the maintenance of a gold reserve. The required gold reserve was to cover 50 per cent of the first 600 million rubles of the new State Bank notes and 100 per cent for any amount of paper notes above this level. The requirement of maintaining such a substantial gold reserve raises the problem of the costs of convertibility in terms of the alternatives to which an excess reserve could have been put. And although there is no reason to deny the considerable costs of the convertibility of the ruble, one ought not to dismiss the benefits of the gold standard. A brief list of such benefits would include the increased security provided to foreign investors, the decrease of transaction costs in foreign trade, and a narrowing of the fluctuations of the value of the ruble by letting the gold standard mechanism correct the changes in relative purchasing power of the ruble and other currencies.

Two more observations might be pertinent to the monetary policies under the gold standard. First, the gold reserves of the State Bank and Ministry of Finance kept on growing beyond the required levels, which led the institutions to maintain reserves of gold and foreign exchange abroad, supposedly for the purpose of facilitating transactions, but actually in part at least to support the ruble on foreign exchanges in order to raise the confidence of foreign creditors. Second, gold coins were introduced into circulation on a massive scale, a curious development that could be explained more in terms of Russia's cultural backwardness than economic necessity. Perhaps there was a need to meet the psychological demand for a "stable" currency on the part of Russian peasants and petty businessmen by minting and circulating hundreds of millions worth of gold coins. If this interpretation is correct, the monetary authorities of Russia displayed not only a good understanding of the demand for money by increasing the money supply on a cyclical basis around the time of the harvest and heaviest trade in grains, but also an understanding that a price has to be paid to create a climate of trust in their new monetary system.

Historians and economists disagree with regard to their appraisal of Russian monetary policy, especially with respect to whether the anti-inflationist bias was detrimental to the growth of the Russian economy. Without trying to resolve the controversy, which would require a separate treatment and comprehensive analysis of monetary, fiscal, and investment policies, one observation might be in order. The architects of Russian monetary policies were not simply ordinary managers of the Russian currency; their functions as ministers of finance included responsibility for monitoring and determining the whole area of government economic policies. It is true that their measures required in some instances the approval of the State Council and, in most cases, of the Emperor; therefore they cannot be absolved of the mistakes and inconsistencies of the whole set of economic policies, and could not claim that monetary policy could be at loggerheads with the policies in adjacent areas. If this analysis is correct, the anti-inflationary bias was probably detrimental to accelerated economic growth. The major question, however, remains: to what extent was economic growth an exclusive goal, overriding the goals of internal political stability and military political aggrandizement in the area of foreign relations? The answer is outside the scope of this essay.

The Banking System

Although the monetary system and monetary policies of the government had a profound impact on the functioning of the banking system in Russia, it is still possible to draw a distinction between the two and to focus on the prevailing banking institutions that both collected the savings of the population and served as intermediaries in the transactions between borrowers and lenders in the Russian economy.

In a purely formal or legal sense, one can distinguish three basic types of institutions operating in the field of banking. The first and foremost were the government banks, with the State Bank, *Gosudarstvennyi Bank,* at the center of the system. The State Bank was simultaneously a bank of issue, the chief agent of the Treasury, a central bank, and a commercial bank. The two other government banks were basically land mortgage banks: the Nobility Bank specialized in loans to landowners and members of the Russian nobility; the Peasant Bank provided credits for land acquisition or resold purchased land to the peasants (individuals or associations). Both the Nobility and Peasant banks derived their capital from bond issues floated periodically, whose yields were guaranteed by the government. Both operated under supervision of the respective government departments concerned with problems of rural credit. While the State Bank was set up in 1860, and in accordance with the spirit of the "Great Reforms," took over the assets and liabilities of the previous institutions, the Nobility and Peasant Banks both started their operations in the 1880s. The savings institutions, *Sberegatel'nye Kassy,* were another type of government banking institution that developed an urban network in the 1860s and extended their activities in the rural areas by the early 1880s. Their network consisted either of separate offices or of adjuncts to the postal offices, where they accepted deposits, paid interest or made payments against savings accounts. They collected the savings of a large number of small savers, kept their balances in the State Bank offices, and invested the savings in a portfolio that consisted of a variety of government loans, government-guaranteed securities, like railroad bonds, and bonds of the Nobility and Peasant Banks. Thus, ultimately the savings of these institutions augmented the flow of funds into the economic activities of the state or state-supported sectors of the economy with particular reference to state-guaranteed securities.

The second category of banking institutions comprised the commercial banks, operating both as private and joint stock companies. The first joint stock commercial banks were founded in the 1870s but achieved prominence only in the 1890s. They were organized along the model of German commercial banks and started out with modest amounts of share capital as well as a relatively modest volume of deposits. The area of their activity was primarily the discount of short term commercial paper before they embarked on a wide use of current accounts as a form of extending credits for both short term and long term loans to firms engaged in commercial and industrial activities. It was only upon reaching a certain level of maturity and relative success that the Russian joint stock commercial banks were able to secure for themselves credits with foreign banks and with the Russian State Bank, both of which contributed to the subsequent rapid growth of this type of bank. Joint stock land banks provided mortgage credits for the rural sector of the economy. Their activities were complementary to the activities of the state-sponsored land banks and, by providing loans against urban real estate assets, they complemented the activities of emerging municipal banks.

The third category of banking institutions embraces a relatively large number of cooperative banks and mutual assistance institutions, the so-called small credit sector in which small savers pooled resources in order to provide themselves with short term credits, in many cases borrowers who might constitute either too large a risk for the commercial banks or where the costs of the transactions might be too high by comparison with the expected return at the customary rates of interest. The growth of such institutions of "small credit" was impressive in terms of their clientele. After the turn of the century, the State Bank served many of them by rediscounting their commercial loans or providing them with credit.

Thus one of the characteristics of the Russian banking system was the degree of specialization of the various banks. Land mortgage credit was provided by the private land banks and by the two government-sponsored land banks. Commercial credit for trade and industry was provided by the joint stock and private banking institutions, engaged in the discount of commercial paper and later in lending for industrial investment. Typically, credit for wholesale traders and industrialists would be provided by the joint stock and private banks, while credit for retail traders, artisans, as well as for some categories of the peasantry (for loans other than land acquisition) would be provided by mutual credit associations and other institutions labeled in the contemporary terminology as institutions of "small credit." To a large extent the relative size of the share and reserve capital of the banking institutions was congruent with the relative size of the demand for credit on the part of their respective clientele.

It might not be fair to pose the question of the extent to which the banks met the need for credit on the part of the business community or the various sectors of the Russian economy. We know that the banking system, as described, was a strictly post-emancipation phenomenon, that there was hardly any tradition of banking (except for land banks) providing loans to an economy that was diversifying and industrializing, where capital was scarce relative to the economically advanced countries of Western Europe. The Russian government exercised control over the various activities of the newly established institutions. The world financial crisis of 1873 dampened bolder attempts to expand the areas of bank activities for some time. Thus, the proverbial conservatism of bankers was reinforced by a traumatic experience at the very beginning of modern banking in Russia.

Nevertheless, the overall impression one gets by looking a little closer at the operations of the Russian banks is that the banking policies were directed toward meeting the demands for short term and long term credits in the economy. It is true that in terms of territorial coverage the major commercial and industrial centers prevailed by getting perhaps more than their share of credit for industrial production or trade. Perhaps there were economies of scale that influenced the flow of funds to such places as St. Petersburg, Moscow, Odessa, Baku, and Warsaw at the expense of other less commercialized areas. But, after all, the Russian bankers were not necessarily the initiators of regional economic development, but operated in a milieu in which location was a dependent variable in their profit maximizing calculations.

For a better understanding of the development of the Russian banking system, it is necessary to view it against the background of long term savings on the part of the population. Unfortunately we have continuous data for the period 1893–1914 only and primarily for government-issued and government-guaranteed securities and for joint stock land banks and urban real estate mortgage banks. Nevertheless, in spite of their incompleteness (of which the share capital of industrial and commercial enterprises is the most obvious omission), such data provide an approximation of the growth of the long term savings pattern in Russia (see table 1.27).

It is worth noting that while government bonds increased from 1,405 to 3,445 million rubles, and guaranteed railroad bonds from 174 to 690 million rubles, the volume of the state-controlled land banks (the Nobility and the Peasant Banks) increased from 264 to 1,851 million rubles from January 1893 to January 1914. Thus, out of the enumerated total of 9,377 millions of long term securities held by Russian investors on January 1, 1914, 4,999 were invested in rural land and urban real estate. This indi-

Table 1.27 Long-term Savings Pattern as Reflected by Domestic Holdings of Securities (in Millions of Rubles)

Year (Jan.)	State Bonds & Guaranteed Loans	Mortgage Bonds	Total	Increase	% Increase	Yearly Av. (mill. rubles)
1893	2,273	1,225	3,498			
1896	2,610	1,336	3,946	448	13	149.3
1899	2,938	1,622	4,560	614	16	204.6
1902	3,382	1,970	5,352	792	18	264.0
1905	3,912	2,230	6,142	790	15	263.3
1908	4,906	2,224	7,130	988	16	329.3
1911	5,505	2,561	8,066	936	13	312.0
1914	6,237	3,140	9,377	1,311	16	437.0

cates the quest for security on the part of the Russian investors, in view of increasing land prices during the period under consideration, as well as the demand for investments in agriculture, and it reveals one of the sources of growth of capital in agriculture. In view of the existing demand for investible funds on the part of the land banks and the government, it was necessary for industrial enterprises to present a profit record that would make them an attractive alternative in the minds of potential or actual investors. It was the demand for capital on the part of the industrial sector that indirectly pushed them to demand a higher level of protection as one of the means to ensure a higher profit rate as a source for dividend payments. One also has to realize that bank loans to industrial enterprises marshalled a higher interest rate than the discount rate for commercial paper. Thus for most of the period, credit to industrial enterprises was more expensive than to some other categories of borrowers.

One other comment may be warranted. Not all of the domestically held securities originated with the rich. By the end of our period more than one-sixth of the enumerated securities and certainly a much higher proportion of the state bonds and state-guaranteed bonds were purchased by the savings institutions that typically collected the savings of private and government lower-level employees, workers, and peasants. A portfolio of about 1,671 million rubles of securities held by the savings banks was one of the forms in which the lower-income groups contributed, if not to the development of the credit system, then certainly to capital accumulation in Russia.

The utilization of long term securities for the creation of credit by the banking system started on a larger scale by the middle of the 1890s and provided an excellent opportunity for the expansion of operations by the commercial banks. Originally the share of dealings in long term securities by the commercial banks was very limited indeed, although some of them began already in the 1890s to underwrite various government-guaranteed loans and cooperate in floating some non-guaranteed securities. However, it was not until the beginning of the twentieth century that the commercial banks started to play an increasingly active and prominent role in the credit market. Their growth, which started during the years of stagnation following the turn of the century, became most pronounced during the period of the Russian-Japanese War (1904–5) and especially during the boom years preceding World War I.

The instrument of their expansionist activity was not primarily their own share capital or the growth of demand and time deposits, but, following the German model, the expansion of current accounts provided credits against the collateral of securities and similar assets. The current accounts were a more flexible instrument of credit creation than the time and demand deposits. They were used to provide credits of different time patterns of which one of the most widely used was the "on call" loan.[11] These became increasingly widespread as instruments of short term lending for commercial transactions. Current accounts created against securities and other effects were also instrumental in the acquisition by the bank clientele of non guaranteed securities floated with the assistance of the commercial banks. Thus, in such a manner the current accounts created by the commercial banks not only served the needs of short term borrowings, but they gradually increased the volume of long term investment capital either by the promotion of corporation shares and bonds or by direct long term lending to industrial entrepreneurs. The current accounts were not only significant as a reflection of a more "liberal" credit policy, but they also directly contributed to the increased use of inter-firm clearings and the payments by check or note against current accounts. The sum of such practices and uses of current accounts decreased the transaction costs of firms and individuals and stimulated the further growth of the volume of transactions handled by the banking institutions. Thus, the massive use of securities as a collateral for borrowings marked an intensification in the use of savings that did not violate the preferences of savers for security but enabled the more enterprising among them to use their savings for additional instruments or for diversification of their asset portfolios.

It would be erroneous, however, to attribute the expansion of the private banks solely to the use of current accounts created by the banks themselves. The expansion of the private banks was also due to the credits provided to them by the Russian State Bank and by some foreign banks. The role of the State Bank in supporting the private banks against runs of depositors in times of economic crisis or uncertainty is known and does not require elaboration. However, largely as a result of changes in the statutes of the State Bank and in accordance with its role as a central bank, the volume of credits to the private banks was expanded, congruent with the growth of the banking institutions in Russia. The chief instruments of support by the State Bank took the form of lending against current accounts and promissory notes of the private banks, loans against securities, and rediscounting of commercial paper.

The data in table 1.28, beginning with 1895, provide some insight into the turnover of State Bank credits to the private banks. Thus, the private banks, owing to the support from the State Bank and the liberalization of credit policy, grew and extended their operations to serve the financial needs of the various sectors of the Russian economy. Within the private banking institutions, the commanding heights were occupied by the large joint stock commercial banks that not only amassed a large volume of assets, but extended the bulk of credits to Russian business. Gradually, the

Table 1.28   Yearly Total Turnover of State Bank Credits to Private Banks
(in Millions of Rubles)

Year	No. Private Banks (includ-ing branches) Served	Lending against Current Accounts & Promissory Notes	Lending against Securities	Rediscount of Commercial Paper	Total Lending
1895	237	181.0	20.1	85.6	287
1898	281	145.2	42.0	106.0	293
1901	339	468.4	165.4	230.0	883
1904	427	369.9	60.9	230.1	687
1907	515	922.7	134.0	238.1	1,330
1910	741	1,305.8	272.0	268.4	1,930
1913	1,071	2,777.8	1,037.7	556.7	4,530

Sources: I. N. Slansky, ed., *Gosudarstvennyi bank. Kratkii ocherk deiatel'nosti za 1860–1910 gody* (St. Petersburg, 1910), p. 54. Gosudarstvennyi Bank, *Otchet za 1913* (St. Petersburg, 1914), p. 14.

Russian commercial banks took over the task of financing Russian invest-ments in areas where previously the main reliance was either on foreign capital or on the government.

This brings us to an appraisal of the role of the Russian government, or more specifically the Treasury, in the realm of Russian banking. Apart from the area of statutory regulation of the various types of banks, its most direct impact was on the policies of the State Bank. Leaving aside the "persuasive recommendations" of the Ministry of Finance, under whose jurisdiction the Treasury, *Kaznacheistvo,* found itself, to grant extraordi-nary loans to selected individuals and firms, the financial dealings between the Treasury and the State Bank are obviously of major importance. It would probably be no exaggeration to maintain that well into the 1880s the Treasury was a net debtor of the Bank, thus forcing the State Bank to use its resources otherwise earmarked for commercial operations in order to support the Treasury accounts. Although Treasury deposits appear every year on the books of the State Bank, a closer examination of its foreign exchange and domestic currency operations reveals this inescapable con-clusion. Therefore, the claim by historians or the inference by economists about the Treasury's contribution to the development and expansion of the banking system in Russia can only be applicable to the period of the 1890s and afterward.

A closer examination of the available data, however, casts some serious doubts even on this inference. The so-called Treasury deposits consisted basically of two categories:

1. Special deposits, represented largely by government securities;

2. current accounts, reflecting some features of the cash flow of the government budget.

As can be seen from tables 1.29 and 1.30, the relative shares of these two types of deposits varied over time. But in addition, the quality of the two types for use by the State Bank in extending loans varied greatly. So, for example, the average number of days for a current account deposit by the Treasury in the State Bank was 29 days in 1909 and 38 days in 1910, while the average for the special deposits was 141 days in 1909 and 156 days in 1910.

It is also necessary to keep in mind that the state budget was for most of the period in deficit and could be balanced only with the help of two sources of revenue: 1) the gross revenue of the state railroads, and 2) by foreign loans. While the first source had its peculiar seasonal patterns (just like the seasonal patterns of the other major revenue sources—the alcohol tax and the custom duties), the foreign loans were not seasonally or otherwise predictable and could hardly be synchronized with the pattern of current government expenditures. What follows, therefore, are fluctuations of the volume of Treasury current accounts within each year that would make it difficult for the State Bank to adjust its own volume of lending unless the lowest volume of the Treasury's current accounts is

Table 1.29   Balance of Treasury Deposits with the State Bank for Selected Years (in Millions of Rubles, on January 1)

Year	Balance	Year	Balance
1892	204	1903	354
1893	147	1904	553
1897	332	1905	351
1898	419	1910	427
1902	499	1911	651

Table 1.30   Balance of the Treasury's Current Accounts with the State Bank for Selected Years (in Millions of Rubles, on January 1)

Year	Balance	Year	Balance
1891	63.7	1903	186.9
1892	28.8	1904	374.5
1899	330.2	1905	174.2
1900	449.5	1906	99.9
1901	333.6	1910	174.2
		1911	375.9

Source: I. N. Slansky, ed., *Gosudarstvennyi bank. Kratkii ocherk deiatel'nosti za 1860–1910 gody* (St. Petersburg, 1910), p. 51.

taken as a base. But apart from the fluctuations within each year, there were violent fluctuations between years. This would suggest that it may be rash to make inferences about the Treasury deposits as a crucial element in determining the lending capacity of the State Bank.

What conclusions can be drawn from this short survey of banking activities in Russia during the period under consideration? The first and most general conclusion on the basis of the published secondary sources is that over time an increasing share of financial transactions in Russia was carried out through the banking system. Second, the banks helped to create an ever more integrated money market and expanded their activities to many areas of the Russian economy. Third, one could agree with the outstanding authority on Russian banking, Dr. Iosif Frolovich Gindin, that the banking system suffered from some of the biases of the governmental policies in giving priority to the economic interests of the landowning classes, perhaps at the expense of the more dynamic segments of the economy, such as trade and industry. However, the above view has to be taken within the historical perspective that industry's active demand for loans materialized only during the 1890s and afterward. Thus, the banks could only be faulted, if at all, for not stimulating but only responding, at the beginning sluggishly, to the demands of industrialization in Russia. Once the demand for industrial investment became strong, the banking system assumed a supportive role.

Thirty-five years of the short period of Russian banking (1860–1914) could be described, if not as infancy, then as a difficult and protracted period of learning. The banks' march toward modernity was originally obstructed by archaic structures of legal and institutional norms, by often inconsistent government monetary and banking policies, and by premodern social attitudes. Given this general milieu, the bankers behaved very much like members of the entrepreneurial groups, proceeding sluggishly and slowly and therefore appearing ineffective, especially to proponents of rapid modernization of Russian institutions. Capital remained scarce throughout the whole period, but this related much more to the low levels of incomes out of which savings were forthcoming than to the alleged conservatism of the bankers. Since the growth of banking in Russia was inexorably related to three phenomena—the commercialization of agriculture, the creation of overhead capital by the government, and the expansion of industrial production—this writer would conclude that during the latter part of the period when the banks were expanding, their performance was not only recognized but their role in the dynamics of the Russian economy became crucial.

The System of Taxation

The system of taxation in Russia during the post-emancipation period changed very slowly, preserving many traditional features in spite of the very substantial growth of the state's revenue and expenditures.

The government budget of Russia was more than a narrowly defined account of the government's tax income and expenditures. In fact, it reflected the total transactions conducted by the government, including the sale of goods and charges for services provided by the state, such as the operation of state-owned railroads and the alcohol monopoly. For these reasons it is necessary to distinguish between the "fiscal" and the "entrepreneurial" functions of the state. In our analysis we will focus primarily on the fiscal activities of the government and on the distribution of the two major types of taxes, the indirect and the direct. Of these two the largest share by far belonged to indirect taxes. Within that group, the excise tax on items of mass consumption, such as alcoholic beverages, sugar, tobacco, matches, and petroleum (and salt until 1881), were the most significant. They were levied either at the point of production or at the wholesale level and were therefore less conspicuous to the consumer, although not less regressive in their effect on consumer income. Still another important form of indirect taxation was the revenue from customs duties, many, like those on tea and other food items, designed for fiscal rather than protection purposes. Since their ultimate economic effect was that the Russian consumers paid higher prices on the items on which customs duties were levied, there is sufficient ground to include the customs revenues among indirect taxes.

The preference for indirect taxes can be explained by the greater ease in collecting such taxes, given the cultural level of both the taxpayers and the bureaucracy, and by the fact that they were less injurious to the wealthier classes.

Although the data in table 1.31 do not contain total government revenue, they reflect the changes in the magnitude of direct and indirect taxation in some categories of taxes that can be easily identified and classified as being of one or the other kind. Thus, whatever the data lack in completeness they gain in consistency over time. The indirect taxes represent the sum of the excise taxes paid on the consumption of taxable commodities and the customs revenue. The direct taxes represent the sum of property taxes, income tax revenue, and redemption payments.

If one takes into account the doubling of the population of Russia during this period, the rise in the price level, and the growth of per capita income, the rate of increase of taxation per capita in real terms is much smaller than the unadjusted data of table 1.32 indicate. All these factors cannot,

Table 1.31   Direct and Indirect Taxes (in Millions of Rubles)

Year	Direct Taxes	Indirect Taxes
1861	58.4	169.8
1865	78.6	164.8
1870	110.2	229.6
1875	133.9	282.6
1880	127.9	351.4
1885	177.6	359.7
1890	177.3	475.0
1895	207.3	586.3
1900	228.1	662.9
1905	182.3	848.8
1910	217.0	1,171.5
1913	273.7	1,372.4

Table 1.32   Per Capita Tax Burden

	Total Population (Millions)	Total Taxes	Per Capita Tax	
			In Current Prices	In 1913 Prices
1861	73.7	228.2	3.10	4.73
1890	117.8	552.3	4.69	6.74
1900	132.4	891.0	6.73	8.97
1910	155.0	1,338.5	8.86	9.96
1913	163.4	1,646.1	10.07	10.07

however, counterbalance the fact of the increase of the tax burden during this period and the strong presumption that the tax burden was heavier on the low-income strata of the population.

The second important shift in the pattern of direct taxation was the very gradual transition from a procedure of determining the total of expected tax revenue that required the lower echelons of the bureaucracy to allocate the tax quota among the taxpayers, to a system of setting tax rates on different categories of taxpayers differentiated by the sources or sizes of their incomes. Although the assessment of sizes of incomes was very sketchy and the estimates were based on some notions of average profitability of occupation, the principle of tax differentiation by income groups as a more just system from the viewpoint of the taxpayers' welfare signified change. It helped the state revenue to benefit from increases in incomes of the population in the short run and led to subsequent reporting of various types of taxable incomes by groups of taxpayers themselves. The statutory obligation to report net incomes was first applied to industry, trade, and finance, where taxes were at differential rates. This procedure was to become a statutory obligation for individuals and corporations alike. Among all the direct taxes levied during the period under consideration, the closest approximation to an individual income tax was taxes on apartments in urban areas (although paid as a percentage of the rent, rather than in accordance with the size of personal income) and taxes on salaries of civil servants and salaried employees of joint stock companies and firms liable to public accounting.

The complexity and variety of direct taxes in Russia were sources of frustration and annoyance, apart from the costs of collection not only to the taxpayers but also to the government. Therefore, various proposals to improve the efficiency of direct taxation by the introduction of a personal income tax were discussed during the decade preceding World War I. The likelihood of a final adoption of the idea of a graduated income tax improved with time, but it did not materialize.

Among the indirect taxes, the largest item was the tax on alcoholic beverages. It was not only the largest item among excise taxes but the largest single source of revenue in the state budget. During the period under consideration the volume of this tax increased from 126 million rubles (or 1.71 rubles per capita) in 1861 to 718 million rubles (4.39 rubles per capita) in 1913. On the assumption that prices rose during this period and that 1.71 rubles were worth 2.61 rubles in 1913, the tax in real terms increased 68 per cent.

Another rapidly rising indirect tax was customs duties. Their rise was due both to the growth in the volume and value of foreign trade and to the rising rates of import duties. Table 1.33 illustrates these trends.

Other excise taxes increased from about 11 million rubles in 1861 to 302 million in 1913. While in 1861 the lion's share was from the old gabelle (abolished in 1881), half of the 1913 excise taxes came from sugar, followed by tobacco, petroleum, and matches.

Although the collection of indirect taxes was an easier task in a country like Russia than the collection of direct taxes, the relationship between the two types is also indicative of the relative burden of taxation on various social groups.

As indirect taxes were levied on items of mass consumption, the taxa-

Table 1.33 Value of Foreign Trade and Customs Duties (in Millions of Rubles)

	1861	1913
Value of Exports	177.2	1,520.1
Value of Imports	167.1	1,374.0
Customs Duties	32.8	352.9
Customs Duties as Percent of Imports	19.6	25.7

tion system was regressive with respect to incomes. A good example of the effect of taxation in Russia is provided by the study of the burden of taxation on the Russian peasantry in 1912 covering the fifty provinces of European Russia.[12] The closest estimate of the peasants' taxes—6.36 rubles per capita—constituted 11 per cent of their income, divided between 1.80 rubles of direct taxes and 4.56 rubles of indirect taxes.[13]

These estimates, by themselves, would still be insufficient to indicate the burden of taxation unless we have an estimate not only of the peasants' total incomes (which the author estimates to be 59 rubles per capita) but of the cash income. Since the bulk of the peasants' income was consumed within the households without reaching the market, the share of tax payments as a fraction of the total cash income of the peasants would be higher than the share in total income. An assumption that the tax burden constituted at least 25 per cent of the peasants' cash incomes would be a very generous characteristic of the Russian governmental tax policies. The tax burden was probably higher, since our calculations excluded local taxes and assumed a high proportion of peasants' marketings and other cash incomes. Thus, the Russian system of taxation not only derived the bulk of revenues from taxing the low-income groups, but it also severely limited the purchasing power of those social groups and affected their level of saving and consumption.

At least two more issues ought to be touched on in conjunction with Russian tax policies. One deals with the problem of state budget deficits and the other with the income redistribution effects of the state budgets.

In spite of all the attempts to present the financial policies of the Russian government during this period as "sound," there existed a chronic budget deficit. If we exclude borrowing in the form of government loans and the printing of currency, only seven years within the span of 1860–1913 show an excess of revenues over expenditures.[14] The chief reasons for the budget deficits were war expenditures and some expenses for overhead capital, but we ought to take into account that apart from military expenditures, high even in peacetime, Russian state budgets reflected a high level of expenses for both administration and the apparatus to maintain internal tranquility or oppression, choosing the term according to one's taste. Therefore the existing form of government, its militaristic orientation and authoritarian-bureaucratic mode of governing, clearly influenced the distribution of the state revenues and explains the incessant pressure to increase the volume of taxation from its populace. The priorities of the government relegated economic growth and economic welfare to receive a relatively small residual of government revenues.

In trying to estimate the income redistribution effect of the state budget, there are two possible avenues of analysis. One method would estimate the share of taxation in the income of a particular social group and estimate the benefits this group derives from the expenditures of the budget or the special services provided to the members of the group. If the benefits exceeded the costs (taxes) or if the services rendered by the state were provided at low cost, presumably the state budget would have redistributed income in favor of this group. Unfortunately, our data do not permit such an analysis. The second method would compare the sources of government revenue by social groups with the pattern of expenditures and derive the effects of both on the incomes of the social groups.

Given the extent of our knowledge of the Russian state budgets, there is no trace of a policy to redistribute the incomes of the rich among the poor. We do not find such policies because of the politically dominant positions of the Russian nobility and upper-level bureaucracy, but also because a country interested in capital accumulation does not promote income equalization policies. While during the second half of the period (1860–1913) there is no blatant income redistribution tax policy from the peasants to the wealthy landowners, one can clearly detect a policy that would redistribute income from the peasants to industrial entrepreneurs. In this respect, the policy of tariff protection for the industrial sector was supplemented by a tax policy favoring industrial development. Agriculture received relatively fewer incentives from the state budget than the industrial sector of the economy, and those most affected by these policies were the peasants.

It is difficult in this brief discussion of the taxation system to enumerate alternative policies and their likely effect on the Russian economy and polity, except to say that the existing system of taxation lagged behind rather than led the process of economic change and transformation taking place in Russia.

Summary and Conclusions

How can the above-described development taking place in the various areas of economic activity be summarized? Which are the vectors common to all economic sectors, and how did they help to transform Russian society?

The most obvious observation is the relationship of Russian economic development to the growth of its population. The growth of production in Russia, whether agricultural or industrial, was caused by an increase in demand for goods and services and an increase in the supply of labor, both due to a large extent to the growth of its population. However, the observed pattern of economic growth as measured by the growth rate of national income exceeded the rate of population growth and was therefore due to an increase in productivity of the factors of production, both capital (including land) and labor. For this to take place, conditions existed to assure that not all of the national income would be consumed, that the rate of savings, voluntary or forced, should be high enough to assure a growth of investment in new capital. However, the growth of productivity of the Russian economy cannot be attributed solely to the growth of physical capital. It has also to be attributed to an improvement in the quality of the labor force, due to extension of life expectancy, to better living conditions of the population, to the acquisition of new skills and higher rates of literacy, and to educational achievement. When the higher quality labor force used an increasing volume of capital, and one that embodied a more modern technology in the various branches of mining, manufacturing industries, and construction, the result was a higher level of output at a lower per unit cost. The savings thus achieved served not only to raise the level of consumption but also to invest and to sustain the process of economic growth.

In Russia, as in other developing countries, a major source of economies in the production and distribution of goods was the modernization of transportation facilities by the use of steam power in overland and water transport. Large-scale railroad construction supplemented by the extension of river and canal transportation were the accomplishments of the period under consideration.

The technological revolution accompanying the industrialization process involved the development of new natural resources, among which, for example, the fossil fuels, coal and oil, were important as energy sources as well as raw material for metallurgy and the chemical industries.

However, most important for the growth of demand and for the supply response was the spread of a capitalist, market economy. It was the market with all the inherent characteristics of this major institution, with its anonymity and reliance on self-interest, with its often devastating consequences of severe business fluctuations, but also with its dynamism and quest for improved organization that drew into its orbit an ever-increasing part of the economically active (employed) population.

It is not sufficient to state that the commercial production of agriculture in Russia was growing faster than the total agricultural product. What was really important is that a growing share of the commercial agricultural production was being exported and made up the bulk of Russian exports in international trade. Thus, Russian grain, fibers, and livestock products not only paid for the imports of foreign machinery and consumer goods, but tied the Russian agricultural sector more closely to the international market. There is also no doubt that Russia's involvement in the international commodity markets paved the way for its access to the foreign capital markets.

The increased commercialization of agriculture as well as the growth of an industrial sector in which the output of large-scale factory production was growing at record high rates, demanded a higher rate of labor mobility than the existing political institutions allowed. Thus, a part of Russian socio-political history, the decline of the village commune, can to a large extent be explained by the conflict between modern economic necessity and traditional institutional arrangements. The development of the market and money economy had a number of revolutionary features, among which the substitution of market forces for government regulation and controls exercised in the interest of a landowning elite was not of minor significance. The growth of the market forces within Russia reached at least the level that economic considerations in shaping of governmental policies became a reputable procedure.

The process of accepting the goal of industrial development as a component of policy decision-making on the part of the Russian government is not tantamount to policy-making that is a priori conducive to industrial growth. Thus, one of the two major controversies among economic historians studying the modern period of Russian development concerns the role of the government in the Russian economy, while the other (not unrelated to the first) concerns the role of foreign versus domestic capital invested in the Russian economy during this period.

When we turn to the problem of capital formation, we observe that the resources for the increments in capital and the acquisition of new skills were primarily created domestically, out of the savings of the Russian population. The process of voluntary saving or capital accumulation was a painful one, given the relatively low levels of income and the relatively high levels of government taxation. But government taxation in itself contained an element of forced savings and redistribution of income among various groups of the population, particularly transferring income from the agricultural sector to the industrial one, but affecting mostly the lower-income groups in agriculture, the peasants. While incomes of the population were rising, so was the bulk of savings, while the per capita consumption of the population tended to rise more slowly.

Although the bulk of savings was generated domestically, there was a significant influx of foreign capital over the period. Though during the earlier part of the period most of the foreign investments were directed to support the growth of overhead capital (chiefly railroads), gradually the flow of capital into mining and manufacturing industries increased, with a spillover into the areas of public utilities and services. While the flow of foreign investments (apart from heavy borrowings of the Russian government to cover its budget deficits) was rising, the data are still too imprecise and incomplete to assess the relative importance of foreign investments for the growth of the industrial sector of the Russian economy. A balanced view would certainly not be one which minimized its role, but it might have been less crucial than some Western observers considered it to be. The data suggest that the contribution of foreign skills and organization were at least as important as the impact of fixed capital assets.

While the controversy with respect to the role of foreign investments and their significance hinges on a proper and meaningful method of measuring or quantifying the variables in question, the controversy about the role of the government in the Russian economy is much more difficult to resolve. Historians of the "etatist" school clearly underestimated the role of market forces and attributed the development of both the overhead capital and the modern industrial sector primarily to the policies and actions of the government. Such a view appears to this author to be too extreme, to say the least, since among other things, the proponents of the "etatist" school seem to take into account only one side of the ledger without examining the government policies that were either counterproductive or in conflict with the goals of industrialization.

The tariff policies of the government, coupled with its monetary policies, provide many examples of counterproductive measures. In our analysis, attention was called to the excessive prices that not only Russian consumers but even Russian producers paid for goods as a result of excessive protectionist policies, as well as to the consequences of certain monetary policies of the government. Whether the famous dictum of Finance Minister Vyshnegradskii, "We will starve but we will export grain," did much to further the cause of industrialization has still to be tested—not for its moral connotations, but for its economic effects.[15]

Therefore, on balance it seems to be correct to acknowledge the role of the government as a stimulant and promoter of industrial growth either in particular periods or in specific areas of the industrial sector, but in view of its inconsistent policies, its own inefficiency, and its relative decline in direct economic activity, the Russian government cannot be considered the prime mover in the industrialization effort.

Although even at the end of the period Russia remained largely an agrarian country, nevertheless agriculture made very considerable progress in supplying an increasing share of production for the domestic and foreign markets and in responding much more rapidly and smoothly to the signals and opportunities provided by the market. In addition, Russia built up a respectable amount of overhead capital, important not only in increasing the size of the market and integrating the various economic regions into

Table 1.34   Economic Indicators for Russia, I
1865–1913

Years	Population (in Mill.)	Length of Railways (in 1,000s of Km)	Industrial Output (in 1,000 tons)				Cotton Consumption by Industry (in 1,000s of Tons)
			Coal	Oil	Pig Iron	Sugar	
1865	75.1	3.8	382	9	300	65	26
1870	84.5	10.7	693	33	360	105	46
1875	90.2	19.0	1,700	132	430	130	85
1880	97.7	22.9	3,290	352	450	205	93
1885	108.8	26.0	4,270	1,800	530	340	124
1890	117.8	30.6	6,015	3,700	930	405	136
1895	123.9	37.0	9,100	6,175	1,450	530	201
1900	132.9	53.2	16,155	10,340	2,930	795	262
1905	143.9	61.1	18,668	7,470	2,730	855	298
1910	160.7	66.6	25,000	9,640	3,040	1,030	362
1913	170.9	70.2	36,040	9,200	4,630	1,850	424

Table 1.35   Economic Indicators for Russia, II
1865–1913

Years	Exports (in Mill. Rubles)	Imports (in Mill. Rubles)	Consumer Price Index (Including Rent) (1913 = 100)
1865	209.2	164.3	55.1
1870	360.0	335.9	65.0
1875	382.0	531.1	69.7
1880	498.7	622.8	78.5
1885	537.9	435.4	74.3
1890	692.2	406.6	67.5
1895	689.1	526.1	72.5
1900	716.2	626.4	77.8
1905	1,077.3	635.1	80.9
1910	1,449.4	1,084.4	89.0
1913	1,520.1	1,374.0	100.0

Table 1.36   Agriculture in Fifty Districts of European Russia
1895–1913

Year	Grain Output (in Mill. Tons)	Livestock Numbers (in Mill. Heads)			
		Horses	Cattle	Pigs	Sheep
1895	43.9	17.0	24.5	9.2	38.2
1900	48.3	19.7	31.7	11.8	47.6
1905	48.9	20.8	31.2	11.5	45.4
1910	60.5	21.9	31.3	12.0	40.7
1913	69.4	22.8	32.0	13.5	41.4

one economic organism, but also in creating new networks of communication and transportation that facilitated the mobility of people and ideas as much as the movement of goods. The interaction between the commercialization of agriculture and the creation of overhead capital made it possible for Russian industrialization to become irreversible. Not only did the process itself become irreversible, but as a result of the relatively high rates of investment and growth of industrial production, the industrial sector represented a sizeable pool of physical and human capital on which further development could have been based and expanded.

Unfortunately this was also a period when the Russian government's political and military ambitions came into sharp conflict with the objective of industrialization in the competition for resources. Politics turned out to be stronger than the desire for peaceful economic development, with the result that valuable resources were wasted on the altars of Mars and Moloch. The outbreak of World War I finally brought this remarkable period in the history of Russian economic development to an end, and the gradual, evolutionary process was replaced by a whole series of discontinuities of a cataclysmic nature and force.

The Economy of Congress Poland, 1860–1914

The separate treatment of the economic development of Congress Poland[16] during the period 1860–1914 does not require any special justification. As a territorial component of the Polish Commonwealth prior to the partition by its three neighbors in the eighteenth century, and as the important component of a politically resurrected Poland in 1918, the region presents a number of intellectual challenges. However, the two basic aspects discussed in this section will be the process of integrating the provinces of Congress Poland into the economy of the Russian Empire and the degree of internal economic cohesion within this region itself. The period 1860–1914 is particularly suited for this type of analysis, since it saw the intensive formation of a national market structure in the Russian Empire and the growing interdependence of economic sectors within economic regions under the impact of industrial development.

Population

The territory included an area of 126,955 square kilometers and by the end of 1913, a population of almost 13 million people. Congress Poland had 2.6 per cent of the territory of European Russia; it had about 10.3 per cent of its population, with four times the density. The territory of Congress Poland was larger than such sovereign states as Belgium, the Netherlands, or Denmark, and it was more populous than any of these and any of the Balkan states. Out of the total population, about 4.1 million inhabited the cities and towns; less than 9 million were rural inhabitants. By comparison, the level of urbanization in Poland was about twice as high as in European Russia. The population was not homogeneous in terms of religion: while over 75 per cent were Catholic, 14 per cent were Jewish, 5 per cent Protestant, and 4 per cent Russian Orthodox (including military garrisons).

The rates of population growth in Poland are shown in table 1.37. The variation in the growth rate reflects a number of factors, such as a declining mortality rate and a corresponding adjustment of the birthrate, the impact of cyclical economic upswings or downswings, and emigration. The contrast between the decade of the 1880s and the 1890s most strongly reflects the different states of the economy, while population growth of the 1900s represents the long-run trend of adjustment of the birthrate to a declining deathrate. While the share of the Jews among emigrants was higher than their share in the total population, this did not substantially change the denominational structure of the population in view of the intensified migration of the Polish (Catholic) rural population.

The employment distribution of the population is of crucial importance for our understanding of the economic structure (see table 1.38). The composition of employment reflects an economy in the early stages of industrial development: the relatively large size of the agricultural labor force, the relatively large numbers employed in domestic services and those classified as unskilled laborers. These characteristics were overwhelming for the female labor force, but the male labor force was not free of them either. Even if we should assume, for good reasons, that the number of employed women was underreported in the census, there is no basis to claim that those underreported had a different employment composition. Thus, the female labor force with 34 per cent in agriculture, 28 per cent in domestic

**Table 1.37   Yearly Rates of Population Growth
in Congress Poland**

Decade	Rate of Growth (%)
1861–70	1.9
1871–80	1.8
1881–90	1.5
1891–1900	2.2
1901–10	1.7

Source: Wladyslaw Grabski, ed., *Rocznik Statystyczny Krolestwa Polskiego, Rok 1913*. (Warsaw: Gebethner Wolff, 1913), p. 15.

**Table 1.38   Population and Labor Force in Congress Poland by Employment Groups
(Population Census of 1897)**

Employment Groups	Population	Employed			% of Total	
		Males	Females	Total	Population	Employed
Agriculture	5,327,663	1,081,826	218,823	1,300,649	58.23	47.90
Manufacturing	1,277,977	376,252	76,957	453,209	13.97	16.69
Mining and metallurgy	61,274	21,083	984	22,067	0.67	0.81
Transportation	163,991	43,560	1,387	44,947	1.78	1.65
Construction	151,184	44,109	234	44,343	1.65	1.63
Health and educ. services	73,810	20,137	7,869	28,006	0.81	1.03
Domestic, farm services	462,179	83,437	179,690	263,127	5.05	9.69
Other services	42,521	6,479	11,443	17,922	0.46	0.66
Trade	577,867	121,033	20,371	141,404	6.32	5.21
Trade intermediaries	24,504	5,697	173	5,870	0.27	0.22
Clerical workers	93,588	25,395	6,196	31,591	1.02	1.16
Unskilled labor	406,299	104,537	51,359	155,896	4.44	5.74
Rentiers & capitalists	160,050	30,896	16,747	47,643	1.75	1.75
Clergy & church services	43,535	12,186	361	12,547	0.48	0.46
Govt. employees	99,658	30,880	162	31,042	1.09	1.14
Total*	9,149,024	2,071,218	644,103	2,715,321		

*Exclusive of the military.

Ed. note: The footings of Population and Total Employed exceed the figures listed above by approx. 2 per cent. The corresponding percentages will have small discrepancies.

service, 8 per cent in unskilled labor, but only 12 per cent in manufacturing is a sign of economic and educational underdevelopment. There is no doubt that the employment composition changed over time while the labor force was increasing, but we lack the exact data for the changes that took place outside the industrial sector during the subsequent period.

Agriculture

The largest sector of the economy was agriculture. According to the population census of 1897, 58 per cent of the population depended on agriculture for their livelihood, and 48 per cent of the labor force was employed in agriculture. In fact, population growth during the second half of the nineteenth century exerted a great deal of pressure on the land resources, which resulted in both the expansion of the arable land at the expense of meadows and forests (see table 1.39) and some redistribution of land among groups of owners.

On the one hand, we encounter a high degree of concentration in the

Table 1.39 Size and Distribution of Selected Categories of Land
(in 1000s of Ha)

Type	1859	1894	1909
Arable land	6,018	6,937	7,062
Garden plot	296	420	486
Meadows	1,051	1,080	1,005
Pasture	639	954	847
Total	8,004	9,391	9,400

Table 1.40 Size Distribution of Small Farms

	Up to 1.7 ha	1.8–3.4 ha	3.5–8.6 ha	8.7–17.2 ha	17.3–50 ha	Total
Peasants on reform land*	126,295	139,694	366,898	111,935	33,623	778,445
Peasants on purchased land	29,819	40,138	81,357	21,299	6,463	179,076
Small gentry	5,839	5,963	18,367	11,528	11,296	52,993
Total	161,953	185,795	466,622	144,762	51,382	1,010,514

Source: W. Grabski, *Rocznik Statystyczny Krolestwa Polskiego, Rok 1913* (Warsaw, 1914), pp. 98–99.
*Peasant land as a result of emancipation in 1861.

holdings of 7,417 owners with a 490 hectare average for each farm, and 302 *majorat* holdings (not subject to subdivision) with a 1,255 hectare average for each, together in 1909 about 7,719 private owners with an average of 521 hectares per estate. The state owned 721,335 hectares (of which 573,688 were forest lands).

Thus, while the large holdings (except the state) included 4,356,876 hectares, the total land owned by smallholders was 7,227,101 hectares in 1909, or 6.57 hectares per smallholding.[17] Given this average size, it becomes clear why the smallholding farms were labor intensive and why the shift from grain production to industrial crops, such as sugar beets, flax, and potatoes was pronounced. But even the relatively low average size of the 6.57 hectare farm does not fully reflect the plight of the farmers. A truer impression could be formed only when we consider the distribution of farms within the smallholder category.

The most striking feature of the distribution of farms by size in table 1.40 is the relatively high percentage of farms below the 3.5 hectare size, 34.4 per cent of all smallholdings, and the 16 per cent at the very bottom of the distribution having not more than 1.7 hectares Although it was against the law to subdivide farms below 3.5 hectares, there is no doubt that a substantial number of farms were created as a result of subdivision. This raises the issue of the economic viability of the small farms. But the issue was complicated further by the existence of a relatively large landless rural population which had a prior claim on agricultural work. The alternatives for both groups, in addition to becoming agricultural hired labor on the estates, were either migration to the cities or seasonal and permanent emigration from Poland. For a certain number of the smallholders, land purchases from the estates was another possibility.

Therefore, one of the moving forces behind the relatively high growth rate of the population in the industrializing urban areas was the search for employment on the part of the smallholding peasants, particularly the ones with "dwarf"-sized farms. Migration abroad, especially seasonal migration for agricultural work in Germany, Denmark, or the provinces of European Russia, was an important source of income for the smallholders and landless peasants. Those migrants, however, encountered competition from peasants migrating to Germany from the province of Galicia (then in the Austro-Hungarian Empire). Thus both the demand for labor on the East German Junker estates and the competing supply of Galician seasonal migrants determined the size of seasonal migration into Germany. And while the wages of agricultural laborers rose, especially during the first decade of the twentieth century, the wages which could be obtained abroad, especially in the West, were approximately double what they were paid in Poland. The seasonal migration in fact grew by leaps and bounds and was estimated at about 20,000 in 1890, around 130,000 in 1900, and 268,000 in 1908, of which 85–88 per cent was in Germany. Thus, a combination of nonagricultural employment and remittances of seasonal migrants contributed a very significant source of additional income for the numerous groups of very small farmers.[18] By comparison with other provinces of Russia, Polish agriculture made significant progress in eliminating the multiplicity of field strips and in consolidating fields within the farms, which should have increased the productivity of the land.

The large farms for which data are available for 1909 included 3,984,224 hectares, of which 2,440,645 or 61.3 per cent was land and 29.4 per cent forest.

The large estates used hired labor and substantial capital. The large landowners did not receive as much support from government policies as in Russia, and they suffered not only from the agricultural crisis of the 1880s and 1890s but also from the competition of the expanding agricultural regions of south and southeast Russia. Therefore, the large landowners sold their land. Those who were able to hold on to their land mortgaged a part of their estates in order to meet production expenses, capital investment needs, and sometimes consumption needs. Out of a total of 2,756,083 hectares of mortgaged land with an estimated value of 402 million rubles at the end of 1912, outstanding loans amounted to 173 million rubles or 43 per cent of the land's estimated value; or 63 rubles loan per hectare, valued at 146 rubles per hectare.

While agricultural production suffered from the impact of the landownership relations, from the imperfections of the land market, and from the protracted decline of agricultural prices during the decades of the 1880s and 1890s, output in the subsequent period grew (see table 1.41).

While a part of the increase in agricultural production was due to the expansion of arable land and a better distribution of land under various crops (see table 1.42),[19] a substantial part of the increase in agricultural production can be attributed to the increase in yields per unit of land. The rise in yields resulted from both the intensification of labor and the use of other inputs, such as improved agricultural implements and fertilizer. Table 1.43 illustrates the trend. It is necessary to point out that the increase of yields took place on both large-scale farms and the smallholdings. Although the sources of the yield increases on both types of farm might have differed (perhaps higher investments accounting for the rise in yields of the larger farms, while larger labor inputs on the smaller farms), the important feature was the parallel growth of yield on both types of farms.[20]

The livestock sector of agriculture declined under the impact of the relative increase in arable land at the expense of meadows and pastures and also under the impact of the livestock production in other regions of Russia

Table 1.41   Average Yearly Output of Selected Agricultural Products in Congress Poland (in Million-Quintals)

	1867–70	1891–95	1896–1900	1909–13
Rye	11.7	13.5	16.4	23.0
Oats	5.6	6.4	7.3	11.1
Wheat	3.9	4.9	5.5	6.4
Barley	2.8	3.6	3.9	5.9
Four grains	24.0	28.4	33.2	46.4
Potatoes	30.5	56.0	65.8	101.7
Sugar beets	1.7	7.1	8.1	14.4

Source: I. Kostrowicka, Z. Landau, and J. Tomaszewski, *Historia Gospodarcza Polski, XIX i XX Wieku* (Warsaw, 1975), p. 167.

Table 1.42   The Planted Area of Grains (in 1,000s of Ha) Congress Poland

Year	Rye	Wheat	Barley	Oats	Total
1864	1,641	362	369	898	3,270
1878	1,662	552	458	868	3,540
1887	1,738	376	325	900	3,339
1900	2,005	537	453	1,059	4,054
1913	2,169	531	519	1,170	4,389

Table 1.43   Agricultural Yields in Congress Poland (Quintals per Ha)

	1891–95	1895–1900	1901–5	1906–10	1911–12
Winter rye	8.0	8.3	8.5	9.4	11.3
Winter wheat	10.0	10.9	10.0	11.1	12.9
Barley	9.0	9.0	9.4	10.4	12.5
Oats	7.0	7.0	7.3	8.6	9.9
Potatoes	73.0	80.9	71.8	94.0	76.5
Flax			5.3	6.3	5.7
Sugar beets	173		166.5	198.0	196.5

Sources: I. Kostrowicka, Z. Landau, and J. Tomaszewski, *Historia Gospodarcza Polski, XIX i XX Wieku* (Warsaw, 1975), p. 168; W. Grabski, ed., *Rocznik Statystyczny Krolestwa Polskiego, Rok 1913* (Warsaw, 1914), p. 129.

Table 1.44   The Size and Composition of the Livestock Herd (in 1,000s)

	1870	1899	1907	1913
Total horned cattle	2,231	2,957	2,375	2,224
cows	—	1,973	1,765	—
oxen	735	153	67	—
Total pigs	1,104	1,193	734	554
Total sheep	4,180	2,767	1,050	760
Total horses	754	1,367	1,287	1,117

Source: B. Baranowski, "Chow Zwierzat Gospodarczych," in Polska Akademia Nauk, *Zarys Historii Gospodarstwa Wiejskiego w Polsce*, vol. 3, part 4 (Warsaw, 1970), pp. 490–552.

where it was more profitable (see table 1.44). One of the characteristic features of change in the composition of the livestock herd was the substitution of horses for oxen as the motive power in agriculture. Both the improvement in the breed of horses and their use outside agriculture could account for this substitution. This led to a change in the composition of the cattle herd, which became more specialized toward the production of dairy products and meat. The very sharp decline in the number of sheep and pigs reflected the impact of competition with other provinces of Russia, where the costs of feed were considerably lower. Thus, in spite of the maintenance of exports of livestock products, Poland substantially increased its imports of livestock from other regions of Russia, especially for the purpose of domestic consumption. The diminution of the sheep and pig population was not related to a special situation of small farms, for it affected all types of farms as becomes clear from inspection of the distribution of the livestock herd among various categories of farms (see table 1.45).

Both the improvements in the productivity of the livestock herd and the availability of livestock imports from other regions of Russia tend to deny

Table 1.45 Distribution of the Livestock Herd by Type of Farms, 1899 and 1907 (in Percent) Congress Poland

| | Large Holdings | | Small Holdings | | | |
| | Estates | | Peasants | | Small Gentry | |
	1899	1907	1899	1907	1899	1907
Horned cattle	17.1	18.3	71.7	70.3	6.4	6.8
Pigs	14.3	13.4	71.3	74.4	6.6	5.2
Sheep	68.2	68.6	25.6	24.6	4.6	5.4
Horses	20.3	19.3	66.5	67.6	5.7	5.9

Source: B. Baranowski, "Chow Zwierzat Gospodarczych," in Polska Akademia Nauk, *Zarys Historii Gospodarstwa Wiejskiego w Polsce,* vol. 3, part 4 (Warsaw, 1970), pp. 490–552.

any suggestion about a decline in the consumption of livestock products in Poland in spite of the contraction of the livestock herd as reflected in tables 1.44 and 1.45.

An additional source of income for landowners and agricultural labor was forestry. During the period under investigation, the size of the forests in Poland declined substantially, from 3,328,000 hectares in 1873 to 2,708,000 hectares in 1882 and 2,408,000 hectares in 1909. Thus, by 1909 there were only 72.3 per cent of forest lands by comparison with 1873, and their share in the total area declined from 27 to 20 per cent. Most of the forest lands in 1909 belonged either to the state or to the estate owners; only 14 per cent of all forest lands belonged to the peasants and small gentry. The decline in the size of forest lands reflected not only the conversion to arable, but also the demand, foreign and domestic, for forest products. Although it could be argued that the administration of government forests as well as the estate forests was quite inefficient during the earlier part of the period, there is a great deal of evidence of their growing efficiency. Certainly by comparison with other regions of Russia, the forestry trade of Poland became a model of efficiency and profitability. To the extent that forestry provided employment for labor outside the agricultural season, income for the owners of the forest land, profits for the merchants, and foreign exchange for the country, its development was beneficial even if its utilization fell short of its potential.

Industry

Within the history of Poland's industrialization, one can distinguish three distinct periods of intensified growth. The spurt in industrial activity in the 1870s preceded the industrialization of the other regions of the Russian Empire. The other two upswings coincided with those in the rest of the empire in the 1890s and in 1908–13.

The first period of industrial growth during the 1870s, especially during the last years of the decade, was preceded by a substantial growth of agricultural production. Not only was this marked by an increase in commercial grains and industrial crops, but even by an increase in the grains produced for household consumption, apparently under the impact of population growth. However, the direct stimuli for industrial growth came as a result not only of the growing demand but also of the supply response of capital formation and investment. The expansionist monetary policy during the Balkan War intensified saving and investment, particularly in the metal and textile industries. The banks somewhat recovered from the all-European financial crisis of 1873 and became more involved in the financing of industry. Railroad construction during this period also promoted employment and trade.

But this spurt of industrial activity was limited by a number of factors: the price decline of agricultural products, the discontinuity of railroad construction, and tight monetary policies. It was only in the 1890s that the industries of Poland began to grow again. This time, Poland lagged behind both the southern region of Russia, which forged ahead in the production of coal and metals, and the Moscow and St. Petersburg regions, centers of the textile industry. Protective tariffs, a new and larger railroad construction boom, and greater involvement of the Russian government and banks helped to achieve high rates of growth throughout the 1890s. Within Poland, the growth rates of industrial production were somewhat lower, as one would expect in a region which achieved a higher level of industrial output earlier. However, investments in industry were increasing and imports of capital goods from the West were rising in order to equip the new factories and to expand the existing ones. Alongside the growth of industrial capital was a growth in the numbers of skilled industrial workers. If in capital intensity southern Russian metallurgy overtook the Polish region, in the level of skills the Polish region maintained its lead over other economic regions of the empire. If wage differentials are an indication, the higher wages of Polish industrial workers reflect their higher productivity and skill.

By 1900, industry in Poland and in Russia in general reached a plateau which it maintained for nearly a decade. Neither the Russo-Japanese War nor the revolution of 1905 helped to raise industrial production. But by 1908 a new spurt began. It differed from the one of the 1890s by a diminution of state activity. Although a new railroad boom developed, sustained by government orders for track and equipment, it lacked much of the direct interference which marked the 1890s. The financing of industrial investment came primarily from the banks, which had become much more adept in mobilizing savings of the public, in direct lending to industrial entrepreneurs, and in floating shares of industrial corporations.

The size of industrial production depended to a large extent upon the size of the labor force. The employment data for the industrial sector of the economy reflect different definitions of the industrial sector. The broadest definition, including crafts as well as factory production, is represented by the data of the 1897 Population Census. It is understandable that as an industrializing region Poland had sizeable employment in crafts and small-scale industry. If we compare the total industrial and craft employment of 1897 (in table 1.46) of 475,000 with 139,000 for larger-scale industry (in 1893), even allowing for a substantial growth of the latter employment we would still have 250–300,000 craft workers, a number that is not absorbed in later industrial employment data. And although craft employment perhaps was not growing, it certainly had not yet been displaced by large-scale industrial employment.

Unfortunately, there are no continuous data for the value of industrial production in Poland except for the early period (see table 1.47); therefore one has to rely on indirect data which mirror the pattern and rate of industrial growth (see table 1.48). Apart from qualitative indicators for the production of particular industries, one can use data on the industrial labor force as an indicator of production growth. Such an indicator would provide a lower bound estimate of production growth because it would not include the growth of output from technological change or from the increase of skills of the labor force. Still another problem arises with regard

Table 1.46   **Industry and Craft Employment in Congress Poland, Census Data for 1897**

Industry	Employment			Total Incl. Dependents
	Total	Males	Females	
Mining and metallurgy	22,067	21,083	984	61,274
Apparel	135,138	107,982	27,156	387,419
Textile	103,127	67,584	35,543	234,433
Metal	57,982	56,921	1,061	169,218
Wood	46,247	44,780	1,467	145,500
Food	45,673	42,312	3,361	149,826
Minerals, ceramics	15,604	14,212	1,392	49,429
Livestock products	13,619	13,082	537	43,324
Printing & related	6,970	6,267	703	23,486
Watchmaking, jewelry	6,263	5,979	284	17,001
Chemical & paper	5,063	3,970	1,093	14,429
Other	17,523	13,163	4,360	43,932
Total	475,276	397,335	77,941	1,339,271

Table 1.47   Value of Industrial Production in Congress Poland 1860–95,
5-Year Averages (in Millions of Rubles)

Years	Industrial Production	Years	Industrial Production
1861–65	42	1881–85	182
1866–70	57	1886–90	207
1871–75	82	1891–95	248
1876–80	125		

Source: A. Jezierski, *Handel Zagraniczny Krolestwa Polskiego, 1815–1914* (Warsaw: PWN, 1967), p. 152.

Table 1.48   Estimates of Industrial Production in Congress Poland,
1860–95
(in Millions of Rubles)

Year	Industrial Production	Year	Industrial Production
1860	33	1880	171
1865	57	1885	187
1870	62	1890	216
1875	97	1895	277

Source: A. Jezierski, *Handel Zagraniczny Krolestwa Polskiego, 1815–1914* (Warsaw: PWN, 1967), p. 152.

to the coverage of the labor force: ought it to include enterprises of all sizes or only medium and large industrial enterprises?

For the growth of enterprises with over ten hired workers there are data for two benchmark years, 1893 and 1911 (see table 1.49). These data indicate a number of interesting processes that took place in the industrial sector of the economy. While the number of enterprises doubled (a growth of 118 per cent), the size of the labor force increased even more, by 143 per cent. Thus one finds a tendency of growth of the average labor force per enterprise from 113 workers to 126 workers. Whether this tendency exhibits a higher degree of concentration in the industrial sector is doubtful, since alongside industries which clearly exhibited this tendency—such as mining, metallurgy, and metal industries—we find industries in which the average size of the labor force per enterprise declined—such as food, wood products, paper, and printing. In general, we would expect to find a growth of the labor force per enterprise in some areas in which new technology and increased capital endowment would provide increasing returns to scale in industrial operations. Table 1.49 also indicates that certain interindustry shifts in the labor force took place. While all branches of industry encountered an expansion of the labor force, not all grew in the same proportion. Thus, employment in the metal and mineral industries increased at a faster rate than in the food industry. Given the relatively

Table 1.49   Industrial Enterprises and Industrial Labor Force in Congress Poland, 1893 and 1911

Category	1893		1911	
	Enterprises	Labor Force	Enterprises	Labor Force
Mining	21	5,888	64	27,919
Metallurgy	49	11,247	14	16,135
Metal	160	13,013	368	44,672
Minerals	114	6,881	302	22,021
Chemical	54	1,962	83	6,428
Wood products	89	4,808	270	12,028
Paper & printing	34	3,588	145	9,235
Textile & apparel	460	66,046	982	155,698
Leather & furs	70	2,885	120	7,663
Food	180	22,570	337	35,870
Total	1,231	138,888	2,685	337,669

Source: I Pietrzaak-Pawlowska, ed., *Uprzemyslowienie Ziem Polskich w XIX i XX Wieku* (Warsaw, 1970), p. 104.

favorable conditions for growth of the capital industries with respect to the Russian market, this development reflects the existing opportunities.

The data for 1911 in table 1.49 are reasonably close to the data provided by the Russian inspectors of enterprises with more than 15 workers that used steam power. In fact, the figure of 293,615 workers in manufacturing reported in table 1.49 for 1911 is very close to the 278,165 workers that were reported for 1910, although the factory inspectors included a larger number of enterprises (2,906 instead of 2,685) than in the table. The factory inspectors' report, however, included an estimate of the value of production of the manufacturing industries (excluding mining and metallurgy) for 1910 of 436 million rubles. This report enabled the official government statistics of Russia for 1910 to claim that industry in Poland had 19 per cent of all large-scale industrial enterprises, employed 14 per cent of the manufacturing industrial workers, and produced 16 per cent of the industrial output of the empire.

There is an independent estimate of the total industrial production of Poland for 1910 without regard to the size of enterprises (see table 1.50).[21] Although it is impossible to reconcile the estimated value of the output of this source with that of the factory inspectors, the data are of considerable interest. By extending the coverage of the labor force from about 338,000 to 400,000, the share of the metal industry increased at the expense of the textile industry, and the shares of woodworking, chemical, and paper and printing increased as industries in which the number of small enterprises was significant.

A short review of the performance of some of the major industries

Table 1.50   Enterprises, Workers, and Value of Industrial Output in
Congress Poland in 1910

	Enterprises	Workers	Value of Output (in 1,000s of Rubles)	Percent Output	Percent Workers
Textiles & Apparel	3,084	175,743	389,186	45.3	43.8
Food	3,032	42,458	154,724	18.0	10.6
Metal	1,510	62,027	110,301	12.8	15.5
Mining & metallurgy	479	45,697	60,139	7.0	11.4
Minerals	520	23,075	30,433	3.5	5.8
Chemical	264	9,153	29,831	3.5	2.3
Leather	284	7,034	29,378	3.4	1.8
Wood products	879	17,259	23,215	2.7	4.3
Paper & printing	672	15,402	25,696	3.0	3.8
Mixed	229	3,074	7,246	0.8	0.8
Total	10,953	400,922	860,149	100.0	100.0

would also be helpful to improve our understanding of Poland's industrialization.

The largest industry in terms of employment and value of production was textiles (see table 1.51). Its center of production was the region of Lodz in west-central Poland. The industry in Lodz was founded by foreign entrepreneurs, mostly German, with the strong encouragement of the government in the 1820s. Although the German and Jewish element among the entrepreneurs and the labor force was strong throughout the period, the labor force was increasingly recruited from among the rural population of this region. The textile industry grew slowly during its first fifty years as it gained a foothold in the local as well as the Russian market. It was only in the late 1870s that the Lodz textile industry produced more than was consumed domestically. From this time on the production of the region became increasingly dependent on exports. Its subsequent growth from about 60 million rubles in 1881 to 341 million in 1910 was primarily a result of expansion into the Russian market and such distant markets as China and Persia. Its relative success was due to the high rate of capital investments, the introduction of new technology, and the improvement in skills of the labor force.

Managerial capacities and aggressive marketing skills were combined with an effective industrial organization and contributed to the growth of the industry. The textile industry, of which cotton goods were the largest component, also included woolen and linen goods in which foreign technology and skills contributed to the high quality of the products, which became competitive in the Russian market. Within the textile industry the impact of large-scale production and the economies of scale achieved by a

Table 1.51   Large-Scale Textile Industry in Congress Poland for Selected Years

Year	No. of Enterprises	No. of Workers	Horsepower Installed	Value of Output (in 1,000s of Rubles)
1879	280	29,795	3,010	50,862
1884	316	47,567	8,061	83,327
1893	412	62,471	29,519	90,965
1909	578	143,395	108,912	305,933
1913	438	138,606	119,316	303,500

Source: I. Pietrzaak-Pawlowska, ed., *Uprzemyslowienie Ziem Polskich w XIX i XX Wieku* (Warsaw, 1970), pp. 268–69.

Table 1.52   Production of Coal and Pig Iron for Selected Years
(in 1,000s of tons)

Years	Coal	Pig Iron
1878	906	35
1887	1,986	64
1894	3,355	180
1900	4,109	298
1909	5,584	216
1913	6,819	419

Source: I. Pietrzaak-Pawlowska, ed., *Uprzemyslowienie Ziem Polskich w. XIX i XX Wieku* (Warsaw, 1970), pp. 159–60.

number of large firms tended to hasten the transition from a handloom cottage industry and putting-out system to large scale modern factories. Thus, the impact of the textile industry was not only to increase total employment, but also to increase the concentration and urbanization of the labor force. Lodz itself and the factory towns of the vicinity belonged to the fastest growing population centers of Poland, and other industries, ancillary to textile production, also located there.

Another rapidly growing industry was metal products, and it, in turn, was based on the development of coal mining and metallurgy. Coal production grew rapidly throughout the period, although at varying rates. A rough indication of the production of coal and pig iron is given in table 1.52. Although the growth of coal output was uneven, the growth of pig iron was strikingly so. One of the reasons for this has to be that the coal locally produced was not suited for coke. Thus, coking coal, a vital ingredient in iron production, had to be imported either from Germany or from other distant Russian coalfields. Second, new productive capacity of modern iron working was usually introduced in large production units with a long gestation period of construction; therefore the increase in production appears to be sudden. Third, depending on market conditions, the use of production capacity might vary substantially. In fact, from about 1900 the full production capacity of the iron-works in Poland was rarely utilized due to the competition of the southern Russian ironworks. However, the local output of metallurgy was clearly sufficient to produce the raw materials for the metal industry. The Polish metal industry produced a wide variety of both capital goods (e.g., locomotives, railway equipment, agricultural machinery) and household goods. Depending on the product, the size of the enterprise and the labor force varied. Both metals and textiles were dependent on the Russian market (see table 1.53). The export data for ironworks indicate that the Russian market demand was strongest during the period of the middle 1890s, Russia's industrial spurt, and during the war with Japan, when military orders were placed with all centers of the metal industry.

The success of textiles and metals does not exhaust the list of rapidly growing industries in Poland. Even the slow-growing food industry had a record of substantial achievements. If we take the sugar industry as an example, output grew from almost 20,000 tons in 1870 to 190,000 tons in 1913, and the value of output increased from 8.5 million rubles to 65 million rubles accordingly. An area of 69,000 hectares and a labor force of over 20,000 workers cultivated sugar beets. The technical equipment of the sugar mills was modern and the yields increased continuously, indicating both the improvement in the sugar beet varieties and the efficiency of the sugar mill equipment. However, due to the competition of other sugar-producing regions in Russia, the sugar exports to the Russian market grew at a low rate or actually declined as a share of output.

The limitations of the domestic market and the fierce competition in the Russian market put real constraints on the growth of the industry in Poland. A similar situation prevailed in alcohol distilling and brewing. Al-

Table 1.53   Exports to Russia of Textiles and Metal Products
(in millions of Rubles)

Year	Textiles	Ironwares	Agricultural Machinery
1880	14.6	14.1	
1885	56.8	14.1	
1890	103.9	17.1	1.2
1895	133.8	46.0	
1900	226.3	27.0	1.5
1905	196.6	51.6	3.6
1910	284.8	39.2	4.0

Source: A. Jerzierski, *Handel Zagraniczny Krolestwa Polskiego, 1815–1914* (Warsaw: PWN, 1967), p. 149.

though the output of spirits increased from 0.39 million hectoliters in 1870 to 1.61 million hectoliters in 1913, and the output of breweries increased nearly eightfold, the lack of foreign markets and the still-limited application of alcohol in industrial uses were effective drawbacks for further growth.

On balance, the industrial production of Poland was fairly rapid by the criteria of other industrializing countries. Its industry was balanced between the production of capital goods and consumer goods; its main problem was the limit of the domestic market that was insufficient to sustain a high growth rate; it therefore depended on the demand in external markets, the most important being Russia.

Trade

The economic integration of Poland into the Russian Empire is both most vividly presented and most convincingly demonstrated by the data of exports and imports of this region. Although it was in 1850 that the customs boundary between Poland and Russia proper was abolished, for more than three subsequent decades Western Europe, rather than Russia, dominated Poland's foreign trade. Both as a destination of exports and even more pronounced as a source of imports, England and Germany were more important than the neighboring Russian market. The two shortcomings of the Russian market which prevented Poland's greater participation were the limited purchasing power of the population and the relatively late start of industrialization. Poland, which began to develop its industrial capacity in coal mining, metallurgy, and machine building earlier than Russia proper, could not compete with the countries of Western Europe in the Russian market for capital goods (before industrialization in Russia created a mass demand for capital goods for industry and construction). Being itself a latecomer to industrialization, Poland could not expect to benefit from the Russian demand for railway equipment and rails vis-à-vis the experienced producers in England and Germany. However, by the late 1880s the situation changed and the metal and coal-mining industries of Poland became suppliers to Russian industry. The growth of incomes in Russia combined with the efficiency of cotton and woolen textile production in Poland enabled the textile industry rapidly to expand exports into the Russian market. Table 1.54 presents the changes that took place in the foreign trade of Poland vis-à-vis Russia and vis-à-vis the West.

An additional and not unimportant element in the integration process was the increase in tariff protection awarded some industrial interests in Russia, including Poland. The increasing tariffs not only provided effective protection to the domestic producers, including higher profit margins as well as higher prices for consumers (a mixed blessing of protective

Table 1.54   Trade of Congress Poland (in Millions of Rubles, 1910 prices)

Year	Exports			Imports			Trade Turnover			Trade Balance		
	West	Russia	Total	West	Russia	Total	West	Russia	Total	West	Russia	Total
1850	4.3	1.0	5.3	7.4	2.9	10.3	11.7	3.9	15.6	−3.1	−1.9	−5.0
1865	15.4	11.1	26.5	16.1	14.7	30.8	31.5	25.8	57.3	−.7	−3.6	−4.3
1870	37.6	25.5	63.1	36.5	23.1	59.6	74.1	48.6	122.7	+1.1	+2.4	+3.5
1880	68	47	115	105	26	131	173	73	246	−37	+21	−16
1890	49	194	243	79	93	172	128	287	415	−30	+101	+71
1900	57	395	452	126	232	358	183	627	810	−69	+163	+94
1910	105	515	620	292	301	593	397	816	1,213	−187	+214	+27

Source: A. Jezierski, *Handel Zagraniczny Krolestwa Polskiego, 1815–1914* (Warsaw: PWN, 1967, pp. 91, 151.

tariffs), but they also stimulated foreign investment in Russia and Poland in order to avoid the tariff. In part, therefore, Poland penetrated the Russian market under the tariff umbrella. That the actual history of the expansion of exports in the Russian market was not as simple as outlined here is beyond any doubt. The competition in the Russian market by the textile and iron industries of Poland met with resistance on the part of industrial producers in other industrializing regions of Russia, especially in the southern metallurgy region and in the Moscow textile region. Although it is beyond the scope of this essay to go into a detailed examination of what was labeled "the trade war" between Lodz and Moscow, it should be mentioned that, by and large, the imperial government through railway rate policies and other measures attempted to favor the Russian regions. In addition, tariffs on industrial raw materials forced the industrialists of Poland to obtain them from distant sources in the empire instead of from neighboring countries.

The significance of the trade with Russia becomes even more intelligible when one examines the balance of trade. Almost without exception, the trade of Poland with Western countries showed a deficit. The demand for Western goods, whether capital goods, industrial raw materials, or manufactured consumer goods, exceeded the supply of exportable agricultural goods and forestry products which made up the bulk of Poland's exports to the West. It was, therefore, the opportunity to export manufactured goods to Russia[22] which enabled Poland to obtain desired manufactured goods and industrial raw materials from the West. And perhaps something else should be mentioned here. While Poland exported agricultural products to the West, it became itself increasingly an importer of agricultural goods from Russia, a development which became particularly pronounced in livestock products. Thus, the growing integration of Poland into the

Russian imperial market was not only a necessity, but also a source of advantage for the economy of the region.

The advantage was derived from the fact that Poland was much more industrialized than European Russia and maintained throughout the period its position as one of the three industrial centers of the Russian Empire, the other two being the southern industrial region and the Moscow-St. Petersburg region. As an industrialized region, Poland had a higher value-added ratio to its total production than European Russia. It imported industrial raw materials and exported manufactured goods and thereby earned substantial income. The role of trade was obviously crucial, but industrial development generated the trade. Not only did Poland receive increasing quantities of cotton, tobacco, and other raw materials from Russia, but the import of raw materials for manufacturing from the West also rose. Table 1.55 provides some insight into the composition of the imports from the West and enables one to judge the rising share of raw materials imports.

The significance of foreign trade for the economy of Poland can be summarized by citing estimates compiled by the Polish economic historian Jezierski, which compare data for industrial and agricultural output with the data for foreign trade turnover (see table 1.56). Although the data represent approximations, the order of magnitude appears to be within a reasonable range. The complementary roles of industrial growth and foreign trade turnover is very suggestive; the growth of the markets enabled industrial production to expand and to maintain its dynamic place in the economy.

Table 1.55   Share of Capital Goods and Industrial Raw Materials in Imports from the West, Congress Poland (in Millions of Rubles)

Years	Total Imports	Capital[a] Goods	Raw[b] Materials	Raw[c] Materials	Share in Total Imports (%)
1880	105	5.7	3.6	14.0	22.3
1885	109	2.4	6.1	30.0	35.3
1890	79	1.2	4.8	9.5	19.5
1895	129	23.1	4.2	35.6	48.7
1900	126	39.5	7.8	38.4	68.0
1905	112	17.7	8.6	82.9	97.5
1910	292	15.4	10.8	96.4	42.0

Source: A. Jezierski, *Handel Zagraniczny Krolestwa Polskiego, 1815–1914* (Warsaw: PWN, 1967), pp. 162–63.

[a]Equipment and machinery.
[b]Coal, coke, pig iron.
[c]Cotton, wool, hides.

Table 1.56   The Value of Gross Industrial and Agricultural Production and the
Foreign Trade of Congress Poland, 1882–1913 (in Millions of Rubles)

Year	Value of Industrial Production	Value of Agricultural Production	Total	Foreign Trade Turnover
1882	184	330	514	246
1900	600	400[b]	1,000	810
1913	1,000	600[c]	1,600	1,212

Source: A. Jezierski, *Handel Zagraniczny Krolestwa Polskiego, 1815–1914* (Warsaw: PWN, 1967), p. 153.
[a]Data for 1880.
[b]Data for 1899.
[c]Data for 1912.

The Capital Stock

Our review would be incomplete without some insight into the area of the infrastructure and the role of human capital in the growth of Poland's economy. Among the elements of the infrastructure which are of considerable importance for the economy, the various forms of transportation occupy a strategic position. However, by the standards of Western Europe the state of the transportation facilities in Poland was not satisfactory. By 1910 Poland had 3,810 kilometers of railroads, 8,343 kilometers of highways, and 3,141 kilometers of waterways of which 1,407 were usable for steamboats. Needless to say, by comparison with 1870, when there were only about 960 kilometers of railway track, some progress was achieved. The lack of a more densely developed transportation network can be explained partly by the ambiguities of governmental policies. The geopolitical situation of Poland required a transportation network which could serve the military purposes of defense and communication lines with the Russian hinterland. But a dense network could conceivably aid a potential enemy in the penetration of Russian territory. This ambiguity led the Russian government not to encourage private railroad construction beyond a few basic trunk lines and to extend some lines of a primarily strategic nature at government expense. The government was also eager to take over the privately operated railroads and to incorporate them into the state-operated network. Although the railroads in Poland were profitable and capital for further railroad construction could be raised domestically or abroad, no major expansion was envisaged. Thus, given the low density of railways and improved paved roads, the economic integration of the region suffered because many of the smaller towns, and certainly the rural areas, depended on primitive wagon roads that were barely passable during parts of the year.

The dearth of public capital for railway construction was also matched by minimal government expenditures in public building. However, whereas private railroad construction could be effectively stopped by the government, private expenditures in housing construction or factory construction could not be. Thus, Poland experienced a rapid growth of construction of factory and business buildings and of dwellings, particularly in the fast-growing cities. While the population of the forty-three cities which had more than 10,000 inhabitants increased from about 1,230,000 in 1893 to 2,317,000 in 1909, one would expect a growth in demand for housing and other amenities. The stock of urban housing increased and was valued in 1910 at about 484 million rubles, factory buildings at about 65 million rubles, a total of 633 million (including also the smaller towns). Private expenditures were also directed toward the construction of various institutions such as hospitals and schools.

This raises the important issue of health care and education. Health care in Poland, as in most regions of Russia, was on a very low level and mostly confined to the major cities. A total of 1,965 physicians and some paramedical personnel served the total population, but of the total number of physicians, 1,608 practiced in the cities. The 347 hospitals, which varied in size, had a total of 10,379 beds, clearly inadequate. While in the cities there was 1 physician per 1,500 population (in Warsaw 1 per 760 population), in the rural areas there was only 1 per 30,000 population. One therefore wonders whether it was under the impact of health care that infant mortality declined and the mortality rate of epidemics fell.

Serious deficiencies also existed in the area of education. Literacy was low, especially among the rural population and among women. And, although the 1897 Census data show a higher literacy rate in Poland than in European Russia, the acquisition of literacy during the subsequent period proceeded faster in the Russian provinces than in Poland. There is no doubt that Poland suffered from discrimination as far as government educational policies were concerned. Russification of the population was at variance with the cultural aspirations of the Polish population and the Jewish population. The application of the Russian government's national and social policies in the field of education had dire consequences, since it not only was discriminatory in terms of government support for the school network, but it also prohibited educational activities to be conducted in their native language, desired by private individuals and the majority of the society.

One- and two-grade schools constituted the base of the government-supported school network. By 1911 there were 4,659 such schools with 338,433 pupils, while the total of such elementary schools (including private and church supported) was 5,091 with 359,000 pupils. This last number of pupils already was an improvement, since in 1895 there were only

3,565 schools with 206,282 pupils. The growth of about 50 per cent over a fifteen-year period, although impressive, lagged behind the increase of a similar school population in European Russia in this period. The difference in the growth of schools in Poland and European Russia could be explained not only by government subsidies and expenditures but also by the fact that, while in Russia a part of the increase was achieved by the parish schools of the Russian Orthodox church, the Catholic church in Poland was much more restricted in its educational activities.

Therefore, if one would try to explain the growth of human capital embodied in the labor force in Poland, the increase in literacy from elementary education would account for some, but not most, of the improvement of the quality of the labor force. For the acquisition of skills, the existence of urban trade schools was important as well as the Sunday trade schools, where apparently workers were able to augment their general education and skill training. In both types of schools the enrollment in 1911 was about 12,000. At the level of secondary education, apart from the over 26,000 enrolled in the general secondary schools, we encounter about 17,800 enrolled in basically commercial and technical types of secondary schools. There is no doubt that the latter provided a supply of trained technicians, lower management, and supervisory personnel. The existence of a polytechnical institution of higher education in Warsaw assured a minimum supply of trained engineers. It is true that the authorities favored Russians over Poles and Jews at the Polytechnic, but nevertheless a modicum of locally trained, highly skilled manpower existed. In fact, Polish industry imported foreign specialists who were acquainted with the most modern technology and often "exported" its locally trained engineers to the factories, mills, and railroads of other regions of Russia.

But when one adds up all the sources of formal education, there still remains a residual of skill acquisition which the employees in industry, craft, and commerce achieved through on-the-job training. The modern factories were the substitutes of the apprenticeship training of previous periods. It was the on-the-job training which contributed a great deal to the skills of the workers in Poland and which made them more productive than the workers in other regions of Russia. Perhaps the longer history of industrialization in Poland created a larger number of hereditary workers who were familiar with the modern factory system and could adjust to it more easily.

Therefore, it is possible to conclude that the economy of Congress Poland underwent a far-reaching transformation toward becoming industrialized from 1860 to 1914. The indicators pertaining to capital, to labor, and to the nature of enterprise support this conclusion.

TWO

Government Policies and
the Industrialization of Russia

If we were to reconstruct a blueprint of the Russian government's goals and priorities for industrial development in the late nineteenth century, it would include the following: 1) development of a network of internal transportation, 2) stabilization of the ruble in foreign exchanges through convertibility and the building up of an export surplus as a prerequisite for enabling the Russian government to borrow abroad, and 3) stimulation of the development of new industries in Russia and their protection in their "infancy." Given the relative success of Russia's industrialization during the end of the nineteenth and beginning of the twentieth centuries and the important role that the government played in this effort, there is no justification for outright rejection or condemnation of Russian government economic policies. There were, however, serious shortcomings in particular government policies, and the presumed effects that they had on the industrialization were not always desirable. This essay is a modest attempt to reexamine Russian government policies on the assumption that the industrialization of Russia was a continuing goal of the state's policies beginning with the 1880s, and one of relatively high priority. The implication of the analysis is that if some of the defects of the state's policies had been avoided, the process of industrialization would have proceeded at least at as fast a pace and the economic costs to Russian society would probably have been smaller.

The following features of Russian economic policies have been selected for discussion:

I have benefited from general discussions with my colleagues Harry G. Johnson and Robert Mundell. A certain familiarity with the data was acquired during the tenure of a National Science Foundation grant. Responsibility for the views and possible errors, however, cannot be shared with anyone.

1) fiscal policy and its impact on the domestic demand for industrial goods;
2) government borrowings and their impact on private investment in industry;
3) government tariff policy, its fiscal characteristics, its protective features, and the welfare loss to the consumers resulting from the tariff; and
4) monetary policy and its possible costs to the Russian economy.

For the discussion of the first point data for the period 1885–1913 are used, for the second and third points the period 1880–1900 is examined, and for the fourth point the period 1897–1913 is used.

It is assumed here that the underlying complicating factors and problems of Russian industrialization can be attributed to the state of Russian agriculture and its slow progress in transforming and modernizing itself,[1] and that state policies which were committed to the preservation of some "traditional" features of Russian agriculture were incompatible with a bold program of industrialization. Thus, whether right or wrong, the implicit assumption is that the industrialization process in Russia required a much more radical and constructive policy toward agriculture than was pursued by the Russian government. The very tentative conclusions drawn in this essay must be considered in the context of the larger issue raised by these assumptions.

I

The process of industrialization accelerates either when there is an increase of domestic demand for industrial goods or when the government conducts a vigorous policy of industrialization. In my opinion, the second alternative was chosen in Russia because the first was not given an opportunity to assert itself under the conditions of the existing political regime.

When one talks about an increase of domestic demand for industrial goods, one implicitly assumes a sustained rise in per capita incomes that stimulates the demand for goods with a relatively high income elasticity, although perhaps also with a substantial price elasticity. I assume that an increasing demand for industrial consumer goods would tend to stimulate their mass production; that this would be accompanied by a fall in their prices due to economies of scale; that import substitution would follow; and that as a secondary effect the demand for capital goods would increase. If the economy had any long-run comparative advantage in the production of these capital goods, their domestic production would tend to increase.

This type of industrialization, perhaps idealized and simplified in its "organic" gradual development, was not, however, permitted to be tried simply because government policies assigned higher priorities to fiscal revenues than to increases in consumption and the accumulation of personal savings.

Table 2.1 attempts to estimate the volume of taxes paid to the government (except for other forms of taxation levied by various local government authorities, which constituted an additional 15 per cent of the taxes paid to the government) and their changes over time.[2]

In order to have some yardstick to judge the size and impact of taxation in Russia, we ought to compare it with two measures: per capita national income and the value of retail trade. For the years for which estimates (although far from satisfactory) are available we have the relationships shown in table 2.2.

Table 2.1   Per Capita Taxation (in Rubles)

Year	Total Taxes[a]	Excise Taxes[b]
1885	6.41	2.43
1890	7.12	2.83
1895	8.15	3.29
1900	8.83	4.10
1905	9.53	5.59
1910	11.79	6.69
1913	11.43	7.34

[a]Excluded from the total reported tax revenue were the gross revenues from the operation of the state railroads and state forests.

[b]The data for 1900, 1905, 1910, and 1913 include the net profits of the state's alcohol monopoly.

Table 2.2   Relationship between Per Capita Taxes, National Income, and Value of Retail Trade

Year	Taxes as % of National Income[a]	Taxes as % of Retail Trade[b]
1885	12.8	—
1899	—	25.9
1900	13.2	27.4
1905	—	27.6
1910	—	32.3
1913	12.85	27.4

[a]The estimates of per capita income for 1900 and 1913 are from S. N. Prokopovich, *Opyt ischisleniia narodnogo dokhoda 50 gubernii Europeiskoi Rossii V 1900–1913* (Petrograd, 1918). The 1885 estimate is a preliminary estimate by me; it was derived in an attempt to reevaluate the changes of Russian GNP and national income for the prerevolutionary period.

[b]The estimates of the value of retail sales are by S. G. Strumilin. See G. A. Dikhtiar, *Vnutrenniaia torgovlia v dorevolutsionnoi Rossii* (Moscow, 1960), p. 79.

Given the fact that the larger part of peasant income was still in the form of income in-kind, mostly agricultural products consumed within the farm households, and that local taxes ought to be added, the burden of taxation on the majority of the population becomes more significant.

One should also not leave out of sight the skewness of the income distribution in Russia[3] as well as the fact that excise taxes constituted a large share of the total burden of taxation. Excise taxes of the "Russian type" were regressive in their nature and thereby burdened the lower income groups.

Thus one would have to conclude that the burden of taxation left relatively little room for substantial increases in demand for goods and services of the type that would stimulate industrial development. This also explains why some Russian industries would frequently "hit the ceiling" of effective demand for their products under the conditions of the limitations on the population's purchasing power.

The volume of taxes, when compared with the gross value of output of Russian industry, provides an interesting insight into the quantitative relationship of the two (see table 2.3). Although it indicates a sharp decline in the ratio of taxes to the gross value of industrial output, nevertheless it does not decrease to a level at which the fiscal policies would have had a minor effect on the demand for industrial goods.

Therefore, one would have to acquiesce in the conclusion that it was the government, by taxing the incomes of the consumers, that deprived Russia of an alternative pattern of industrialization, thus usurping for itself the role of an active participant and stimulant of this process. It is therefore incumbent on the economic historian to investigate the basic tendencies of government economic activity in order to detect the elements which facilitated or intensified the process of industrialization. The primacy of fiscal policies in the government's activities in Russia appears to be established beyond any reasonable doubt.

Table 2.3   **Taxes as a Percent of the Gross Value of Industrial Output**

Year	Ratio[a]
1885	51.3
1890	46.2
1900	27.3
1905	29.2
1910	34.4
1913	25.5

[a]The gross value of industrial output estimates are from S. G. Strumilin, *Problema promyshlennogo kapitala v SSSR* (Moscow, 1925), pp. 12–13; the taxes are from note 2.

To expect that fiscal considerations would be overruled by long-run in-dustrialization policies is too much to expect of most governments, and to expect it from the government of Tsarist Russia is to misinterpret the na-ture of this particular political regime and thereby to have to assume that its subsequent fall was the work of a *deus ex machina.*

Nevertheless, historians often tend to disregard the existing features of the reality of government policy and to pass judgment on the basis of general pronouncements or misleading government statistics. Let me illus-trate this contention by an example from the work of a generally respected historian of the period under consideration, Theodore Von Laue, who was victimized by his admiration for the Russian minister of finance and by his misreading of Russian budget reports.

> How much the government spent for its various economic activities in these years may come as a surprise. Roughly totaled, the appropriations for all economic ministries (Finance, Agriculture, Communications) and the service of the government debt (contracted largely for railroad construction) amounted to over 52 per cent of the combined ordinary and extraordinary budgets in 1894 and 55 per cent in the following year. The army and navy combined claimed about half as much, nearly 29 per cent in 1894, but only 22.5 per cent in 1895. What was left went to the administrative agencies, the Ministry of Interior with its extensive organization and its police, diplomatic service, schools and universities, the Church, the courts of law, the Ministry of Justice and the Imperial household. Obviously the economy rather than defense was the benefi-ciary of Witte's financial management[4].

A closer inspection of the data used by our historian reveals that the dis-tribution which he constructs is grossly misleading for two reasons. First, the official budget figures he uses include the gross expenditures of such public enterprises as the government railways, and later of the state-operated alcohol monopoly; these expenditures should obviously not be classed as expenditures embodying an economic policy. Second, Von Laue overlooks the fact that the category of expenditures on administration in-cludes only a part of the overhead expenses of the government apparatus; much of the expenditures of the "economic ministries" were for pure ad-ministration.

The fallacy of Von Laue's method can be illustrated by the fact that, applied to the budgets of 1887 and 1888—before Witte assumed control of policy—it shows that respectively, 52.5 and 52.2 per cent of total gov-ernment expenditures were on the economic ministries. The same method when applied to 1913 reduces the share of defense expenditures from 36 per cent, to 24.4 per cent of the total budget expenditures. An official distribution of the 1903 government budget expenditures (still Witte's brainchild) gives the following shares of different expense categories (in per cent):[5]

Economy and cultural expenses	16
Interest and the redemption of public debt	22
National defense	36
Administration	25

One could probably also argue with Von Laue about whether railroad construction or various wars were primarily responsible for the growth of the national debt and its service charges.

In addition, the category labeled "economy and cultural expenses" included for fifteen years, 1892–1912, a total of 692 million rubles of famine relief and food reserves purchases (of which 565 million was direct famine relief). How productive such an expense was from the point of view of industrialization is difficult to assess. It is, however, even more difficult to absolve the government of Russia and her fiscal and economic policies from coresponsibility for the necessity of such expenses. There is no doubt that the total government spending in manufacturing and mining never even came close to the expenses of famine relief.

The fiscal policies of the government would be justified from the point of view of the objectives of industrialization if the forced savings siphoned off by the fiscal authorities had been used to a large extent to finance industrial investment. The specific criticism which can be brought against the Russian government is that only a minute part of its budget expenditures went directly for purposes of developing the industrial sector.

The area given heaviest financial support by the government was that of railroad construction. Major criticisms of the Russian railroad network as a form of social overhead have pointed out that much of it was constructed to serve the needs of troop movements, in case of war mobilization, rather than the economic needs of freight and passenger service. Even in view of the recent attempts to revise downward the previously exaggerated claims of the magnitude of social savings by railroads, the Russian railroads beyond any doubt contributed to the process of economic and cultural transformation of the country.

However, we find that internal and external borrowing were the overwhelming sources of financing railroad construction rather than straight budget financing. It is difficult to find one's way in the maze of Russian railroad statistics for a number of reasons, but the rough approximation for expenses in direct railroad construction and for subsidizing private railroad construction would not exceed by much a total of 1 billion rubles for the 1880s and 1890s. For a comparison, this corresponds very closely to the government customs revenue from imports of tea, coffee, alcoholic beverages, salt, and herring. If we take into account that the interest payments of railroad bonds were paid from the gross revenue of the government-operated railroads and certain surcharges for their services, the expenditures by the state budget proper were not excessive.

But while the expenditures for railroad construction were the government's single largest item for industrialization purposes, the direct subsidies to industrial entrepreneurs did not come to an even close second within the total expenditures for "development of the economy" for the last two decades of the nineteenth century.

In addition, the substitution of government demand for goods and services from the industrial sector, as well as the flow of government investment, was highly irregular and uneven. This had an adverse effect on the economy, which also moved in an erratic fashion, intensifying in some instances the business cycle and adversely affecting business expectations in some crucial industries. This created a situation in which the growth of industrial capital and output was all but smooth; among its results were the industrial boom of the late 1890s and virtual stagnation in 1900–1906.

II

One of the often-voiced criticisms of the Russian pattern of investment, typical of many criticisms in less-developed economies and in the minds of critics justifying strong government intervention, is the relatively low preference of investors for providing funds for the industrial sector of the economy.

As in many criticisms of this type, there is a grain of truth in this observation, and two phenomena particularly call for further investigation. One is that a substantial part of the savings was provided by successful landowners under conditions of an imperfect money market and banking system. This might explain, in part at least, their preference for investment in land mortgages under conditions of rising land prices. The greater familiarity with the agricultural sector, the relative security of funds invested in mortgage loans, and the favorable attitude of the government to this particular type of loan, expressed by its interest in the workings of the Bank of the Nobility and the Peasant Bank, made this type of investment a powerful competitor to industrial investments. But one ought not to forget that during the period 1880–1900 the government was not a newcomer in the money market but was a long-standing competitor for investible funds.

Unfortunately, we have very sketchy and imprecise estimates from which to judge the relative competitive situation of the demand for investment by industry. The data are insufficient even to state with any degree of certainty whether we are dealing with a unified market or with a few separated markets for industrial funds. However, some available estimates will indicate the general trend. Using the estimates provided by Brzheskii, who provides a breakdown of changes in the stock of some elements of the primarily domestic process of capital formation,[6] we can roughly distribute the investment flow among three major claimants: 1) the government, 2) the land mortgage banks and companies, and 3) the corporations engaged in industrial, mercantile, and other nonagricultural activity.[7] Although the third group is amorphous, we can assume that in broad categories the increase of the stock of capital of such enterprises and institutions was a favorable element for the process of industrialization.[8] Table 2.4 presents the yearly changes in the capital stock of the major claimants of domestic investment funds. The role of the government as a competitor

Table 2.4 Yearly Increase of Some Elements of Domestic Investment,
Estimates of Changes in Capital Stock (in Millions of Rubles)

Year	Total	Domestic Public Debt	Mortgage Capital	Capital of Dividend-Paying Firms and Share Capital of Industrial Corporations
1882	206	91	71	44
1883	62	−11	39	34
1884	96	13	41	42
1885	69	−12	47	34
1886	548	463	56	29
1887	217	91	104	22
1888	345	208	98	39
1889	68	−19	52	35
1890	−59	−37	−58	36
1891	319	−25	278	66
1892	−33	8	−75	34
1893	92	−20	77	35
1894	169	79	54	36
1895	289	131	82	76
1896	143	54	−40	129
1897	385	77	127	181
1898	359	50	161	148
1899	559	67	203	289
1900	625	84	220	321
1882–1900	4,459	1,292	1,537	1,630
Percentage distribution of the total increase	100.0	29.0	34.5	36.5

for savings appears very clearly in this table. While during 1882–90 the government borrowed 787 million rubles, out of a total of 1,552 million, or one-half, during the subsequent period the government borrowed 505 million out of 2,907 million, only 17 per cent. Therefore, one is inclined to believe that not only might the preference for gilt-edge government bonds in the domestic market have declined in favor of other types of securities, but that the decreased government demand for savings in the domestic capital market (which was in part substituted by heavy borrowings abroad) enabled Russian industrial entrepreneurs to borrow more freely.

As imperfect as the underlying estimates may be, they tend to indicate that the difficulties (real or alleged) encountered by industrial entrepreneurs in obtaining the capital funds for profitable investments depended to some extent not on the presence but on the absence of the government as a borrower in the domestic money market. That its stepping down as the major claimant of investable funds indirectly helped the industrial entrepreneurs is also hinted at by the imperfect data at our disposal.

III

Russian tariff policy was as much revenue oriented as protection oriented, the upward tendency in tariff rates being sustained by fiscal needs as much as by the clamor for protection from imports. Of course there were differences in the timing of both factors, as well as distinctions between the tariffs on various groups of commodities, but the general nature of the policy can be established without much difficulty.[9]

Customs duties as a per cent of total direct and indirect taxes collected by the government increased from 18 per cent in 1881 to an average of 28 per cent for the years 1897–1900. The revenue features of the tariff were most clearly reflected in the rates of the tariff on imported foodstuffs, which increased in the same period from 30 per cent of the value of imports in 1881 to 69 per cent in 1897–1900. The chief sources of revenue among foodstuffs were tea, coffee, alcoholic beverages, tobacco, salt, and herring, thus complementing the state revenues from the excise taxes. That the fiscal features of the tariff policies were not limited to the importation of foodstuffs becomes evident in view of the parallel upward tendency of tariff rates on raw materials and semi-manufactured goods.

This of course represented a conflict between short run fiscal interests and the objectives of industrialization, since the tariff tended to increase the costs of raw materials, imported or domestically produced (like cotton, wool, iron), to the domestic manufacturing industries. These rising costs in turn "justified" the increase in tariff rates for cotton yarn, woolen cloth, and metal products. The result of this chain reaction was that fiscal considerations contributed to the raising of the tariff umbrella over an increasing number of manufactured goods—tools, machinery, and capital goods in general not excluded.

Although the government stimulated the development of some capital goods industries (like locomotives and railway equipment, shipbuilding, etc.) by direct placing of supply contracts, a tariff was levied on some capital goods imports, presumably in the expectation of the establishment or expansion of domestic output. In the meantime, a period which in some cases lasted rather long, Russia's capital goods importers[10] experienced the paradox of having to pay higher prices for the imports which were to foster industrialization. This lack of refinement and discrimination in tariff policies (and many examples can be cited to support this claim) cannot be attributed either to ignorance or to bureaucratic routine, but it resulted from the overriding priorities of fiscal needs.

No one would deny that the Russian tariff had a number of stimulating effects on the growth of domestic industrial output, employment, and incomes. This is indisputable. Very seldom, however, have economic historians asked the question: How much did it cost the Russian consumer, the ultimate payer of the tariff?

There are two ways of measuring the impact of the tariff. One is simply to assess the customs revenues and add them on to the costs of the consumers. From the point of view of economic theory, however, customs duties, being a government income, cannot be assumed to constitute a loss to the consumers' welfare.

Another method, however, allows us to make some estimates of consumers' welfare losses. The tariff levied on foreign imported goods raised their costs to the Russian consumers and allowed the domestic producers to charge for domestic substitutes a price equal to the foreign price plus the tariff. By artificially increasing the price of foreign imports to the consumers, the tariff distorted the allocation of consumer expenditures (the consumption cost of the tariff); by providing a subsidy to domestic producers, the tariff distorted the allocation of resources that would have taken place under the conditions of a free market (the production cost of the tariff).

The consumption costs may be estimated as follows: if it is assumed that the demand elasticity for the goods protected by the tariff is unity, the consumption cost of the Russian tariff can be calculated using the formula $C = 1/2T^2P \cdot Q$, where T equals the percentage of the Russian tariff of the foreign price, and $P \cdot Q$ equals the value of the total domestic output and imports of the commodity at the domestic price.[11] The consumption costs were calculated for the following commodities: coal, pig iron, iron, steel, cotton, and cotton yarn. This selection was dictated by the ready availability of data and the relative importance of these commodities for the process of industrialization.

Table 2.5 summarizes the results of the calculation (in millions of rubles). The preliminary results of the calculation indicate that the consumption cost of the Russian tariff on coal was negligible for the period 1880–1900, but the costs to the consumer of the products of the metal and cotton textile industries, the two major industries of Russia, were considerable. These results should be compared with the customs revenue from the enumerated commodities for a particular year (see table 2.6).

Even if one assumed that the estimates of consumption costs tend to have an upward bias—the foreign goods imported being of higher quality—because of the use of domestic prices in the calculation instead of the average between domestic and foreign prices, or because the actual demand elasticity was less than unity, it would still probably be correct to assume that in terms of the loss to the economy in the long run, consumers' losses exceeded the short-run benefits to the Treasury. Despite benefits in the growth of industrial employment (which involves the wage differential between industrial wages and alternatives, let us say, farm wages),

Table 2.5 Estimated Consumption Costs of the Tariff
(in Millions of Rubles, Current Prices)

Year	Coal	Pig Iron	Iron	Steel	Cotton	Cotton Yarn
1880	—	0.2	1.3	1.2	0.1	n.a.
1881	—	0.2	3.8	2.3	0.2	n.a.
1882	—	0.2	4.2	1.3	0.2	n.a.
1883	—	0.2	4.5	1.1	0.2	n.a.
1884	—	0.3	3.2	1.0	0.2	n.a.
1885	0.1	0.9	6.1	1.1	0.2	n.a.
1886	0.1	2.2	4.8	1.2	0.3	n.a.
1887	0.2	5.0	9.1	2.3	0.6	n.a.
1888	0.4	13.5	8.2	1.8	1.4	n.a.
1889	0.5	10.0	8.3	1.9	1.5	n.a.
1890	0.4	10.2	8.7	2.9	1.1	12.8
1891	0.5	18.2	11.5	4.4	1.8	13.9
1892	0.3	21.0	16.1	7.5	2.5	14.0
1893	0.4	20.7	16.4	11.9	3.8	16.2
1894	0.4	22.4	12.1	5.8	3.9	15.0
1895	0.5	22.5	11.2	8.6	10.0	17.0
1896	0.4	27.3	13.8	12.9	10.0	19.7
1897	0.7	44.1	18.6	17.5	12.3	20.0
1898	1.4	62.2	28.9	29.1	13.4	16.3
1899	1.9	64.0	n.a.	61.3	20.1	44.1
1900	0.8	53.6	n.a.	57.4	20.6	44.0

Table 2.6 Consumption Cost and Customs Revenue of Selected Commodities, 1897 (in Millions of Rubles)

Commodity	Consumption Cost	Customs Revenue
Pig iron	44.1	2.6
Iron	18.6	15.5
Steel	17.5	3.4
Cotton	12.3	27.8
Cotton yarn	20.0	1.6
Total	112.5	50.9

one would suspect that, at least for some industries, the tendency would be for the consumption cost to increase.

With regard to the production cost, in 1906 the Russian economist N. N. Savvin estimated the cost of the tariff to the Russian consumers of manufactured goods in 1900. He estimated the customs duties for imported manufactured goods as 141 million rubles and the "excess payment" for domestically produced goods as 238 millions, or about 22 per cent of the estimated net output of Russian manufactures in 1900.[12] Apparently Savvin's estimate did not include such commodities as cotton, wool, and pig iron, since Sobolev (who quotes Savvin's estimates) provides an additional calculation of "additional excess payments for raw materials" totaling 253 millions and views Savvin's estimates as "moderate."[13] Although no attempt was made to estimate the consumption or production costs of the tariff beyond 1900, the circumstantial evidence pertaining to both the metal industries and some branches of the cotton textile industries would indicate that the continuing tariff protection during the decade to come did not succeed in bringing them nearer to a position of competitiveness.

The first decade of the twentieth century was marked by a growth of monopolistic tendencies in the metal-producing industries. Monopolistic activities, such as price-setting collusion and quota setting for output, became widespread in the Russian iron and steel industries with the organization of such producers' associations as "Prodamet," "Krovlia," "Prodvagon," and "Provoloka." Although attempts were made to organize the cotton textile producers in order to maintain prices and to divide markets, they were less successful than in the case of the iron industries.

Thus the tariff policies of the government, by imposing losses on the consumers, not only limited the demand for industrial goods, but in addition shielded the producers from real competition which would have forced them to innovate and decrease production costs. By allowing the producers to engage in monopolistic practices, the government permitted them to inflict more losses on the consumers.

As more data become available to the historian, it will perhaps be possible to calculate with greater precision the costs (direct and indirect) of the government's tariff policies. At the moment we can only state that the protective features of the tariff were a mixed blessing, interpretation of which requires a balance sheet that would record the benefits as well as the costs.

IV

One of the goals of Russian economic policy was to achieve a state of convertibility of its currency into gold at a fixed price. After a number of years of accumulation of substantial gold reserves by the Treasury and the State Bank, a monetary reform was carried out in August 1897. The new notes of the State Bank were convertible in gold on demand at the rate of 66.67 gold kopeks for a paper ruble. Under the new arrangement the gold reserves for the bank notes were set at 50 per cent for the amount below 600 million rubles and at 100 per cent for any sum above 600 million. In addition, the mint started to put into circulation an increasing volume of gold and high-value silver coins.

The benefits of the monetary reform, apart from the elimination of the fluctuating exchange rate, were a greater facility in foreign borrowing for the Russian government and an influx of private foreign capital.[14]

Many economists and historians have sung praises to the Russian government or to the architects of their monetary policy for the introduction of the gold standard in Russia. Very few, if any, have asked about the economic costs of the gold standard as it was applied in Russia during the subsequent seventeen years.[15] It has been said that in general the defects of the State Bank's organization with respect to note issue are in a sense analogous to those of Sir Robert Peel's Bank Act.[16] I believe that a question could be raised about the policy of keeping such high gold reserves (see table 2.7). During the period 1897–1913 an excess of 443 million rubles in gold, on the average, was held by the State Bank over and above the requirements of its statutes. In fact, if one would take into account the fact that gold in coins and reserves increased from 1,131 million in 1897 to 2,185 million in 1913 (or from 895 million in 1894 when the exchange rate of the paper ruble was 67 gold kopeks), or by over 1 billion rubles, one could perhaps question the wisdom of such policies.

However, if the Russian government had instead kept a gold reserve of two-thirds of the total currency in circulation, the average yearly holdings in gold could have been less by about 590 millions.[17] If we assumed that variations in the note circulation within each year would require about 100 million rubles in gold as an internal reserve, and an additional 100 million

Table 2.7   Notes in Circulation, Gold in Circulation, and the
Gold Reserves of the State Bank
(In Millions of Rubles)

Year	Notes in Circulation	Gold in Circulation	State Bank Gold Reserve	Total Gold
1892	1,055	—	642	642
1893	1,074	—	852	852
1894	1,072	—	895	895
1895	1,048	—	912	912
1896	1,055	—	964	964
1897	1,068	36	1,095	1,131
1898	901	148	1,185	1,333
1899	662	451	1,008	1,459
1900	491	641	843	1,484
1901	555	683	737	1,420
1902	542	694	709	1,403
1903	554	732	796	1,528
1904	578	775	909	1,684
1905	854	684	1,032	1,716
1906	1,207	838	927	1,765
1907	1,195	642	1,191	1,833
1908	1,155	622	1,169	1,791
1909	1,087	561	1,220	1,781
1910	1,174	581	1,415	1,996
1911	1,234	642	1,450	2,092
1912	1,327	656	1,436	2,092
1913	1,495	629	1,550	2,185

rubles deposited in foreign banks to facilitate balance of payments problems, it would still leave us with an excess gold reserve of about 400 millions yearly on the average. When invested instead of kept as a reserve by the State Bank, even at a 5 per cent rate of interest, the income yield during the seventeen years of the gold standard would have been at least 340 million rubles, a sum that a country as capital poor as Russia could not have ignored. Yet the price of 20 million rubles per annum was not an unacceptable price to pay for the convenience and stability of operating under the gold standard.

V

From the above discussion the following tentative conclusions may be drawn:

1) There existed an inherent conflict between the fiscal interests and demands of the Russian state and the requirements of a vigorous long-range policy of industrialization. In most cases when choices of sub-

stantial magnitude of resources were involved, the primacy of short-run fiscal interests seemed to prevail.

2) To resolve the conflict, at least in part, the Russian government attempted to obtain funds from abroad, both in the form of straight government borrowings and foreign investments in Russian industries.

3) As a means of facilitating borrowing from abroad, the Russian government was willing to pay the price imposed by its conservative monetary policy and was probably correct in following this course.

4) The success of the effort to secure foreign capital relieved the government of dependence on internal savings and allowed for a substantial increase in private funds for industrial development.

5) The tariff policy of the government had a very significant fiscal impact that could be added to the direct impact of excise taxes on the majority of Russian consumers.

6) The losses in welfare to the Russian consumers imposed by the tariff were considerable in comparison with the employment effects and benefits enjoyed by the protected industries.

7) The burden of taxation to support the Russian political regime appears to have been the chief obstacle to a more vigorous industrial development of Russia.

Appendix

Excerpts from review of Theodore H. Von Laue, *Sergei Witte and the Industrialization of Russia.*[18]

It is no accident that students of nineteenth-century Russia are much more attracted by the leading figures in Russia's intellectual history than by those whose names fill the annals of her political history: for almost a century the Russian political system bred pygmies not giants.

Among such political personalities, the figure of Sergei Witte, the resourceful Minister of Finance at the turn of the century, assumes towering proportions in the book under review where it was Witte who attempted to hook the locomotive of industrial development to the primitive Russian economy and pull it along the newly laid railroad tracks toward the goal of transformation.

Von Laue's book is not a substitute for a history of the industrialization of Tsarist Russia but rather an attempt to analyze a particular phase of Russian economic policy under the regime that has become known as the "Witte system." The problem of industrialization is set next to Witte's personality and activity in the center of the author's discussion.

Industrialization is a much more complex social process than the mere accumulation of resources for the purpose of erecting industrial structures, mounting machinery, manning the machines, and turning out manufactured goods for distribution and sale at a profit. Industrialization involves, on the one hand, sets of cultural phenomena that entail the creation of wants resulting from the acceptance of a new value system, the willingness to change traditional patterns of life, perseverance in the pursuit of particular goals, acceptance of new behavioral norms, the assumption of responsibilities and risks, and new types of decision making by a multitude of people, and, on the other hand, significant and grave political decisions. We are confronted with a mystery of industrialization that has a single prime mover: government policy with Witte's hand on the throttle. Granted, it is easier to describe the results of the process of industrialization than to define its necessary conditions, or to describe the economic continuities or discontinuities, or to analyze the particularities of the process within a given country or milieu. But this is precisely the area where originality of insight can be displayed and a genuine contribution made. By failing to define the problems with precision and in detail, Von Laue, as it were, invites the reader to use whatever image of industrialization he possesses and to plug into the Russian historical realities anything ranging from the British-American industrialization experience to that of Guinea and Mali. Similarly, the lack of definition of industrialization made it possible for the author to refer to Witte as "one of the giants in the succession from Peter the Great to Lenin" (p. 36), a reference which might very easily, perhaps even against the author's intention, be transformed into "a link in a historical chain" of industrialization, modernization, and what not. In spite of its obvious appeal to the uninitiated, such a chain explains very little and as a generalization, in addition to being obscure, might also be confusing. But no author should be severely criticized for implications drawn from errors of omission.

Furthermore, an historian should clearly distinguish between the political motives behind a government policy favoring industrialization and the type of political decisions used to implement it. Peter the Great and Frederick II, Alexander Hamilton and Friedrich List, Bismarck as well as Witte and Lenin, recognized the development of industry and trade as a means of strengthening the political status of a country in the field of international relations or of preserving its national sovereignty. But what distinguished Witte from most of these others was his inability to perceive the role of political institutions in bringing about industrialization. Von Laue does not sufficiently elaborate on his hero's notions of the adjustments that the state or ruling groups have to make in order for industrialization to succeed. In fact, I would suggest that for Witte this would have presented itself much more as an administrative than as a real political problem, which in turn raises the nagging question about Witte as putting a wager on the capitalists, the businessmen. He fails, however, to follow up the logic and consistency of this view by inquiring into the role Witte assigned to the capitalists. Did Witte see the businessman as an unfettered agent, or preferably as a tool of government policy, without much political influence and even with little guarantee of the continuation of favorable policies? No radical changes in the political system were envisaged in Witte's scheme of industrialization. Von Laue probably comes closest to the truth when he suggests that Witte felt most secure under the system of autocracy, which assured him, at least for a while, what was perhaps an inefficient but certainly an obedient execution of his orders. This might reveal the real Witte, the high-level bureaucrat, the superbly skillful technician in need of a political autocracy (or even a command economy) for the realization of his objectives, a mind inclined toward mechanistic views of social problems, of somewhat limited intellectual capacity and therefore drawn toward administrative solutions.

On the positive side, one should give due credit to Witte's sense of the time dimensions involved in the duration of protectionist trade policies and infant industry protection as well as of the utilization by the government of periods of peace for the diversion of resources to the support of private industry. On balance, Witte appears to be a product of his social environment, an able representative of the upper echelons of the Russian bureaucracy, the group that contributed so much to the perpetuation of an archaic political regime. The socially subordinate role of this group in the power structure of the Russian political system conditioned even its most able representatives to such an extent that they could not conceive of a change in the system that would replace the traditional primary decision makers. This was the general weakness of this class, including Sergei Witte.

THREE

The Tsar "Hunger"
in the Land of the Tsars

In nineteenth-century Russia famines were frequent, despite large areas of arable land. During such occasions, hunger and deprivation reigned. The purpose of this paper is to portray and analyze the governmental measures designed to prevent some of the most detrimental effects and provide relief from the consequences of the frequent famines.

The first task is to ascertain the frequency of significantly deficient grain harvests and to place them in a chronological sequence. This requires the use of a plausible measure of grain yields in nineteenth-century Russia which would pinpoint the years of significantly reduced grain harvests.[1] Table 3.1 provides the dates of harvest failures for nineteenth-century Russia. These data, based on crop reports, were also cross-checked with available grain price data. When the available price data were adjusted for changes in the general price level, the association of low prices with good harvests and high prices with short harvests can be established.

There is, however, a complicating factor in assessing the likely effects of deficient harvests. For a country the size of Russia, a harvest deficiency represents a host of possible patterns of regional harvests. A yield decline might be more or less evenly distributed among regions. It may, however, affect primarily the winter or the spring grains; thus it may be more heavily concentrated in one region while not affecting other regions at all. At some

Table 3.1 Years of Significant Deficiencies in the Size of the Grain Harvest in Russia during 1801–1914

1801	1833	1859	1889
1805	1839	1865	1891
1811	1840	1867	1897
1823	1848	1875	1901
1830	1850	1880	1906
1832	1855	1885	1911

level of analysis and disaggregation, certain methodological problems become crucial in terms of the interpretation of their effects. However, since we will not discuss the causes of the frequent famines and harvest shortages, this set of considerations will also be left outside our analysis.

The degree of commercialization of grain farming in Russia during this period is one of the characteristics which bears a direct relation to our analysis. The division of agricultural producers into two categories—one outside any market activity and the other connected with the market—also creates a differential response to the issue of holding reserves on the farm or relying on off-farm grain reserves. Commercialized agriculture presupposes the existence of a communication and transportation network which permits movement of grain from surplus to deficit areas. The development of the grain market and its basic characteristics, such as fragmentation into local markets, regional integration (involving interregional trade), export orientation, or the development of a full-fledged national market, obviously make significant differences to the nature of the effects of grain harvest deficiencies and the means of dealing with particular aspects of the effects.

For example, during the eighteenth century when commercial output was limited to the supply of major urban areas, in some selected regions of low local production (such as the North of European Russia and Siberia) and heavily concentrated in the export trade in others, grain exporting was frequently prohibited by the government in order to deal with internal shortages. This repeatedly used government policy might have been mistaken and ineffective on a number of grounds; it nevertheless persisted for a long time.[2]

One can clearly detect in the reasoning about fixed demand, or for that matter fixed supply of marketable grain the elements of mercantilist thought.[3] That the policies of export embargoes would not have achieved their objectives under conditions of a developed national grain market is also clear from the size of Russian grain exports in the eighteenth century relative to the grain consumption of the military, the urban population, and the alcohol distilling in some of the grain-deficit areas.[4] Whether the grain export embargoes worked, even under the existing conditions of the fragmentation of the market and its many imperfections, is still debatable.

The alternatives to grain trade embargoes that did not work were grain storage and grain reserve schemes initiated by the government. One can distinguish three broad areas of government concern—the military, the urban population, and the grain producers. All European governments enacted measures to protect army and urban consumers. The concern for the third category, the grain producers, in Russia originates not only in general welfare considerations, but also in the proprietary relationship—the ownership of government serfs. Thus we find government measures designed specifically to lower the effect of harvest deficiencies on the state-owned serfs.

The problems of grain-supply effects on the armed forces received the highest priority already in the eighteenth century as a result of the modernization of the army, the creation of a navy, and emphasis on an active foreign policy. The system of assuring an adequate grain supply both for current consumption and for stored reserves affected the location of military garrisons, the purchases in less expensive markets in order not to exceed the budgetary allowances at times of rising prices, the logistics of contracts and grain transportation, and the varying size of emergency reserves. However interesting the different aspects of the grain policies for the armed services supplies were, they are only of secondary interest for our analysis. What matters at this point is the scope of grain purchases for the military, in itself a function of the size of the armed forces, and the experience of the bureaucrats and suppliers that could be transferred to other areas of handling reserves and storing grain. With the exception of a few districts, or for a few years when taxation in-kind was applied to augment the army grain reserves, the supply of grain was handled through cash purchases and a system of forward contracts awarded to grain merchants who traded in the grain surplus areas. In other words, both the current supply as well as maintenance of the grain reserve became routine procedures conducted in the market. Protracted wars, rather than crop failures, created logistic problems for the armed forces. To the extent that the demand of the armed forces was predictable and budgetary constraints never too stringent, the flexible use of access to the market and the existing reserves sheltered the armed forces from the impacts of deficiencies in grain yields. See tables 3.2 and 3.3 for data on government assistance.

The government's grain reserve policies applied to the urban population were an outgrowth of its military grain supply experience and, at the same time, were determined by the size and distribution pattern of the urban population. The urban population constituted at the beginning of the nineteenth century between 8 and 10 per cent of the total population and rose slowly until the last decades of the century when its growth accelerated to reach 11.5 per cent in 1913. The bifurcation of its distribution, with its high concentration in the capital cities and a few other population centers and its dispersion over a large number of settlements with a relatively small population, eased the task of the government. Apart from the cities in the North of Russia and in Siberia which were supplied by grain shipped from other regions, most of the smaller cities depended on local or regional or interregional markets for their supply, a major problem at times of famines and serious yield deficiencies.

110

Table 3.2
Government Assistance to Victims of Crop Failure, 1867–1908,
by Districts of European Russia

	1867	1868	1869	1870	1871	1872	1873	1874	1875	1876	1877	1878	1879
Tavria			x	x			x	x			x		
Samara					x	x	x	x					
Penza	x		x	x								x	
Orenburg								x					x
Novgorod	x												
Viatka											x		
Saratov						x							x
Pskov	x	x		x						x			
Kazan'											x	x	
Simbirsk													
Ekaterinoslav													x
Kherson							x	x	x	x			
Oriol	x												
Ufa													
Voronezh													
Nizhnii-Novgorod			x										
Smolensk	x	x	x		x	x							
Tambov						x							
Vologda	x	x											
Olonets	x	x											
Tula													
Bessarabia									x				
Perm'													
St. Petersburg	x	x											
Tver'													
Kaluga													
Kursk													
Riazan'	x					x							
Vitebsk	x												
Kharkov													
Stavropol													
Vladimir						x							
Chernigov													x
Astrakhan													
Arkhangel	x												
Kostroma													
Don Military													
Vilno	x												
Poltava													
Volyn													
Kiev													
Kovno	x												
Mogilev	x												
Lifland													
Estland	x												
Podol'e													
Iaroslavl													
Grodno													
Kurland													
Kirsk													
Moscow													

Table 3.2 (continued)

	1880	1881	1882	1883	1884	1885	1886	1887	1888	1889	1890	1891	1892
Tavria	x	x	x	x			x		x			x	
Samara	x	x									x	x	x
Penza		x		x	x	x		x	x	x	x	x	
Orenburg	x	x			x				x	x	x	x	
Novgorod	x	x				x	x			x			
Viatka					x	x						x	x
Saratov	x	x										x	x
Pskov	x	x					x						
Kazan'				x	x	x						x	x
Simbirsk	x		x	x							x	x	x
Ekaterinoslav	x	x				x	x	x					
Kherson				x		x						x	x
Oriol					x	x						x	x
Ufa					x				x	x		x	x
Voronezh												x	x
Nizhnii-Novgorod					x							x	x
Smolensk						x	x						
Tambov												x	
Vologda					x	x				x	x		
Olonets		x	x									x	
Tula												x	x
Bessarabia													
Perm'												x	x
St. Petersburg		x					x						
Tver'	x					x	x						
Kaluga						x						x	
Kursk												x	x
Riazan'												x	x
Vitebsk													
Kharkov				x								x	x
Stavropol													
Vladimir													
Chernigov	x	x											
Astrakhan	x											x	
Arkhangel												x	
Kostroma												x	
Don Military												x	
Vilno													
Poltava												x	x
Volyn													
Kiev													x
Kovno													
Mogilev													
Lifland													
Estland													
Podol'e													x
Iaroslavl													
Grodno													
Kurland													
Kirsk													
Moscow													

1893	1894	1895	1896	1897	1898	1899	1900	1901	1902	1903	1904	1905	1906	1907	1908
						x	x	x	x	x		x	x	x	x
					x	x	x	x	x		x	x	x	x	x
					x				x		x	x	x		
								x	x	x			x	x	x
x	x	x					x		x	x	x	x	x	x	x
					x	x		x	x	x	x	x	x	x	x
					x	x		x	x		x	x	x	x	x
	x	x								x	x	x	x	x	x
					x	x		x	x			x	x	x	
					x	x		x	x			x	x	x	x
								x	x	x	x	x	x	x	
			x				x	x	x						
				x	x							x	x	x	x
					x	x		x	x				x	x	
				x				x	x	x		x	x	x	x
					x	x		x	x			x	x		
													x	x	x
				x	x			x	x		x	x	x	x	
											x	x		x	
x							x			x	x				
				x	x	x				x		x	x	x	
x						x	x	x		x	x	x	x	x	
					x	x		x	x	x		x			
x	x											x	x		
			x							x	x	x			
					x	x						x		x	x
					x	x						x		x	x
					x							x	x		
										x	x	x	x	x	
								x					x	x	
				x	x								x	x	
										x	x		x	x	
														x	x
													x	x	
													x	x	
												x	x	x	
														x	x
										x					
									x						
														x	

Table 3.3   Receipt of Government Assistance by Selected Districts, 1891–1908

Districts	No. of Years	Assistance in 1,000s of Rubles	Indebtedness on 1 Jan. 1909 in 1,000s of Rubles	Assistance per capita in Rubles	Indebtedness per capita in Rubles
Samara	12	64,473	29,810	24.87	11.50
Saratov	11	60,709	23,131	28.96	11.03
Kazan'	9	52,365	21,775	26.38	10.97
Simbirsk	10	32,134	12,714	22.63	8.95
Ufa	8	28,282	11,205	13.54	5.36
Tambov	9	27,561	11,500	11.21	4.68
Voronezh	10	26,518	12,981	11.23	5.50
Tula	9	24,755	12,343	19.84	9.89
Penza	6	24,495	10,957	18.41	8.24
Nizhnii-Novgorod	8	19,926	8,950	13.82	6.21
Viatka	12	18,979	8,223	6.47	2.80
Oriol	8	16,920	8,754	9.45	4.89
Riazan'	5	16,544	5,544	10.14	3.40
Orenburg	9	12,758	2,388	8.81	1.65
Perm'	8	9,097	1,073	3.23	0.38
Pskov	8	8,524	3,449	8.14	3.29
Kherson	6	7,384	3,283	3.80	1.69
Kursk	7	5,201	587	2.42	0.27
Novgorod	11	4,294	2,123	3.35	1.66
Tavria	10	4,008	1,785	3.46	1.54
Don Military	3	2,899	2,555	1.29	1.14
Vitebsk	5	2,035	2,035	1.60	1.60
Bessarabia	7	2,003	854	1.22	0.52
Kaluga	6	1,802	1,174	1.74	1.13
Chernigov	2	1,745	805	0.84	0.39

Obviously, during times of yield deficiencies and high grain prices, the low-income groups in the cities required relief and support. Because of the narrow jurisdiction and limited authority of the municipal bodies in Russia, the functions of relief or supply had to be assumed by the central administrative authorities. Thus, already in the eighteenth century, grain reserves for the supply of the urban population were established in the capitals and two dozen other urban centers. They emerged originally as adjuncts of military stocks or reserves and initially used the turnover (or renewal) of the military grain stock (every two or three years) as the supply base for urban grain stores. Such stocks, managed by officers of the central administration, were used to sell grain to urban dwellers when the regular supply was seriously disturbed and at below-market prices during times of famine and rising prices. Created primarily as a response to the grain deficiencies of the middle 1780s, the urban reserves were little used during the eighteenth century but underwent substantial change in the nineteenth century.

The creation of compulsory grain stocks by and for state-owned serfs on a major scale was decreed by Tsar Paul I at the turn of the century and was followed by a decree ordering the private serfowners to follow the government's example.

Perhaps at this point it is appropriate to pose the general question of why the Russian government had to force the agricultural population to hold grain stocks if the historical record of famines in Russia itself recommended such a course of action on the part of the mass of grain producers. The answer to this question is not readily available and could be arrived at only by consideration of some permanent and some changing features of the Russian agricultural scene. Among the general characteristics of Russian agriculture, the following are significant: 1) the low output-seed ratio in Russian grain production, 2) the high costs of grain storage, 3) the distribution between market-oriented and nonmarket-oriented farm regions, 4) the frequency of famines and severe grain deficiencies, and 5) the income levels of the mass of producers.

The generally low output-seed ratio in Russian grain production required the expenditure of a significant volume of output for seeding purposes, which involved the maintenance on the farms not only of the volume of ordinary seed requirements but also of an additional seed reserve for protection against winterkill. Thus the low output-seed ratio not only determined the difference between the gross and net output of grain but exacerbated the problem of stock maintenance over and above the situation faced by producers with a higher output-seed ratio.

The costs of grain storage vary among different regions in the world, and they varied also among different climatic zones in Russia. The costs of grain storage were relatively high in the central region with ample precipitation, where the grain had to be protected from excessive moisture. In the normally dry areas, however, where there was precipitation during the harvest season, the grains to be stored had to be intensively dried. Thus, apart from the investment in storage capacity, labor expenditures to bring the grains into proper conditions for storage were relatively high. One might also add that the economic costs of storage tend to be high in countries in which there is a capital scarcity or a high rate of interest. Russia was such a country, where both the direct costs of storage and the indirect costs of storage tended to be relatively high.

Russian agriculture during the nineteenth century possessed a growing but still relatively small sector of commercialized agriculture. While the commercial output of fiber crops, sugar beets, and livestock was fairly developed, the bulk of the grains were produced and consumed within the farms, outside the market. The size of the country with an underdeveloped road network, the relatively small size of the urban population, and other factors kept substantial regions of potential surplus grain producers outside market channels. On the other hand, some farms were too small to produce a marketable surplus.

One would like to assume that farms not connected to the market by reason of distance could have maintained larger on-the-farm grain reserves than market-oriented ones. The latter would presumably dispose of their surplus during years of high yields and rely on their money savings for the purchase of grains during years of poor harvests. Thus money savings became a substitute for the actual reserves of grain on their part.

Obviously the decision about the maintenance of on-the-farm grain stocks, although circumscribed by the output-seed ratios and costs of storage, was shaped to a large extent by the actual experience of the frequency and severity of the grain deficiencies. In this respect the geographical distribution of farms was important. The frequency of crop failures tended to increase with the expansion of farmland in the dry, blacksoil regions where the grain yields were higher but also the frequency of droughts was above that of the nonblacksoil region. Since nineteenth-century Russian agriculture was marked by southward and eastward expansion of its grain area, the frequency of crop failures tended to increase and the severity of their effects rose accordingly. It can be safely assumed, however, that as a general rule the Russian grain farmers maintained on the average a year's stock of grain for their seed, food, and feed requirements. This stock would act as a buffer even in case of a single-year crop disaster. The situation would become grave in cases of two consecutive crop failures, or two crop failures within a span of a few years, because the replenishment of stocks took considerably longer than one or two years. This inability to replenish the on-the-farm stocks within a relatively short period following a crop failure was clearly related not only to the output-seed ratio and the low level of agricultural technology resulting in low productivity of Russian grain output, but also to the low level of agricultural incomes of the Russian serfs or peasants. Apart from the high share of seed in the gross income of the producers, the share of rents under the condition of serfdom and after emancipation was considerable. Whether the rent was paid in kind, in money, or in labor services is less material than the relation of the rent to the output of the grain producers. Given generally low net agricultural incomes, high rents, and even assuming stable consumption demand, there was little room for savings earmarked to build up a high level of grain reserves.

If one adds the legal obligations of serfowners to feed their serfs at times of famines and the government's relief actions as a historical legacy of earlier periods, the behavior of most grain producers in not holding the maximum stocks that would suffice to supply them with grain under repeated grain failures becomes intelligible.

The relatively low level of grain reserves maintained in the trade network of Russia can be explained by the high costs and the lack of capital and facilities to maintain such reserves. Needless to say, the existing reserves in commercial channels tended to smooth out the price fluctuations during "normal" years. They were, however, insufficient in size to affect strongly the price peaks during years of sufficient yields. The only "constraint" of the violent upward price movements at times of repeated famines came from the grain supplies of outlying isolated regions which entered the market when the rising prices "overcame" the high transportation costs.

Given the behavior of the producers and the middlemen in grain trade, the Russian government remained in the grain storage business, even following emancipation of the serfs. It remained a permanent feature and dominant factor in the relief from grain deficiencies. Given the active role of the government, it is possible to venture an opinion about its relative effectiveness in performing the tasks.

The government activity can be distinguished in four areas: 1) in forcing the producers to create reserves and maintain stocks over and above the ones they were holding voluntarily, 2) providing grain and money loans for those affected by grain harvest failures, 3) providing relief for the population victimized by the crop failures, and 4) supplying incomes to those affected by harvest failures by means of instituting public works.

The enforcement of government decrees to create grain reserves in the urban and rural areas was viewed by the population as an additional tax which they reluctantly paid. During the existence of serfdom, the serfowners resisted the measures which they perceived as competitive to the rent payments.

As a lender, the government, given its resources, could lend grain and money in quantities over and above what private lenders were willing to lend and at lower interest rates.[5] The high private rates of interest were not only a result of general capital scarcity in Russia, but also of the absence of equity, legal assurances, and guarantees by many borrowers. A serious crop failure in a particular region might have caused the demand for loans to exceed the capacity of the private lenders. It might be also of interest to note that food grain loans were combined often with seed loans, in which case the lenders, or the government, considered the seed loan as a surety of some kind that the food loan would be repaid. In the case of government loans, it was assumed that the loans would be repaid because of the government's power of taxation and enforcement of contract. That this was not universally true will become apparent from the examination of the record.

Although there was a distinction drawn between loans and gifts, or general relief, prevailing realities and attitudes on the part of the victims of crop failures tended to obscure the distinction. Numerous cases of loans that were "forgiven" at various occasions (coronation, birth of a royal successor, etc.) often served to obliterate the distinction. However, there were cases when the relief provided by the government was explicitly termed as gifts and was invariably accompanied by a campaign calling for public participation in the relief operations. Eliciting private gifts combined with extensive government relief was practiced during times of famines encompassing large regions of the country. In order to evoke a response of solidarity and charity from the public, the government felt obliged to set an example of the charitable spirit. Prior to the abolition of serfdom, the government appealed to the semi-legal obligations of the serfowners and to the moral obligations of the mercantile class. After the emancipation it could appeal to the sense of civic duty, morality, and compassion. Although there was hardly any institutionalized system of private philanthropy, such appeals would strike a sympathetic cord.

One of the forms of government relief for the population in regions stricken by crop failures was employment in public works. It was a time-honored measure used in different areas of the country since the first half of the nineteenth century. The prevailing characteristic of the public works was their haphazard nature, the lack of previous preparation and planning, and their poor timing. A typical example was the public works instituted in 1906 and 1911 for which the "unfinished" tasks of the 1891 public works were automatically "revived" and the plans dug out of the state archives. Typically also, the public works would start late, when the affected population was already weakened by malnutrition, or when they interfered with work on the farms. Almost as a rule, the public works were concentrated in road and railroad construction and avoided agricultural improvements. It was not even clear whether the objects of the public works were of high priority as components of overhead capital, although for the population of many areas stricken by crop failures the public works involved travel of considerable distances. Although the agricultural specialists of Russia had very clear ideas about remedies against drought and soil erosion, and when shelter belts in the steppe regions and drainage in the areas of high precipitation were recognized as useful measures, or when people concerned with overhead capital knew the significance of improving certain riverbeds or particular road networks to facilitate the flow of agricultural goods to the markets, the public works that were undertaken did not contribute to those objectives. As a result, the public works did not appear to the population as meaningful projects that would affect their welfare in the long run, but simply as a means to provide them with income and purchasing power as a form of relief in exchange for which they had to expend energy.

To the extent that the governmental policy of interference in the grain economy in the nineteenth century had as its point of departure the enforced maintenance of grain stocks, the discussion of policy issues and the assessment of their effectiveness could conveniently start with the state of grain stocks ordered by Paul I at the turn of the century. The immediate response to Paul's decree was either noncompliance or only reluctant compliance.[6] While the existence of such grain reserves had no effect on the deficient grain supplies during the first two decades of the century, rural grain reserves kept on rising in the yearly policy reports submitted to the government, if not in reality. The figures rose to 68,756 rural storage places with 17,795 thousands *chetverti* of available grain and 4,700 thousand *chetverti* of loans and arrears outstanding for the beginning of 1816, or almost one *chetvert'* per male of the rural population in those regions. That this was largely a figment of a bureaucratic imagination became clear and a policy review was ordered. In defense of its gross negligence or reflecting the resistance of the serfowning class, the Council of Ministers unanimously reported to the Tsar that given conditions of free trade, uninterrupted transportation, and communication, thirty-five districts of Russia did not require any grain reserves, twelve districts needed to purchase grain from neighboring districts only in case of famine, and only six districts had a chronic deficiency in meeting their normal grain requirements. It may be of interest to note that among the forty-seven districts described as self- sufficient in grain or requiring some additional purchases during famines, twenty-three were classified as suffering from grain shortages when there were slight declines in the grain yields later in the century. What followed was an interesting dichotomy between the views of the Council of Ministers and the perception of the ruling monarch (Alexander I), who disagreed with his government and refused to dismantle the existing structure of rural grain storage. Moreover, the Tsar ordered the use of the proposed substitute for grain storage, a 25 kopek tax, in only twelve districts with developed grain marketing while preserving the physical grain stocks in forty districts of the Empire.

The system created by the decree of April 14, 1822 introduced a decentralized, district-based administration of the grain storage and grain disbursement measures. The decision-making authority at the district level consisted of representatives of the government administration and district nobility, who had to review the grain supply situation yearly, determine the size of the grain stocks, and make the appropriate recommendation to the district bureaucrats. The desired level of grain stocks kept in special granaries was determined by the decree as two *chetverti* of grain per male, of which one-half *chetvert'* was to be spring grains. The reserve had to be accumulated through yearly payments (of four *garntsy* of grain [one garnéts = 1/64 chetvert', equivalent to 5 pounds of rye in the 1820s—ed.]) over a thirty-two year period and stored in granaries which would be erected in villages of over fifty households. For the districts in which a tax in money was substituted for grain, the target was the money equivalent of one *chetvert'* of grain at the five-year average price and was collected roughly over a forty-eight year period. A special permission by the Ministry of the Imperial Court for court serfs enabled them to substitute the grain or money payments by labor on one-sixteenth of a *desiatina* of land per male, the grain output of which would be turned over to the special reserve granaries. Grain and money loans carried a 6 per cent annual rate of interest.

The grain shortages, especially the famine in Byelorussia of 1822, justified the decree of the same year in the eyes of the public, and the data in tables 3.4 and 3.5 provide some impression of the relative progress of the system.

That the 1822 system had its shortcomings in terms of effectiveness is clear from the targets, which were half of the minimum per capita yearly requirements, and from the long time period during which they had to be accumulated, as well as from the assumption that the loans would be repaid within a reasonably short period of time.

A few reasons can be cited why the 1822 system did not satisfy the

Table 3.4 Accumulation of Monetary Reserve for Harvest-Failure
Relief, 1823–32

Year	Amount	Areas
1823	1,813,860	265,370
1824	3,043,950	537,657
1825	4,277,110	615,245
1826	5,539,774	743,207
1827	7,265,016	696,273
1828	8,518,873	755,431
1829	9,981,327	826,974
1830	11,449,845	847,132
1831	12,844,620	738,913
1832	14,366,991	738,683

Source: Ministerstvo vnutrennykh, Khoziaistvennyi departament, *Istoricheskii obzor pravitelstvennykh meropriatii po narodnomu prodovol'stviu v Rossii,* vol. 1 (St. Petersburg 1892), p. 259.

Table 3.5   Grain Reserves in Rural Granaries, 1822–32 (in Chetvert')

Year	No. of Granaries	Grain in Available Reserves	Grain On Loan	Total	Areas
1822		4,327,310	2,579,758	6,907,068	270,887
1823	29,568	5,437,508	2,569,644	8,007,152	343,552
1824	31,560	5,876,380	3,236,754	9,113,134	516,127
1825	32,124	6,407,059	3,340,699	9,747,758	655,761
1826	33,025	7,198,960	3,227,985	10,426,945	692,619
1827	34,512	7,480,348	3,590,148	11,070,496	829,367
1828	33,405	7,795,806	3,041,604	10,837,410	866,886
1829	36,149	8,194,756	3,199,139	11,393,895	915,072
1830	33,000	8,750,177	3,417,011	12,167,188	1,000,000
1831	32,398	7,737,540	4,471,088	12,208,628	1,374,212
1832*	32,311	7,968,052	4,601,550	12,569,602	1,445,554

*The granaries and their contents in 1832 belonged to the following categories of peasants:

Private	14,937	3,649,350	1,713,485	5,362,835	586,206
State	15,355	4,035,077	2,786,042	6,821,119	831,366
Free	1,237	18,282	5,522	23,804	3,821
Other	782	265,343	96,501	361,844	24,161
Total	32,311	7,968,052	4,601,550	12,569,602	1,445,554

Source: Ministerstvo vnutrennykh, Khoziaistvennyi departament, *Istoricheskii obzor pravitel'stvennykh meropriatii po narodnomu prodovol'stviu v Rossii,* vol. 1 (St. Petersburg, 1892), pp. 258–59.

governing circles of Russia. For the "free traders" it was excessively interventionist; for the authoritarian minded expecting quick results it was too lax in terms of its time horizon and enforcement. To the extent that the 1820s were characterized by a price decline in grains and presumably relatively bountiful harvests (with the exception of 1822–23), those officials expected higher rates of grain stock formation, both in the private and in the government-enforced sectors. The data indicate that as far as the government-sponsored grain reserves were concerned, this was hardly the case. The famines of 1832 and 1833 clearly exhausted the existing reserves and exacted a heavy toll of malnutrition and suffering of the affected rural population. As a response to the shock of 1833, especially severe in southern Russia, a revision of the system of grain stocks took place by the so-called rules of July 5, 1834. The 1834 rules both lowered the targets (from 2 to 1½ *chetverti* per male) and shortened the time period allotted to collect the grain to sixteen years. The collection of money as a substitute for grain was also reduced to sixteen years. For all practical purposes, this signified the increase of the yearly payment and added to the tax burden on the peasants' incomes. In order to assure an adequate grain supply for the city dwellers in times of crop failures and rising grain prices, the urban population had to create a special fund of 3 rubles per inhabitant, which would assure some minimum grain supply. The creation of the urban "grain capital" was allowed to take place over a twenty-year period, or by the payment of the assessed 15 kopeks per inhabitant.

Although the direct responsibility for the augmentation and maintenance of the rural grain stocks was assigned to the serfowners and to the village communes of the state serfs, the rules of July 5, 1834 increased the role of governmental controls over the administration and disbursement of grain stocks. The previous district authorities who permitted a modicum of local autonomy and influence by the local nobility were now subordinated to more centralized administrative controls, the result being a further centralization and bureaucratization of decision making. The Ministry of Interior, which controlled the operations of the grain stocks, published data that indicate a rapid growth of granaries and available reserves during the rest of the 1830s.[7] However, the famines of 1839–40 and 1849–50 reduced the accumulated reserves. The chief cause of the reduction of available reserves was not only the distribution of grain and money to the affected population, but the tardiness in the repayment of food and seed loans, to some extent a problem of the government's own making. Some of the government's instructions required the repayment of the grain loans in money. While the prices of grain at the times of borrowing were high, the monetary value of even a small loan was considerable. In order to repay this amount of money, the borrower had to sell much more grain at considerably lower prices. Needless to say, this created serious problems.

The evidence for the period up to the serf emancipation (1861) indicates the continuous attempts to build up the grain reserves and their reduction during the relatively frequent crop failures. Since the actual reserves were inadequate to assure a normal grain supply to the affected regions, they could at best mitigate the crisis.

Considerable changes were brought about by the emancipation of the serfs. The quasi-legal obligations of the landowners expired, and the reliance either on private initiative or on government actions increased. The existing grain stocks were liquidated as a by-product of the distribution of common property among the emancipated serfs. It took a number of years for the government to devise and implement a new system of grain reserves. The administration of the "revived" grain stocks was turned over to the organization of local, predominantly noble autonomy (*zemstvo*). Thus the pendulum swung from centralized to decentralized administration and control.

However, more important were the changes that took place in the structure of Russian agriculture. In spite of the obstacles to mobility and the reluctance to grant private property rights to the peasantry, the commercialization of Russian agriculture and factor mobility were constantly gaining ground. The expansion of grain production in new areas, the growth of foreign demand and Russian grain exports, the impact of railroad construction on the scope and shape of the markets—all this took place without regard to periodic crop failures and famines. The recurring famines affecting smaller or larger areas tended to heighten the public's awareness of the effects, resulting in hunger and misery. The volume of government and private relief tended to rise secularly during this period, especially because of the social and political dimensions of the problem, but the concerns were of a short-term nature. Neither the government nor Russian society was ready to make an extraordinary effort to deal with the problem of yield fluctuations and their effects. Perhaps the existence of the peasant commune was one of the obstacles to sufficient investment in effective antifamine measures. One would suspect that improvements in crop rotation, in superior seed varieties, and in land drainage were difficult to make under conditions of communal proprietorship. On the other hand, not much was achieved by owners of large agricultural estates who very often had the choice of leasing their land to tenants who bore the excessive costs of the yield fluctuations. Thus, one would not have expected much progress prior to the Stolypin reforms (1906–10) that tried to replace communal proprietorship by private ownership in the peasant sector.

Thus during the period 1867–1913 the Russian government "muddled through" with its policies of rural grain storage, government relief, and public works.

Government expenditures for famine relief grew rapidly as seen in table 3.6. The reported sums of government relief were not spent equally within all regions of the country, and it is necessary to take cognizance of the pattern of distribution. This pattern we will assume was developed as a result of the frequency and severity of grain yield deficiencies in the various districts of Russia, perhaps mitigated by the volume of savings of the rural population. In order to correct the ranking of the districts by sheer size of receipts of relief, a per capita relief figure was calculated using the size of the rural population according to the 1897 population census. How-

Table 3.6 State Expenditures for Famine Relief

Period	Expenditures (in 1,000s of Rubles)
1867–90	32,226
1891–1900	236,671
1901–July 1906	128,694
July 1906–1908	197,462
1911–12	136,297

ever, the most important data, the relief per capita of population receiving assistance are missing. Since the archival data will not reveal those figures, we will remain in the dark about the real effectiveness of government relief. The presently available data can offer only a very general impression, let us say, when the money expenditures are converted into quantities of grain, but they are inadequate to express how much additional foodstuffs could have been bought by the ones most directly affected by the calamities, since we do not know the exact number of people on the relief rolls.

The data of the post-emancipation period permit us to view the relief effort as consisting of a central government source and sources under the control of local governmental and nongovernmental institutions, with the share of central government resources growing over time. In this connection, it is possible to distinguish two patterns of behavior, one marked by the reliance almost exclusively on central government resources and the other relying largely on local resources. This distinction of the two patterns coincided with the distinction between normally grain-surplus producing regions and nonsurplus producing regions, or as some observers noted, between predominantly private landholders and predominantly communal landholders.

Toward the end of the period, the size of the assets (liabilities) of the grain stock and relief programs reached over 400 million rubles or over 2 per cent of the GNP. It is difficult to assess the significance of the size of programs under such circumstances. It appears to be low given the frequency of the calamities, but high in terms of its continuous growth. But most of all, it conveys a sense of utility, since no basic improvement was in sight. A basic incongruity existed between the substantial sums spent for relief under the various government-sponsored schemes and programs and the lack of real remedies. No agro-technical measures were developed for particular regions, no special varieties of seeds or crop rotations were developed to mitigate the impact of the weather or to ameliorate the influence of the crop failures.

It is commonplace to state that the costs of famines and crop failures in Russia were high. Pitirim Sorokin dealt with Russia in his admirable work, *Hunger as a Factor in Human Affairs,* which still makes interesting reading fifty-five years after its publication.[8] However, social scientists do not have a rigorously defined methodology to measure the social, or for that matter even, private costs, of such calamities. We usually include in such costs the unrealized output measured as deviations from the long-term trend of "normal" weather output. We include the effects of malnutrition on the rate of population growth and on the labor effort of the population, and sometimes we might include the effects of forced short-term migration movements in search of food and work.

When viewed against this background, the various government efforts in Russia appear to be of relatively little effectiveness. Although many would blame the Russian government for its acceptance of crop failures as a datum and dealing with the symptoms and some of the effects but not with the core of the problem, it may be necessary to point out that the government reflected to an extent the view of the society at large.

The dynamics of social and economic development of Russia were insufficient to stimulate either an overall national effort or a ceaseless activity on the part of individuals who for their own interest would be willing, capable, or have the resources to deal with the problem. The acceptance of the tsar "Hunger" accompanied the acceptance of the other tsars.

Natural Calamities and Their Effect on the Food Supply in Russia

The catalog of natural calamities in appendix table 3A includes the type of exogenous effects on agriculture and the population's food supply which were independent of human action and affected the population, regardless of human circumspection.[9] Throughout this period the impact of a natural calamity primarily affected the grain output. Grain constituted the food staple of the agricultural population; therefore any change in the size of the grain harvest directly affected the consumption level of the vast majority of the population.

The presentation of a catalog of natural calamities which affected the food supply of any country makes sense only if accompanied by an explanation of some of their characteristics and an analysis of the socioeconomic consequences of such calamities. The longer the period covered by the catalog, the more general the analysis is likely to be.

Given the length of the period in this catalog (1757–1965), an attempt will be made to present some of the more general observations and conclusions based on it.

The Catalog

The records underlying the catalog of natural calamities are of five basic types:

1. Chronicle data, selected by the compilers of various chronicle texts from the oral tradition or from records kept by contemporaries.
2. Records and correspondence of government institutions, including descriptive reports from local officials and responses of the central administration.
3. Grain yield data of scattered farm units for various crops.

4. Data indicating the size of the harvest compiled for administrative regions or the whole country.
5. Meteorological observations in various localities, collected in a systematic fashion, which permit the analysis of the nature of the particular natural calamity.

The most reliable records belong to the fourth and fifth categories, and a combination of these latter types yields a more accurate insight into the nature of the calamity and the likely scope of its effects.

The incidence of natural calamities for the earlier periods, until the middle of the eighteenth century, could not be verified, for the most part, by yield reports, which were simply not collected. Thus the evidence available from documentary sources or chronicles could only be checked against other independent contemporary documents describing the same phenomenon, or by the use of scattered food price data for particular localities, to the extent that such data are available. From the middle of the eighteenth century to the middle of the nineteenth century, the yield data are inadequate to provide a sufficiently reliable check. It was only from the second half of the nineteenth century that systematically collected yield data and meteorological reports could verify the observations from other sources.

A singularly difficult problem presented by the sources is the identification of the calamities. Whenever a recorded single natural phenomenon or combination of two phenomena to which the effect could be attributed were listed in the sources, it was included in the catalog. Whenever there was proof of an effect upon the food supply but the cause was either unknown or could not be linked or attributed to a single cause, the effect rather than its cause was recorded. Therefore, along with such calamities as droughts, floods, fires, frost, hail, windstorm, and locust, famines are also recorded as effects of original calamities. Thus the choice of classification of calamities in the catalog itself was partially determined by the availability of information in the primary and secondary sources.

Similarly, in determining the geographic location the sources often do not allow more than a transcription of the description as found. Thus, it is difficult to delineate such descriptions as "area," or "region," and one is certainly puzzled by a location described as "Russian land" (the area around Kiev), which reflects the geographic horizon (and perhaps the political concept) of the early chronicle rather than the modern era. Therefore, in following the sources one is exposed to the terminology of Russian historical geography rather than to modern political geography.

The limitations imposed by the nature of the sources are also apparent in the evaluation of the scope of the effects of the calamities, being either local or nationwide. For the earlier historical periods the "nationwide" scope of the effect of particular calamities could be estimated as the sum total of causes and effects recorded in a number of localities, encompassing a wide range of severity of local effects and thus making the classification dependent very much upon the discretion of the historian. For the latter period the "nationwide" scope could be computed in terms of the deviation of grain production from the national average yield for the decade, thus leaving less room for impressionistic freedom of the historian.

But apart from the decision to classify the effects of such calamities as of local or nationwide scope, one cannot on the basis of the sources pass judgment about the relative degree of intensity of the effects of the calamities. How does one compare the messages conveyed by phrases like "very severe," or "people died" with "many died"? Thus, whenever quantitative data were missing (as in most instances), reliance had to be put upon the phrase in the general description which reflected the impressionistic impact upon contemporaries.[10]

All the above adds up to the conclusion that much additional research is needed to make a foolproof case for each of the dates in the catalog. Yet even in its present form, the catalog represents historical evidence for the seriousness of the impact of natural calamities upon the food supply in Russia.

The Causes and Nature of the Famines in Russia

Although Russia is by no means an exception, yet among the major European countries it experienced for much longer and in a most severe fashion the vagaries of its climate. In each century of recorded history, Russia had to cope with problems of natural calamities which caused famines.

A number of factors appear to be co-responsible for the seriousness of the effects of natural calamities upon the food supply in Russian history. The foremost is the relatively low output-seed ratio of most of the grains, which can be seen from table 3.7. Although the output-seed ratio rose over time, it still remained one of the lowest among European countries. During the post–1914 period the output-seed ratio remained low, rising above the 6.0 level in a few bumper crop years only. The significance of such a low output-seed ratio under conditions of natural calamities is indicated by the fact that a loss of the seed constitutes a high percentage loss of the yearly crop, or that a sharp decrease in yield meant a higher share of the current crop would need to be used as seed in the next crop year. In other words, a low output-seed ratio under conditions of climatic variability indicates a high susceptibility of the other (except seed) components of gross output of grain to the variations of the weather. Given the relatively modest shares

Table 3.7   Output-Seed Ratio of Grains in Russia 1800–1914
(8-Year Averages)

1801–6	3.49	1863–70	3.47
1807–14	3.47	1871–78	3.95
1815–22	3.50	1879–86	4.09
1823–30	3.47	1887–94	4.49
1831–38	3.49	1895–1902	4.90
1839–46	3.29	1903–10	5.30
1847–54	3.52	1911–15[a]	5.78
1855–62	3.45		

Source: Mikhailnskii, *Urozhai v Rossii,* pp. 2–4.

of feed grain and the marketed output in the gross output of grains during the nineteenth century in Russia, the impact of a particular natural calamity which results in a lower-than-average grain crop is much stronger upon the food supply than if the other components of gross output were larger and could play the role of a buffer. Thus as long as Russian grain output, at a low output-seed ratio, remained close to the subsistence level, variations in yield produced even greater variations in the consumption of the agricultural producers. The distribution of the gross output of grains for most of the period was such that under conditions of natural calamities the effects on human consumption were accentuated rather than mollified. In addition, a severe famine could also adversely affect the next year's crop by causing a scarcity of grain for seed.

If the grain output consisted of winter grains only, and a natural calamity like winterkill affected a sizeable territory, it would still be replanted with spring crops. This would involve substantial additional cost of grain seeds and labor and adversely affect the level of yields, but the effect would probably not be so disastrous as to cause a famine. But one of the characteristics of Russian agriculture was the growing share of spring grains in the total grain area. Under such conditions, a combination of winterkill followed by drought (the typical, most widespread form of natural calamity) adversely affected not only the winter crops but also the replanted area or the area of the original spring crop with much more serious results for the total grain crop. This growing share of spring grains in the total grain area, which increased rather than diminished the frequency of natural calamities in the nineteenth and twentieth centuries,[11] was a result of the territorial expansion of Russian agriculture (chiefly grain acreage) toward the south and southeast, into the areas of the steppes and semiarid regions. These were the regions more severely affected by drought than other regions and with the highest frequency of droughts. Any expansion toward the south and southeast from a line drawn from Poltava through Khar'kov to Voronezh and Penza increased the probability of droughts, as can be seen from table 3.8, which summarizes the observations from the 1880s to the 1940s for this region.

One could raise the question why, given the likelihood of frequent droughts and losses in yields, the expansion of the planted area and the migration toward those areas took place. The answer is to be found in the pressure of labor against arable land within the central areas of European Russia. On the southern and eastern fringes of the Russian Empire the landowners received lavish land grants and the serfs worked land at higher land-labor ratios than in the areas of their old habitat. These were also lands where commercial grain output was being developed on estates to a larger extent than in the old, traditional areas of Russian agriculture.

Another factor contributing to the severity of the impact of droughts, even if it had not contributed to their increased frequency, was the deforestation of the southern and eastern regions of European Russia. Although, conservationists traditionally tend to overstate the significance of deforestation in explaining its impact on agriculture, it appears that there is some validity to their claim with regard to these particular areas in Russia. The deforestation in south and eastern Russia was carried out partly to meet the demand for construction lumber and firewood, and partly for land clearing and expansion of the planted area. Higher population density in other regions resulted not only in deforestation but also in the plowing up of meadows. Deforestation, by destroying the natural shelter belts against drought, and the plowing up of meadows, which affected the texture of the soils, made the impact of droughts on the level of grain yields more severe.

The yardstick in measuring the impact of a particular natural calamity or combination of them is the deviation from the "normal" or long-term average grain yield forthcoming or expected on a particular territory, or

Table 3.8   **Observations on the Frequency of Drought in South and Southeastern Regions**

Observation Point	Total Years	Years of Droughts
Poltava	61	14
Chaŕkov	53	12
Voronež	58	14
Penza	53	12
Nikolaev	57	26
Rostov on the Don	62	21
Saratov	60	33
Volgograd	56	39
Uralsk	58	45

Source: Rudenko, *Zasukhi v SSSR*, p. 172.

the size of reduction of the grain output. But even a cursory glance at the catalog demonstrates that very seldom did a single year's decrease of the grain yield or grain output produce a famine in Russia. In the majority of cases a famine took place as a result of a repetition of adverse conditions within a short time span (two to three years).

Thus even more than the geographic spread of adverse weather, its repetition within a large territory was a precondition of famine. There are areas in Russia where the frequency of certain weather conditions or the recurrence of some types of natural calamities within given time periods can be predicted with a higher probability than in others. So, for example, the repetitiveness of droughts in some of the "new land" areas[12] was observed during a period from forty to sixty years and is summarized in table 3.9.

Given, therefore, some regularity in the repetitiveness of droughts in some areas, the coincidence with a simultaneous natural calamity in another area is likely to produce a sizeable reduction of the grain harvest on a national scale, and if repeated the following year, might result in a famine.[13]

But apart from the factors mentioned above, which contributed to the impact of natural calamities on Russian agriculture and the food supply, the economic structure of agriculture itself and the social conditions of the agricultural population were of utmost importance in determining the effects of the natural calamities upon the food supply of the population.

Table 3.9   Repetition of Droughts in the New Land Area

Observation Point	5 Years	4 Years	3 Years	2 Years	Number of Years of Observation
Celinograd	1929–1933		1935–1937	1900–01	49
				1926–27	
				1940–41	
Orenburg		1888–1891	1906–1908	1901–02	62
				1932–33	
				1938–39	
				1948–49	
Kustanaj			1931–1933	1903–04	44
				1936–37	
				1942–43	
				1951–52	
Kokčetav				1911–12	39
				1929–30	

Source: Rudenko, *Zasukhi v SSSR*, p. 100.

Consequences and Effects of the Natural Calamities on the Food Supply

The table of grain yields in Russia during 1801–1914, compiled by Mikhailovskii, appendix table 3B, provides an approximate measure of the deviation from the eight-year average grain yield for the years of natural calamities in Russia during the nineteenth and the first decade of the twentieth century. The results are presented in table 3.10.

Although the indicated range of deviations from the average yield was very wide (from 8.6 to 31.8 per cent), the data suggest that a yield decrease of over 20 per cent from the average resulted almost invariably in a nationwide famine (with the exception of the years 1906 and 1911 under special circumstances). They also suggest how close to the point of disaster Russian agriculture found itself (15–20 per cent deviation) for most of the years when stricken by natural calamities.

For a discussion of the effects of natural calamities on the food supply, it is convenient to distinguish between the effects on urban dwellers and on the main agricultural producers, the peasants.

A decrease in the total output of grain, given unchanged seed requirements, had the primary effect of decreasing the volume of marketable supply on the part of some producers, which would lead to an increase in the price of grain. The increase in price, however, probably had a secondary effect of drawing additional grain to the market.

In terms of the Russian reality, the peasants would have decreased their marketings not only because of a reduced supply but also because a rise in the price of grain would enable them to obtain the minimum of their re-

Table 3.10   Percent Deviation of Grain Yields from 8-Year Averages
during Selected Years (Based on Output-Seed Ratios)

Year	Percent Deviation	Year	Percent Deviation
1811	− 17.9	1867	− 17.1
1822	− 11.4	1875	− 14.4
1823	− 16.3	1879	− 8.6
1830	− 16.1	1880	− 10.8
1832	− 19.8	1885	− 10.8
1833	− 31.8	1889	− 18.7
1839	− 18.9	1891	− 27.4
1848	− 22.7	1892	− 10.1
1850	− 19.3	1897	− 15.9
1855	− 24.6	1901	− 16.7
1859	− 16.8	1906	− 23.6
1865	− 19.5	1911	− 27.9

Sources: Mikhailnskii, *Urozhai v Rossi,* pp. 2–4; Semenov, *K voprosu o zakonomernosti,* pp. 57–95.

quired monetary income (for tax payments and purchase of some manufactured consumer goods) from a lower quantity of grain sold. The higher grain prices, however, would induce the landowners to market a higher proportion of their grain production. Thus, given a reduction in grain output and grain marketings, the commercial grain producers were the ones who benefited most from the price increases and the income transfers from the buyers to the sellers of grain.

Thus, in order to understand the effect of reductions in the grain output on urban dwellers, one has to inquire into the connection of agriculture with the domestic and international market.

It is difficult to speak about a national market for grains in Russia prior to the middle of the eighteenth century. During the earlier periods, the size of the country and the high costs of transportation for such a relatively bulky commodity as grain kept the market fragmented, and most regions (except Siberia) relied upon supply drawn from a relatively limited area. In addition, until 1753, internal duty payments and tolls increased the costs of trade between regions, thus shortening the radius of grain supply to the centers of demand. Under such circumstances, a decline in the supply of grain within a particular region led to relatively high price increases until shipments of grain from other regions took place. In order to induce such interregional grain shipments in which distances had to be overcome at considerable expense, the price differentials had to be substantial. Thus for particular regions, the price data indicate sharp fluctuations which can be explained primarily in terms of the fragmentation of the market and the virtual absence of what we would call a national market, where prices are uniform if adjusted for the transportation costs.

It was only with the improvement of the waterways, the construction of canals, and the abolition of the internal tolls that grain started to move more freely both among regions and toward the seaports. That creation of a national market and mitigation of regional price differentials were slower than one would expect can perhaps be explained by the forced immobility of the majority of the rural population, the serfs, and the low rate of growth and mobility of the urban population. Gradually the monopoly on grain trade of the urban merchant class was broken up; the influx of both gentry and peasants into the grain trade infused much more competition in the grain market, and under the impact of a growing demand, both the grain output and its marketable share started to grow at a faster pace.

The foreign demand for Russian grain grew considerably after the end of the eighteenth century, when both population growth in Western Europe intensified and Russia absorbed some of the traditional grain export areas of Poland. Russia's share of the export trade in grain on the world market was increasing, and the urban consumers had to compete with the foreign demand. Since there was an export duty on grain, not all price fluctuations in the world market affected the domestic market. During years of low grain output, the government had the discretion of raising the export duty or setting export quotas and thus assuring a greater share of the commercial output for domestic consumption and preventing the prices from rising. It is difficult to assess the success or failure of such measures without much more additional information than is available for each case. The average yearly prices for rye, flour, and bread, which are available for Moscow in 1797–1862 and 1870–1914, indicate that during each year of decline of grain output recorded in the catalog, the domestic price of grain in Moscow rose, although the range of price increases differed widely. The registered deviation of the price from the eight-year average ranges from 15.4 per cent to 72.9 per cent. Fluctuations in supply were lower for the Moscow market than for any other region; the range of deviations therefore appear to be significant.[14] During the eighteenth century and on a few occasions in the nineteenth century, prohibitions of grain exports or special licensing were instituted to assure an adequate supply for domestic consumers. For the nineteenth century, out of a total of twenty-one years with substantially reduced foreign sales of grain, fifteen years can clearly be identified as years of natural calamities or years following such with a diminished grain output.[15]

Since it was only in exceptional cases that the demand of the urban population required the importation of grain, the grain import problems will be dealt with in conjunction with the impact of famines upon the agricultural population. The grain consumption of the agricultural producers was the largest item in the net as well as in gross output of grain until the twentieth century, and therefore was most susceptible to fluctuations in the yield and production of grains.

In order to survive the years of low yields and famine, the rural agricultural population tended to decrease the uses of grain for nonconsumption purposes. Unfortunately, the margins were quite narrow because of the high priorities of saving the workstock on the peasant farms, on the one hand, and the necessity of some grain sales to pay taxes, rents, and redemption fees, on the other, not to speak of the purchases of manufactured consumer goods. The state of grain production in the peasant sector of Russian agriculture was made much more precarious by the natural calamities which in turn not only prevented the development of livestock production based upon the grain supply, but invariably pushed back the peasant farm into a subsistence stage, decreasing the size of its marketable output. Not only did the marketable output shrink, as reflected by the available grain-export data, but during years of famine substantial grain imports became imperative if almost the total grain output would be consumed by the agricultural population.[16] That this was insufficient during years of severe famine is witnessed by evidence of both famine relief and increased mortality attributed to hunger.

Counter-Famine Measures

Assuming that the frequency of natural calamities affecting Russian agriculture could not have been unnoticed by the agricultural producers, even at times when natural calamities were considered a "punishment from heaven," we would expect, in order to minimize the effects on the food supply, that reserve stocks and grain carryovers existed in the agricultural areas.

The accumulation of stocks or of large yearly carryovers of grain by the agricultural producers depends upon their ability to save out of their current income. However, such natural calamities are random phenomena, the frequency of which cannot be predicted, and this creates problems in determining the size of the stocks needed to minimize the effect of such calamities. The costs of maintaining stocks tend also to vary for different localities and regions.

The fact that famines developed in Russia usually during the second consecutive year of adverse climatic conditions indicates the existence of stocks and the approximate period of their exhaustion, which would also suggest their probable size. Let us therefore appraise the burden of carrying stocks against the economic situation of the Russian peasants.

The assumption of one lost crop in ten years requires saving, out of the gross output, of over 10 per cent and of up to 13–14 per cent yearly out of the net output of grain of the peasant household. This is as much as farmers in relatively rich nations presently choose to save under conditions of prosperity. It is also the considered judgment of agricultural historians of Russia that, under the conditions of serfdom, such a saving ratio was an extreme burden upon the peasant economy. It might also be interesting to note that most of the government decrees of the eighteenth century prescribing the establishment of grain stocks for the population in the rural areas required that such stocks be carried by the landlords and not by the peasants.[17] The institution of serfdom itself worked against the accumulation of stocks, even if this would be economically feasible, since any visible surpluses could have been syphoned off either by the serfowners or by the government.

Thus it could be concluded that in most of the regions of Russia during the prevalence of serfdom, a year's stock of grain is the upper limit of what the peasant households could afford (at the price of curtailing current consumption).

That this situation did not change radically in the post-emancipation period, at least certainly not to the better, can be witnessed by the following official conclusion of a government study reporting on food consumption problems of the rural population: "As a general rule, the food supply produced by agricultural labor is sufficient for the satisfaction of current needs and does not leave any surpluses to be saved for a rainy day. . . . In other words, the threat of hunger and death is a likelihood for a substantial number of agricultural inhabitants of Russia."[18] If it is safe to assume that peasants in surplus grain regions carried stocks of less than one year's consumption, in grain-deficit regions the peasants' stocks were minimal, and each substantial price increase reduced their real income and lowered their consumption level, often decreasing their assets when such had to be converted to current expenditures.

There is very little evidence about the maintenance of substantial grain stocks by serfowners or large landowners during the latter period for the purpose of providing famine relief. The repetition of harsh government decrees about requisitions of grain and distribution among the hungry during the seventeenth and eighteenth centuries,[19] and particularly the ensuing involvement on the part of the government in famine relief, suggests that the obligations by the serfowners to provide assistance and relief were fulfilled unsatisfactorily.

The serfowners' high propensity to consume and the proverbial lack of liquid assets on the estates gave high preference for short-term gains versus the long-run protection of their capital assets—the serfs. Following the emancipation of the serfs, a weak sense of moral obligation and the need to protect their capital was replaced by a wishful sense of charity on the part of the landowners to assist their former serfs in times of distress. But the evidence of such a charitable spirit was difficult to detect even by well-trained historians.

It was therefore mandatory for the Russian government either to provide the measures which would minimize the effects of natural calamities on the food supply or to provide on a standby basis actual famine relief. Historical analysis is unequivocal that either by choice or by inability the Russian government performed the second task while failing abysmally in the first.

The government policies moved in two directions, although neither dealt with the fundamental problems.[20] First, the government ordered and supervised the buildup of local stocks in the settlements of state-owned serfs, including emergency stocks in the urban and rural areas;[21] secondly, it provided tax relief loans in grain and subsidies in money and grain to the areas most affected by famine. The supervision of the buildup of grain stocks in various regions was turned over to the Ministry of Interior, and in 1834 the maintenance of stocks was made obligatory on the whole territory of Russia. The available reports indicate that the size of the stocks fell short of the professed goal of about 200 kilograms of grain per male inhabitant registered in the population census. Although the goal had to be reached by the collection of grain on an installment basis over many years, it was never achieved while the recurring decreases of output made their periodic dent in the existing stocks. Since the serfs and later the emancipated peasants were the ones from whom the collections for the buildup of the stocks had to be exacted, and since they were also the most frequent victims of droughts and famines, the task given to the Russian bureaucracy, known better for its cruelty than for its efficiency, turned out to be beyond its capacity. Thus, the government-supervised stocks (during most of the post-emancipation period entrusted to the village commune under the supervision of the local gentry officials) were a form of forced savings imposed upon the peasants and considered by them as a variety of taxation.

Standby relief for famine-stricken regions by the government had a long tradition in Russia. Government appeals and orders to monasteries (maintaining sizeable stocks of grain) to ship and sell grain go back to the fifteenth century. Inventories of grain were ordered and surpluses had to be disposed of according to the decrees by Boris Godunov (1601–1603), Aleksei Mikhailovich (1661), and Peter the Great (1722). Quotas of maximum grain exports were set in 1764, and in famine years during the eighteenth century exports were prohibited. Millions of rubles of scarce state revenues were spent for famine relief during the nineteenth century. Even during the Soviet period, assistance and relief funds were solicited abroad in 1921 and 1946, and grain imports were instituted during 1963, 1965 (and subsequent years).

Another government measure viewed as famine relief was the setting up of public works in famine-stricken areas, providing either payment in grain or money which enabled the peasants to acquire grain at the increased price during years of famine. The peasants were employed at road building, land clearance, forestation, and occasionally on railroad construction by the government.[22] Unfortunately, the scope of the public works was insufficient to provide relief for more than a small fraction of the total in need of such relief. Thus, the policies of income transfer were insufficient to prevent a serious decrease in the consumption of those directly affected.

To the extent that natural calamities and the low harvests that followed them affected the income of the peasants, the main taxpayers in Russia, the government was aware of their impact upon the fiscal income of the state. While tax arrears tended to build up and increase during years of famine, occasional lowering of tax rates for the current year or postponement of tax collections by the government was announced as a measure of famine relief.[23] But while a tax decrease was effective for peasant relief in the eighteenth century, it was much less effective in the nineteenth century with the growth of indirect taxes and of the significance of the production and sale of alcohol for the state revenue. I was unable to find proof that the government attempted either to economize on the grain used in alcohol production (except in the regions where potatoes were normally used for this purpose) during a famine or to curtail alcohol consumption. Apparently faith in the sturdy constitution of the Russian peasant fathered the view that alcohol is after all a substitute for food, particularly if it serves the fiscal needs of the Russian state. Thus while certain measures of famine relief were periodically repeated, the Russian government was quite unable (or unwilling) to institute nationwide programs to mitigate the effects of natural calamities upon the food supply or to change its socioeconomic policies in order to shelter the permanent victims of such calamities.

Some Secondary Effects of the Natural Calamities

The most intriguing secondary effect of the natural calamities via the food supply is the effect on population growth.

In the case of Russia, however, it is difficult to ascertain that the impact of natural calamities upon population can be determined from the available data. Global population growth figures reflect complex social processes; one ought to be careful in attributing changes in population growth to famines rather than to devastating wars, epidemics, or pestilence.

Nevertheless, over longer time periods, there appears to be a correlation and perhaps a causal relationship between the frequencies of natural calamities during a particular period and the changes in the rate of population increase.

By excluding the periods of the most frequent wars within the stretch of 138 years of the eighteenth and nineteenth centuries for which we have crude data, based upon male population censuses taken at irregular intervals, we can distinguish two periods, one from each century, of less-than-average population growth. When combined with the data from the catalog, the results are rather instructive (see table 3.11). A frequency of natural calamities in the neighborhood of every second year can be associated with a lower-than-average population growth rate. And although the effects of the calamities certainly varied in strength, on the average it was sufficient adversely to affect the mortality rate, the birth rate, or both.

During the subsequent period 1858–1914, for which we have consistent, if only relatively reliable, population estimates, seventeen years of natural calamities and nineteen years of significantly lower-than-average population growth were registered. Out of these totals, ten years of natural

Table 3.11 Population Growth (in Percent) and Years of Natural Calamities

	1719–44	1833–50	1719–1857
Average Yearly Rate of Population Growth	0.66	0.64	0.81[a]
Number of Years of Natural Calamities	12	7	38
Frequency of Natural Calamities	0.48	0.41	0.275

Sources: Population data from Kabuzan, *Narodonaselenie Rossii*, pp. 164–65. Years of natural calamities from the catalog.

[a]On a comparable territory.

Table 3.12 Coincidence of Epidemics with Natural Calamities in Russia (Twelfth–Nineteenth Centuries)

Century	Total Natural Calamities	Total Epidemics	Epidemics Following or Coinciding with Natural Calamities
Twelfth	14	5	3
Thirteenth	17	6	4
Fourteenth	14	19	5
Fifteenth	15	10	7
Sixteenth	16	6	5
Seventeenth	15	2	2
Eighteenth	15	11	6
Nineteenth	26	13	8

calamities either coincided or were followed by eleven years of low population growth.[24] Of the remaining eight years of low population growth, at least three could be explained by increased mortality resulting from epidemics.

This brings us to the problem of the relationship between famines and epidemics. There is an old hypothesis that although a famine is not a direct cause of an outbreak of epidemics, one of the effects of malnutrition is the lowering of resistance to contagious diseases among the population, thereby increasing the probability of rapid spread of disease and higher mortality rates.

The comparison of dates of famines and major epidemics in Russia makes it possible to inquire into the coincidence of the two phenomena.[25]

The most general results for major epidemics which either coincided or immediately followed years of natural calamities are presented in table 3.12. Since in most of the presented cases the coincidence between epidemics and famines involved famines on a national scale, the data suggest a more than random relationship. They are, however, insufficient to prove a hypothesis of some causal relationship between the two phenomena.[26] The quest for a social rather than medical link ought to continue when the data both of famines and of epidemics are refined through further research. It is just plausible that the link between a famine and the outbreak of a severe epidemic existed in the situation in which a famine, causing a higher degree of population mobility, destroyed the enforcement of the quarantine system established by the government as the most general anti-epidemic device. This might be sufficient to convert a local outbreak of a contagious disease into a nationwide epidemic.

If such forms of "social causality" between famines and epidemics could be proved to have existed in Russia, the impact of natural calamities upon the rates of population growth, as a secondary effect, could be established with some higher degree of probability.

Appendix

Table 3A   Catalog of Recorded Natural Calamities Affecting Agriculture and Food Supply (Bold Type Denotes Calamities of National Importance)

Year	Type of Calamity	Geographic Location (Region, unless otherwise specified)	Degree of Intensity
1757	Low yields	In most of the Ukraine	
1767	Crop losses caused by July hailstorm, followed by drought	Large areas of the central nonblacksoil and central blacksoil regions	Apparently only summer crops affected
1774	Drought	Left-bank Ukraine, central blacksoil	From the hot wind the grains and grasses dried up.
1778	Drought	Nonblacksoil	
1780	Drought		
1781	Famine caused by drought in previous year	"Sixteen gubernii"	"Severe."
1785–86	Low yields	Nonblacksoil	
1788	Low yields	Southern Ukraine, Tauria	
1799	Low yields	Kiev, Poltava, Kherson	
1812	Low yield	Moscow, Siberia	
1817	Drought	Nonblacksoil	Rise in prices
1821	Heavy rains, hail, and drought	Belorussia	
1822	Famine caused by drought and locust	Most of European Russia, particularly south and southeast	Very severe: "People ate pine cones, oil-cake. Many died."
1823	Low yields	Central and Eastern Russia	
1830	Low yields caused by cold spring, summer drought	Most of European Russia	
1832–33	Famine caused by cold spring, followed by drought and early snows	Central blacksoil, Ukraine, Lower Volga, Northern Caucasus	Large scale grain imports, slaughter of cattle

Catalog (continued)

Year	Type of Calamity	Geographic Location (region, unless otherwise specified)	Degree of Intensity
1839	Famine caused by drought followed by hailstorms	Central blacksoil, Ukraine	
1840	Crop failure of winter grains due to cold spring and rains. Drought affected spring grains	Central nonblacksoil, Central and Lower Volga, central blacksoil	Rise in grain prices
1846	Low yields caused by hailstorms. Severe	West, Central, and Northcentral Russia	
1847	Low yields caused by spring frosts	Central Russia	Grain imports
1848	Famine caused by spring frosts and droughts	All Russia except western region	Rise in prices, population movements in search of food
1850	Low yields caused by spring frosts, rains, and drought	Northeast and south	High grain prices
1852	Low yields caused by rainy, cold spring	All Russia	
1855	Low yields caused by hot winds and drought in spring and early summer rains and hail in July–August. Locust	Eastern Belorussia, western blacksoil, South and Western Ukraine	
1859	Low yields caused by spring and early summer drought	Volga, eastern blacksoil, eastern nonblacksoil, Northern Ukraine	
1864	Low yields	West and central nonblacksoil	
1865	Drought	Eastern blacksoil, eastern nonblacksoil	
1867	Frost and drought	Smolensk, nonblacksoil	
1875	Drought	Ukraine, nonblacksoil, North Caucasus	
1879	Drought	Middle Volga, Central Ukraine	
1885	Drought	South and East Ukraine, Middle and Lower Volga, North Caucasus	
1889	Drought	Ukraine, Lower Volga	
1890	Drought	Lower Volga, Ural	
1891	Famine caused by drought	Blacksoil, all of Volga, Southern Ukraine, North Caucasus	
1892	Drought	Ukraine, central blacksoil, Lower Volga, North Caucasus	
1897	Drought	South Ukraine, Lower Volga	
1900	Frost and drought	Ukraine, Western Siberia	

Catalog (continued)

Year	Type of Calamity	Geographic Location (region, unless otherwise specified)	Degree of Intensity
1901	Drought	Eastern Ukraine, Ural, Lower and Middle Volga	
1906	Drought and heavy rains	Eastern Ukraine, Volga	
1911	Drought	European Russia, Ukraine, West Siberia	
1914	Drought	Volga, Ukraine	
1920	Drought	Ukraine, Volga	
1921	Famine	European Russia, Ukraine, Volga, Western Siberia	Accompanied by starvation
1924	Drought	Central blacksoil, Lower Volga	
1931	Drought	Western Siberia, Ural, central blacksoil	
1934	Drought	Central blacksoil, Ukraine, North Caucasus	
1936	Drought	Ukraine, Volga, Western Siberia	
1938	Drought	Central blacksoil, Eastern Ukraine	
1939	Drought	Lower Volga, Upper Volga, Southeast Ukraine	
1946	Famine	Ukraine, central blacksoil, Volga, North Caucasus	
1948	Drought	Middle Volga, Ural	
1950	Drought	Eastern Ukraine, Middle and Lower Volga, eastern central blacksoil	
1951	Drought	Ukraine, Lower Volga	
1953	Drought	Ukraine, Volga	
1954	Drought	Southern Ukraine, Lower Volga	
1955	Drought	Western Siberia, Lower Volga	
1955	Drought	Western Siberia, Kazakhstan, Lower Volga	
1963	Drought	Western Siberia, Kazakhstan, Ural, Eastern Ukraine	
1965	Drought	Western Siberia, Kazakhstan, Central Asia, Ural, Volga	

Table 3B Output-Seed Ratios of Grain Production, 1801–1915

Year	Output-Seed Ratio	Year	Output-Seed Ratio
1801	3.04	1844	3.81
1802	3.4	1845	3.42
1803	3.65	1846	3.38
1804	4.04	1847	3.6
1805	3.2	1848	2.72
1806	3.47	1849	4.03
1807	3.73	1850	2.84
1808	3.89	1851	4.0
1809	3.33	1852	3.83
1810	3.4	1853	3.61
1811	2.85	1854	3.51
1812	3.1	1855	2.6
1813	3.43	1856	3.26
1814	4.0	1857	3.95
1815	3.1	1858	4.08
1816	3.4	1859	2.87
1817	3.7	1860	3.78
1818	4.1	1861	3.51
1819	4.0	1862	3.57
1820	3.4	1863	4.26
1821	3.25	1864	3.28
1822	3.1	1865	3.01
1823	2.9	1866	3.84
1824	3.5	1867	3.1
1825	3.5	1868	3.75
1826	3.67	1869	4.06
1827	3.61	1870	4.59
1828	3.9	1871	3.52
1829	3.75	1872	3.88
1830	2.91	1873	3.94
1831	3.2	1874	4.34
1832	2.8	1875	3.38
1833	2.38	1876	3.85
1834	3.62	1877	4.26
1835	3.92	1878	4.49
1836	4.1	1879	3.78
1837	3.98	1880	3.65
1838	3.93	1881	4.73
1839	2.67	1882	4.31
1840[a]	3.32	1883	4.04
1841	3.4	1884	4.3
1842[b]	4.39	1885	3.65
1843[c]	4.36	1886	4.28

Table 3B   (continued)

Year	Output-Seed Ratio	Year	Output-Seed Ratio
1887	4.87	1902	5.77
1888	4.69	1903	5.2
1889	3.65	1904	6.13
1890	4.14	1905	4.86
1891	3.26	1906	4.05
1892	4.0	1907	4.88
1893	5.63	1908	5.04
1894	5.68	1909	6.33
1895	5.04	1910	5.87
1896	5.04	1911	4.17
1897	4.12	1912	6.24
1898	4.76	1913	6.75
1899	5.4	1914	5.06
1900	5.01	1915	6.70
1901	4.08		

Sources: Mikhailnskii, *Urozhai v Rossii,* pp. 2–4; Semenov, *K voprosu o zakonomer-nosti,* pp. 57–95.

[a]Output-seed ratios 1.82 according to Semenov.
[b]Output-seed ratios 3.73 according to Semenov.
[c]Output-seed ratios 4.07 according to Semenov.

Bibliography

Buchinskii, I. E. *O klimate proshlogo russkoi ravniny.* Leningrad: Gidrometeoizdat, 1957.

Bucinskij, I. E. "O zasukhakh na russkoi ravnine za polednee tysiachiletie." In *Suchovei, ikh proiskhozdenie i bor'ba s nimi.* Izdat. Moscow: AN SSSR, 1957.

Ivanov, B. K. "Uslovija vozniknovenija i charakter suchoveev Zapadnoj Sibiri." In Suchovei, *ikh proiskhozdenie i bor'ba s nimi.*

Kabuzan, V. M. *Narodonaselenie Rossii v XVIII-pervoi polovine XIX vv.* Moscow, 1963.

Maksimov, V. *Ocherki po istorii obshchestvennykh rabot v Rossii.* St. Petersburg, 1905.

Mikhailovskii, V. G. "Urozhai v Rossii 1801–1914 gg." In *Biulleten Tsentral'nogo statisticheskogo upravleniia RSFSR* (Moscow), no. 50, (1921).

Pasuto, V. T. "Golodnye gody v Drevnei Rusi." In *Ezegodnik po agrarnoj istorii Vostochnoi Evropy, 1962 g.,* Minsk, 1964.

Pokrovskii, V. I. *Sbornik svedenii po istorii i statistike vnesnei torgovli Rossii.* St. Petersburg, 1902.

Rudenko, A. I. *Zasukhi v SSSR, ikh proisckhozhdenie, povtoriaemost' i vliianie na urozai.* Leningrad: Gidrometeoizdat, 1958.

Russia, Ministerstvo vnutrennikh del. *Zhurnal Ministerstva vnutrennikh del.* St. Petersburg, 1856.

Shcherbatov, M. M. "Rassuzhdeniia o nyneshnem v 1778 g. pochti povsednevom golode v Rossii." In *Sochineniia,* vol. 1. St. Petersburg, 1896.

Semenov, M. I. "K voprosu o zakonomernosti kolebanii urozhaev." In *Vestnik statistiki* (Moscow), no. 11 (1925).

Polnoe sobranie russkikh letopisei. Various volumes.

Polnoe sobranie zakonov Rossiiskoi Imperii (cited as PSZ). St. Petersburg, 1830-.

Stanislavkii, L. M. "Khronika golodnykh godov." In A. V. Chaianov (ed.), *Problemy urozaia.* Moscow, 1927.

Vainshtein, A. L. "Evoliutsiia urozhainosti zernovykh khlebov v Rossii." In *Planovoe khoziaistvo* (Moscow), nos. 7, 8 (1927).

Varadinov, N. V. *Istoriia Ministerstva vnutrennikh del.* vols. 1–3. St. Petersburg, 1858–63.

Volkov, E. Z. *Dinamika narodonaseleniia SSSR.* Moscow and Leningrad, 1930.

FOUR

Notes on Serfdom in
Western and Eastern Europe

The purpose of these observations on serfdom in Western and Eastern Europe is to call attention to some of the problems, in part methodological ones, that arise in attempts to analyze the system of serfdom as a social institution.[1]

Both the variety of historical experience in the process of formation, functioning, and duration of the institution of serfdom and the voluminous sources and secondary literature on this subject defy an attempt to deal with its implications. It would be wrong, however, even while laboring under the constraints of space, to obliterate the significant differences of the forms of serfdom that resulted from various economic and political conditions. It might also be futile, given our present state of knowledge, to produce a "distilled, pure essence" of the serf economy. Therefore, for the purpose of emphasizing some possibilities for further research, specifically research by economic historians, only a few topics will be treated here.

Serfdom, legally defined, represented a variety of forms of limited ownership of human beings or legal claims to varying parts of their wealth, income, or services. To a certain extent one could therefore, by analogy with slavery, view the institution of serfdom as representing ownership capital, that is, ownership of an income-generating asset.

By further analogy with slavery, one could enter a discussion of the profitability of serfdom to the serfowners. Discussing the problem of profitability of serfdom in various countries, one might observe, as in the case of slavery, that serfdom at the time of its abolition was still profitable to many serfowners when measured in terms of private returns, and it did not disappear as an economic institution when it ceased to be socially profitable.[2] Apparently involuntary labor, while it exists, can be profitable to its beneficiaries under various circumstances, or it can be made profitable by a number of policies.

In viewing serfdom from the perspective of American slavery, however, one tacitly assumes that the economic environment of serfdom was one of a capitalist market economy, and that the behavioral parameters of the serfowner are those of an asset holder in the modern sense. I must admit my uneasiness with assuming for thirteenth- or sixteenth-century serfowners the attributes of capitalist entrepreneurs, and I would therefore not wish to support the attempts to link the characteristics of medieval or early modern serfowners to the behavior of American slaveholders of the nineteenth century. It is methodologically dubious to use an analytical apparatus designed to study the market economy for the analysis of a society in which only a relatively small volume of resources was available in a market.[3] But the real difficulty with using a free market analytical framework is more complex than the quantitative volume of resources entering the market. Two out of a host of institutional arrangements are at the roots of market behavior, namely property rights and the possibility of entering into and enforcing free contracts. Unless the definition of the exact form of property rights in serfs is made clear, the distinctions between the various forms of a serf economy and a market economy will be obscured.

Property rights existed within a number of institutional arrangements. For example, property rights in movables existed within a communal setting side-by-side with quite different principles of common property of immovables. Property rights in men existed in both nonmarket and market economies. Property rights in immovables (for example, land) existed in the minds of their holders or users and might or might not be explicitly recognized by custom or customary law. Such rights rested on the power of the proprietor or the community to protect them or to prevent their transgression by outsiders. They were sometimes granted by the state authorities and enforced in a discriminatory fashion. Finally, property rights, including the ability to acquire and dispose of the rights, could be elevated to a general principle of the polity and enforced by the authorities of the state in a nondiscriminatory way.

What follows from this is that property rights or private ownership is a historical category, and its scope and nature depended on the particular historical setting. Therefore, it is important to identify the guarantor of property rights, to recognize, that is, where the power of enforcement of such rights resided—with which institution, public body, or private group.

The methodological problems of contracts raise similar issues, such as the degree of freedom of entering into contractual obligations, the adjudication and enforcement of contracts, and so forth. The economic historian must look into these problems before using a particular model or analytical framework in discussing aspects of the serf economy.

I am suggesting that to understand the operation of the serf economy we need a different economic model from the usual one and that the mechanical application of components from our conventional analytical apparatus to the institution of serfdom will provide only severely limited comprehension of the process of formation, growth, decline, and transformation of the institution. In the absence of a general model of the serf economy, I will propose a set of parameters—some easily quantifiable, some perhaps nonquantifiable—that an explanatory model of a serf economy ought to contain.[4]

Thus, I would like to suggest that a model of the serf economy or of the system of serfdom ought to include information about the following areas and relationships:

1) The relative size of the serfowner class and of the serf population and their changes in the context of population growth;
2) the land-labor ratio in agriculture and the relative prices of both factors;
3) the distribution of land between the serf households and the demesne, the level of yields, and the state of the art in agriculture;
4) the growth of the social product of agriculture and its distribution between the serfowners, the serfs, and the state, and the changes in the real incomes of the serfs;
5) the relative size of the prevailing forms of rent payments by the serfs—in kind, labor services, money;
6) the degree of spatial and social mobility of the serf population and the effectiveness of barriers to mobility;
7) the degree to which legal norms limited the economic decision making of the serfowners on their estates with regard to their serfs;
8) the areas of government interference in the economy and in particular in the relations between the serfowners and the serfs;
9) the intensity of dissatisfaction of the serfs with their status and the forms of resistance to impositions of increased burdens on their income and to limitations on the autonomy of their economic decision making;
10) the degree of commercialization of agriculture and the availability of markets for products, for land, and for labor; and
11) the changes in the general price level and the relative movement of agricultural and nonagricultural prices, the terms of trade between agricultural producers and the nonagricultural sector of the economy, and the long term changes in the terms of trade for the various social groups participating in the exchange.

When one turns to some of the basic characteristics of the serf economy, it is necessary to recognize that serfdom was an institution that combined limited ownership of human beings with ownership of another resource, chiefly land, for the purpose of providing revenue for the owners of those resources from the combination of the two. Thus, serfdom presupposed ownership of land. We can therefore assume that a precondition of the process of enserfment involved the alienation of or extinguishing of rights to the land occupied by the objects of enserfment. The acknowledgment of property rights to the land held or acquired by private individuals, institutions (churches or other corporate institutions), or state authorities by the future objects of enserfment was a necessary step in the process. Whether this acknowledgment or consensus was a voluntary one or an involuntary one on the part of the future serfs is a problem belonging to the area of political relations, which I shall discuss later. A further necessary step in the process of enserfment was the establishment of a system of dependency, whether personal or territorial, which imposed on the serfs enforceable obligations of payments and services for the use of land that they were tilling. These two steps did not necessarily appear in a determined sequence and in fact often developed simultaneously over a period of decades or centuries.

The effectiveness of these institutional arrangements depended to a large extent on the degree of control exercised by the legal owners of the land. This is a central point. The most effective utilization of serfdom as an institution, in terms of the share of revenue or volume of services, depended on the degree to which land ownership, and by extension serf ownership, was made a monopoly of a well-defined and limited group. Thus, while serfdom, as an institution to acquire revenue by extending property rights over human beings, could under certain circumstances function without monopoly, its effectiveness was greatly increased by collusion or outright monopoly. The elimination of competition among serf-owners for serfs extended and expanded the right of ownership over additional areas of the serfs' economic and noneconomic activities.

Much of the literature produced by historians and economists, while apparently centered around such problems as the impact of the land-labor ratio on the institution of serfdom, is, in fact, centered around the stage of development of the institution at which the monopoly of serf ownership is being enforced. The special fascination for historians held out by the tying of the serfs to the soil—the prohibition of serf mobility, enacted in the law and enforced by a central authority of the state—is in essence the legal sanctioning of the monopoly which imposes monopolistic behavior on its participants. The impression that the institution of serfdom was permeated by monopoly (or near-monopoly) elements is strengthened when we consider the numerous instances in which the economic reward of the institution (for the serfowners) was increased by the expansion of monopoly rights outside of land ownership or even outside of the production process in agriculture itself.

One example of such a monopoly, which provided a large share of the incomes of serfowners in times of a decline in agricultural incomes from the demesne, was the monopoly sale of alcohol to the serfs. Whether viewed as a special consumption tax or some other form of income transfer, the monopoly characteristics of the alcohol sales were paramount. Another example is provided by the struggle of the serfholding nobility to establish monopolies in the grain trade to the ports; this is especially apparent in Eastern Europe. There is no doubt that the monopoly of the grain trade, where established and enforced, augmented the incomes of the serfowners and, in turn, led to a whole set of economic and political developments that affected the nature and duration of serfdom.[5]

A corollary of monopoly rights in other parts of the system of serfdom was the monopoly of judicial power over the serfs acquired by the serfowners. Given the state of law at the time, in particular the frequent overlap of the functions of public and private law, the judiciary power of the serfowners over their serfs became an important vehicle of economic advantage and exercise of power on the part of the serfowners. Very often what could not be achieved by legislation was instituted by the manorial courts.[6] Certainly contractual relations are not very meaningful when their adjudication is left to one of the contracting parties.

My preliminary reading of the materials pertaining to the serf economy, then, suggests that perhaps a useful alternative approach to those followed by other economic historians would be to emphasize the central role of the serfowning monopoly and the circumstances of its creation and development. The monopoly, sanctioned by the power of the supreme authorities and embodied in the legal system, not only established and transformed property rights to land, to human beings, and to part of their labor, but also restricted the rights of entry into the privileged group that owned these rights, restricted the mobility of the serfs, and maintained the subordinate position of other groups, such as the burghers. This institutional arrangement at any rate describes the functioning of serfdom, if not completely explaining its inception or demise.

To pursue the argument of a unifying framework for the serf economy further, one has to recognize the political framework within which the institution of serfdom functioned. Political scientists and historians have focused much attention to the power of a central authority in the state as against diffusion of power within the state. Clearly, this is an important issue for any interpretation of the process of enserfment. Enserfment of the peasants would be impossible to enforce in the absence of an established monopoly of serfholding as an exclusive privilege of a defined serf-owning class, and in the absence of sanctions enabling the members of this social group to behave as monopolists. Such a "monopolistic discipline" has to be either developed by the group itself or enforced by a powerful authority. Thus, the relationship between the supreme authority in the state and the prospective or actual serfowners was of crucial importance, particularly when serfdom was expanding or contracting.[7]

There are a number of possible alternative combinations (or political alliances) that could characterize such a relationship. Consider a few examples from a host of possibilities. One could visualize a relationship between a powerful central authority and a gentry class, under the terms of which the central authority, depending on the gentry for military service, would find it more convenient to allow the gentry to enserf the peasants as an alternative to imposing a system of taxation to maintain a hired standing army. One could envisage a relationship between a weak central authority and a strong oligarchy, which would lead to the enserfment of the peasants by the oligarchy, dividing the revenue from serf labor between the oligarchy and the state in proportions that would vary according to the changing power relationship between the two. One could also imagine, or perhaps deduce from historical evidence, a central authority setting itself up as an arbiter between an oligarchy and a numerous gentry, where the proceeds from serf labor would be divided among the three parties according to a formula, which would presumably reflect the power relationships of the parties involved. Finally, not to exhaust but to emphasize the broad spectrum of possible relationships, the central authority might ally itself with nonagricultural interests in order to gain independence of action from a landed oligarchy or gentry and perhaps to curtail the process of enserfment.

Three points ought to be emphasized about these examples. First, among the forms of serfdom encountered in the history of Europe, very few conform to any single one of the simple types enumerated. This historical sequence of events and the changing social relationships challenged the political process and by extension the legal framework and thereby forced on them a dynamics and complexity in the development of serfdom as an institution. Second, it would be fair to assume that for the period under investigation some of the central authorities themselves were not only major owners of land, but also owners of serfs. Thus, a decision or policy to enserf the peasants, or to expand or contract serfdom, involved for the central authorities a consideration of political and economic advantages with respect to its own resources and revenues. Third, there is no presumption about the durability of such combinations. We know from historical experience that some were eroded by long-term demographic or economic processes, some were influenced by calamities of various kinds (e.g., the Black Death, the Hundred Years War, etc.), some were affected by random variables (e.g., the change of a ruling dynasty). Therefore, we have to be able to distinguish between what appear to be patterns of long-run political change and what are particular turns in the policies with respect to serfdom.

It has been claimed by some historians that the political power of an oligarchy is positively correlated with the strengthening of serfdom, and that the demise of such an oligarchy leads to a weakening if not a withering away of serfdom. Other historians, however, insist that the survival of serfdom until the nineteenth century would have been impossible in the absence of a powerful central authority that helped to maintain or abolish serfdom for reasons of its own.

Regardless of the accuracy of these two generalizations—and they ought not to be considered as mutually exclusive—it is clear that serfdom could probably survive longer in a political situation in which the equilibrium of conflicting forces was stable. In this respect, the sixteenth through the eighteenth centuries, with their growth of centralized authority, were more stable than the thirteenth or fourteenth century in Europe.

When we turn to a comparison of the institutional arrangements of the serf economy in Western and Eastern Europe, it appears to be necessary to deal with two assumptions common in the popular literature. One of them pertains to the establishment of serfdom in Western Europe and portrays right of land tenure subject only to the constraints of an extended family, clan, or tribe constituting a peasant commune. Even if correct, this notion of the peasant commune, supposedly derived from historical sources pertaining to the early social organization of Germanic tribes, did not have the decisive impact on the system of land tenure or organization of agricultural production that is commonly ascribed to it.

First, let us remember that the conquest of Western Europe by Germanic tribes found an indigenous population at least as numerous as the conquerors, with a system of landholding that was perhaps altered by the conquerors but not discarded in its entirety. The Roman colonate or other forms of dependency prevailed at the time of the conquests. The Germanic tribal society at this time was already much more differentiated than is suggested by Tacitus's earlier portrayal, which has often served for many historians as definitive of the social organization of the Germanic tribes. Thus, two socially differentiated societies clashed politically, and one was subjugated by the other. There is no reason to believe that the upper class of the conquerors granted property rights in land to the subjugated tillers of the soil. And while in some areas the indigenous Celtic-Roman upper class was physically destroyed, in other areas it assimilated itself with the upper class of the conquerors. If we assume that the conquerors were socially differentiated at the time of the conquest, it might also be logical to assume that the gradual limitations on the land tenure rights of the allodial holders were exacted not primarily by the commune, but by the upper classes. The question still remains whether in the areas of settlement of the Germanic tribes the previous group of allodial holders rose to the estate of unlimited land proprietors or descended to the status of dependents. In fact one would suspect that in areas where the Celtic-Roman elements were culturally and economically strong and where a fusion of the native upper social groups with the upper groups of the conquerors took place, the descent of the majority of the allodial holders to a subordinated, dependent status was the more likely outcome.

In the early centuries of serfdom, moreover, the institution of slavery still existed in Western Europe, and the convergence of the status of former slaves with the status of dependent peasants was one of the spectacular legal and economic feats of the institution of serfdom. It would, therefore, be a historical mistake to look for the origins of serfdom in England so late as the time of the Norman conquest or in France and Western Germany so late as the eleventh century. The institution goes back centuries earlier.

Thus, the later development of the manor, as one of the chief institutions of landholding accompanying the development of serfdom, took place neither in a political nor social-institutional vacuum. One has to be keenly aware of the degree of continuity of the old and preconquest elements, the dynamics of the social relations arising from the social differentiation established after the conquest (a large part of which was later reflected in the so-called customary law), the role that the central authorities of the state played in modifying serfdom, and the actual relations of landholding and the distribution of land as well as of the claims to the property of and in men. The authority of the state could often seize legal property rights over the land and distribute them on primarily political criteria. It is worth emphasizing that the first beneficiaries of these land distribution policies were the church and monasteries, followed by the lay nobles of the king's entourage. But land alone was not of significant intrinsic value unless it was cultivated by its tillers; therefore, we can observe simultaneously the formation of a hierarchical system of dependence and services. The fusion of the two assured that there would be income derived from the land and influenced its distribution from the start.

Thus the manor at its inception cannot be viewed as an independent institution free to enter into contractual arrangements with individuals or groups of agricultural producers. In fact, in most cases there was probably no need for the manor to enter into a contractual relationship since status and power enabled it to impose its interests on the social groups that were politically inferior and economically weaker.[8] The manor had obligations toward the church, as did the peasants. The success of the early history of the manor consisted in its ability to shift onto the serfs most of the burdens and obligations that the manor owed to the crown. Unless the obligations toward the crown were extinguished in favor of the lord of the manor, the serfs remained henceforth under a double burden.

And even in cases when the obligations of the prospective or actual serfs toward the state were extinguished in favor of the manor, it is doubtful that one could label the lord-serf relationship as a contractual one. If simple personal dependency provided both parties with a modicum of choice, a system of territorial dependency as exemplified by the later development of the manorial system provided very little choice to at least one of the parties—the objects of serfdom. The enforcement of monopoly rights, where successfully maintained, did the rest, completely destroying the facade of a contractual relationship.

The second popular assumption is the notion of the "reintroduction" of serfdom in Eastern Europe, as though serfdom existed in Eastern Europe, was abolished, and subsequently was reintroduced. I believe that this myth ought to be laid to rest as entirely erroneous. In fact, the history of serfdom in Eastern Europe, although imperfectly synchronized with that in the West, nevertheless exhibits a logical and sequential development of its own.

Economic historians can draw on a voluminous literature which describes many features of the development of serfdom in Eastern Europe. One can easily trace the development of the concepts of the manor both in the area of public law and in the rules of administration of the manor as categories of private law. As in the West, there was a hierarchy of sovereignty, within which there existed rules and behavioral norms regulating the relations between the upper and lower strata. The variations of the forms of land rent—with quitrent, labor services, and payments in kind appearing in different combinations, determined by the region, period, or market demand—remind one of Western Europe. But serfdom in Eastern Europe was not a mere repetition, at a later date, of Western European experience. It certainly did not try to copy a vanishing model. Eastern Europe experienced its early phase of political integration at a later date than the West (it was also converted to Christianity at a much later date than Western Europe); the pace of economic development was slower; and some consequences of political events (the calamitous effects of the Tatar invasions, to cite one example) were detrimental to population growth and to the development of the economy. Therefore, the process of enserfment proceeded slower in Eastern Europe than in the West. But the fourteenth and fifteenth centuries witnessed an acceleration of the process of enserf-ment, which moved eastward and which was accompanied in some coun-tries of Eastern Europe by renewed efforts at political integration. Political integration, in turn, made it easier to further the process of enserfment. In short, the spectacular expansion of serfdom in the sixteenth and seven-teenth centuries in Eastern Europe was a result of the previous pattern of development coupled with a set of special circumstances, among which the changing land-labor ratios, the demand for grain in Western Europe, and the political developments inside the countries of Eastern Europe cer-tainly played an important role. The result was an expansion of serfdom but not a reintroduction, not a "second serfdom."

Serfdom in Eastern and Western Europe, regardless of the differences in the chronology of origin, development, and decline, exhibited many com-mon features, sufficient to consider them similar, if not entirely identical. The locus of productive activity was in both cases the agricultural sector of the economy; the dependency of the serfs on the serfowners was fixed in the law; and the limited ownership of both the humans and the land by the serfowners constituted the basis for a distribution of agricultural in-come that favored the serfowners.[9]

But because the institution of serfdom reached its apogee in Western Europe at a different time than in Eastern Europe, there were significant differences. As a result of a smaller size of the market, and perhaps a different land-labor ratio, the size of the demesne in the Western European manor was considerably smaller than on Eastern European serfowning es-tates. This had at least two major consequences for the serf economy in Western Europe. On the one hand, the limited size of the demesne in Western Europe probably provided less scope for the managerial or entre-preneurial activity of the manorial lord, and on the other hand, it enabled the landholdings of the villeins to provide a larger share of the marketable product than that of the serfs in Eastern Europe. Thus, involvement in the local and domestic markets and in the money economy permeated and also undermined the institution of serfdom in the West to a larger extent than it did in the East, where the serfowners rather than the serfs engaged in trading activities, primarily for a foreign market. The role of the cities was also different in Western and Eastern Europe. While in the West most of the cities developed into corporate bodies with charters guaranteeing the freedom of the city dwellers (*Stadtluft macht frei* was the West's maxim) and therefore sometimes served as an escape route, in Eastern Europe many of the cities did not possess such charters or were owned by large serfowners and could not provide this means of escape. This situation presented less of a threat to the institution of serfdom and to the enforce-ment of the serfowners' monopoly than the Western European situation.

Last, but not least, it appears that it was difficult for the Western European serfowners to impose a monopolistic code of behavior, with the result that substantial costs to individual serfowners were entailed in retrieving fugitive serfs. In most countries of Eastern Europe, the state assumed the costs of returning fugitive serfs to their owners, and the monopoly was imposed by the state on the serfowning class, thus eliminating most of the nonmarket competition for serfs.

In contrast to the relative abundance of detailed records and secondary literature dealing with the manorial economy of the twelfth and thirteenth centuries in Western Europe, the literature dealing with the fourteenth and fifteenth centuries is thin. There is, however, little doubt that the manorial system in Western Europe during the fourteenth and fifteenth centuries was under severe stress. Grain prices declined while wages rose. Given the scarcity of wage labor and of capital, changes in the value of money and shrinkage of the market led to a decline of real income to the manor. The inability of the serfowners to impose an effective monopoly on other areas of the serfs' activities also followed. In view of the peasant resistance (such as the Jacquerie in France and Wat Tyler in England), the decline of income led to the decline of the demesne as a producing unit and its gradual shrinkage by leasing out the land on easier terms than the ones existing under the system of serfdom. In other words, the solution was to provide incentives, which ultimately transformed serf rent-payers into tenants and freeholders.[10]

The decline of ownership rights in men that took place for both economic and political reasons in Western Europe was not accompanied by a general rejection of such rights as a socially and legally acceptable institution of Western European society. The institution of property rights in men was exported from the metropolis to the colonies. This time, not grains but crops that were even more labor intensive, such as sugar and tobacco, were the output of a system of servitude. Although serfdom failed whenever attempted in the colonies, slavery took its place. It lasted there for centuries until, as a result of the development of a new economic and political system, it became morally abhorrent.

The situation in the sixteenth through the eighteenth centuries in Eastern Europe was different in many ways. Serfdom in the sixteenth century was stimulated not only by a favorable land-labor ratio but to a large extent by the growth of Western European demand for grain from the Baltic region, thus including Eastern Europe in the world market economy. Grain prices were rising throughout the period of the so-called price revolution, and although productivity in Eastern European agriculture was not high, the monopoly power of the serfowners made the production of grain relatively cheap. Thus, although in the West two centuries earlier the declining prices of grain and the expense of the major inputs caused a shift from cereals to livestock and sheep, in the East relative prices favored the production of cereals produced by serfowning estates. Serfdom was by this set of circumstances given a relatively long lease on life.

The institution of serfdom, beginning with favorable economic conditions and later strengthened by the power of the state, was capable of surviving during economically adverse periods. It was able to shift the impact of declining incomes onto the serfs and to keep the majority of them at a subsistence level for extended periods. In the process of preserving the institution intact, the serfowners not only became brutalized but the whole body politic became dehumanized and permeated by elements of lawlessness. Thus, the changes imposed on Eastern Europe in the nineteenth century found neither the basic legal institutions nor the prevailing social attitudes ready to accept them. The political authorities were primarily responsible for the abolition of serfdom. And as a political act, it had to signify a break with the institutions of the past, the most visible and perhaps the most obnoxious symbol of which was serfdom.

FIVE

Forms of Social Protest by the Agrarian Population in Russia

The record of social protest by the agrarian population of Russia has been studied superficially by historians who have focused primarily on spectacular features like peasant rebellions and peasant wars of the seventeenth and eighteenth centuries. Particularly during the Soviet period historians felt obliged to draw comparisons with the "classic" examples of similar phenomena in Western Europe, with Wat Tyler in England, the Jacquerie in France, the Peasant War of 1525 in Germany, and the like.

Until relatively recently not much attention was paid to the less spectacular forms of social protest of the peasants, to the incessant struggle against the legal framework and institutions which kept the peasants in a position of second-class citizens not only by virtue of their low position on the income scale but primarily because of their exclusion from political power in the state.

I would therefore define the term "social protest" as used in this essay as any collective action by peasants, legal and illegal, which expressed dissatisfaction with and grievances against their social adversaries; as their adversaries I would not necessarily consider the groups classified as such by modern sociological or political analysis, but primarily the ones so designated by the peasants and against whom their wrath was directed.

The historical record of the peasants' social protest in Russia indicates—and I do not believe it to be a peculiarity of Russia—that agrarian protests are not sporadic events but a continuous process and ought to be studied as such. Peasant unrest in Russia will be treated as a continuum, the forms of which were changing, depending on conditions and circumstances, and expressed in a variety of types of collective action.

The Russian experience, or the experience of eastern and southeastern Europe (which differed from Russia slightly in scope and intensity), when viewed as a continuing process, has a definite validity in the study of social relations in agriculture in the presently developing countries. The primary

157

reason for using Eastern Europe's experience to test certain hypotheses is that this region not long ago lagged substantially behind Western Europe and the United States in its political and economic development, and therefore was in a similar position to that of the developing countries vis-á-vis the developed, industrialized part of the world.

It recently became possible for scholars both in Russia and in the West to engage in a series of studies of social protest owing to the publication of a monumental, eleven-volume collection of documents which, although not complete, provide a catalogue of incidents of social protest of the agrarian population for the period 1796–1917.[1] The period can be divided into roughly two halves, with the emancipation of the serfs in 1861 as the dividing line.

I assume that a discussion of the causes of peasant dissatisfaction with the institution of serfdom is redundant. Apart from the economically oppressive and psychologically degrading features of serfdom as an institution, I find the prohibition of personal mobility the most significant among the causes of serf unrest in Russia before 1861.

In addition to the problems of personal mobility either during or after the period of emancipation, there existed still another problem of general mobility, of upward social mobility. In spite of the existence of serfdom, with its leveling attitudes toward the peasants, or the village commune, which favored equality in income distribution, income inequalities developed within the peasant milieu. Employment in rural crafts and industry and in trade and money lending provided opportunities for capital accumulation. However, the prevalence of serfdom (and difficulties of manumission) and the inflexible legal stratification of Russian society made upward social mobility difficult for the peasants.

The uncertainty of ownership under serfdom and the social barriers maintained afterwards by a gentry-dominated polity, coupled with bureaucratic inertia and lack of respect for the law, made it extremely difficult for individuals to raise themselves from the lower strata. Since the social status of richer peasants was hardly higher than that of poor peasants, the investment of accumulated capital in agriculture was looked on as a second-best solution, and peasant savings were in the form of hoarding rather than improvements in agriculture.

The above contention might explain not only the slow growth of a strong middle-income peasantry but also the fact that, until the twentieth century, in so many cases of peasant unrest it is difficult to draw any line of distinction between the richer and poorer peasants, and the participation in various forms of protest cannot be attributed to the relative economic position within the peasant population. The process of differentiation within the peasantry with respect to choice of forms of social protest and the emergence of conflicts of interest, which affected both the participation in such protests as well as the goals of such, were slow in coming. Such differentiation became visible at a relatively late period, at the stage of intense "politicization" of peasant movements and after gaining political experience in established peasant organizations with a mass following. For most of the period, Russian peasant protest was dominated by a chain of spontaneous, violent, and often destructive actions.

The classification of the various forms of social protest involves problems both of methodology and choice.

It is possible to use a legal-historical viewpoint and adopt a classification which provides the spectrum of actions in a strictly legal sense from petitions and court litigations to the most offensive actions (according to the legal code). This does not necessarily imply that the classification will follow a gradation of violence, since legal codes could be much harsher in punishment for political propaganda than for manslaughter.

A classification which systematically distinguishes certain groups of causes of social protest possesses a great deal of merit. Students of social history are interested in the nature of peasant grievances which involved conflicts of ownership, relations among landlord, estate steward, and peasants, the conditions of hire and work, the terms of land lease, the level of rents, and so forth. It is therefore possible to set up a classification which would distinguish the relationship between the estate and the peasant farm from the relationship between the landlord and the peasant and attempt to systematize each in terms of socio-economic or socio-psychological analysis. It is also possible to classify the various forms of social protest in terms of the adversaries against whom the particular protests were directed. We may learn a great deal from studying the intensity of social protests (however defined) depending on whether they were directed against representatives of a particular social stratum (in most cases the gentry-landlords) or against the institutions of the state.[2]

The preference of one type of classification over another involves two considerations. One is the primary interest of the student and the analytical toolbox at his disposal; the second is the volume of information at his disposal which he chooses to absorb.

I personally found it very useful in the choice of classification to have at hand the information on the number of participants, the duration of the various actions, the forms of legal response or retaliation on the part of the authorities, and in some cases, the extent of victimization of the participants.[3] This information, which reveals not only the occurrence of peasant unrest (which varied between periods) but also its distribution among regions, could reveal the relationship between such peasant actions and other social parameters.[4]

For illustrative purposes, let me present a modified version of a classification adopted by my former student Eugene Vinogradoff of Columbia
University, in a paper on "Peasant Protests in Russia, 1850–1860." It is a
legal-historical classification:

1. Collective petitions
2. Collective litigation
3. Disobedience and passive resistance
4. Flights
5. Illegal assembly and active resistance
6. Violation of property rights
7. Violent crimes against persons

Collective petitions were the most innocuous form of peasant protest in
Russia and when, conforming to the requirements of legality, encom-
passed most of the peasant population involved in each dispute. Thus they
were not only the most "legal" but also the most general form of expression of peasant grievances. Petitions, to be legal, had to be adopted by
duly convened assemblies of the village commune and addressed to the
proper authorities (the landlord being considered the first level of authority). Thus, petitions started a long drawn-out process of investigation with
appeals to higher authority following the original petition. But petitions
could also precipitate a violent reaction if they did not follow the proper
channels of bureaucratic procedure. The risk involved in attempting to
reach a higher authority, not to mention the Tsar, was considerable, and
legal norms called for disciplinary action against the "initiators" or the
"messengers" of the petition.[5]

Disobedience and passive resistance as a form of social protest includes
a whole array of actions. Such an action could be precipitated simply as a
follow-up of an earlier peasant petition, when the subscribers were called
on to withdraw or revoke the petition. In most cases, however, disobedience and passive resistance were directed against the orders of the estate
administration (the estate stewards), the estate owners, and the local law
enforcement authorities. During the existence of serfdom, refusing to perform additional (apart from the statutory) work on the estate or refusing to
pay increases in the quitrent were the most common forms of disobedience
and passive resistance. Extraordinary tax collections, corvées, and additional burdens imposed by the local administration ignited peasant protests. That many protests were founded in the ignorance of the peasants of
the existing laws or even of their self-interest can be surmised from the
mass resistance to the orders to destroy cattle in cases of livestock epidemics (e. g., hoof-and-mouth disease).[6]

Disobedience and passive resistance were also used as weapons by the peasants in defending the independence of their institutions of autonomy—the mir (village commune) in particular—from attempts to make them dependent or servile to the commands of either the landowning gentry or the local administrative officers. The refusal to elect officers of the commune who would be meek tools in the hands of the authorities or landlords and the refusal to make the village assemblies rubber-stamp institutions were forms of such social protest. Nevertheless, it was probably rather difficult for the peasants (much more than for the historian concerned with classification) to draw a sharp line between protests of disobedience, passive resistance, and active resistance. The danger that any peasant assembly, or any group of peasants acting in unison, would cross the line toward active resistance was ever present. In most cases, the responsibility for such a turn of events could be attributed not to the original agitation or despair of the peasants but rather to the provocation of their adversaries. In a certain sense, the adversaries of the peasants preferred active to passive resistance. To break passive resistance was much more difficult and time-consuming, while the use of harsh measures against active resistance was both sanctioned by the law and easier to apply. Thus, the frequency of disobedience and passive resistance bears witness to the self-discipline of the peasants rather than to the limits of their objectives.

Individual or group flights of the serfs from their lords was one of the most widespread forms of peasant protest. For about 250 years the phenomenon of fugitive serfs accompanied the institution of serfdom. And although prayers to a special saint (Ivan Voinstvuiushchii) were recommended as an aid in recovering the fugitives, serfowners preferred other measures. The obligation to find and return fugitive serfs to their lawful owners was placed on the state (after 1649). Thus a continuous manhunt was under way on the territory of Russia, primarily in its eastern provinces, which attracted oppressed peasants from the more densely populated areas of central Russia.

There are no exact data on the full extent of peasant flights. For some periods, documents pertaining to the number of serfs apprehended and returned have survived, and they provide an approximate lower estimate for the scope of peasant flights from serfdom. So, for example, from 1719 to 1742 about 526,000 fugitive male serfs were returned to their owners, or about 21,917 per year; from 1816 to 1842, 85,050 fugitive male peasants were found, or 3,150 per year; and from 1851 to 1853, 11,003, or 3,668 fugitives per year were found.

It is true that during this period peasants fled not only from the oppression of their lords but also to avoid military service (of long duration, hardships, and high mortality rate) and sometimes religious persecution.

But it is realistic to assume, even for the eighteenth century, that the data on unsuccessful flights primarily reflect the peasants' protest against their owners and the institution of serfdom, and that in this protest the animosity of the serfs toward their landlords was also transferred to the state authorities, actively engaged on the side of the landowners.

The seriousness of the problem of peasant flights compels one to focus attention on the problems of personal immobility under serfdom. It is particularly important in view of the existing opportunities for colonization on the eastern fringes of the Russian Empire. Thus the absence of serfdom and the freedom of mobility combined with opportunities to acquire land in the east and southeast could have created a very significant safety valve for peasant unrest.

In fact, the preservation of the Russian village commune after the abolition of serfdom (for the purpose of facilitating tax collections for the state and to assure a sufficient labor supply for the estates), effectively limited the mobility of the peasant population and contributed to the continuity of peasant unrest. The same was true for other countries in Eastern Europe, where by economic or, more important, by extra economic means the personal mobility of the peasants was curtailed.

The peasant flights were a primitive form of protest requiring little or no organization. Whatever assistance peasants displayed toward fugitive serfs, they gave spontaneously and without organization. Other forms of peasant protest required much more organizational skill and understanding of the ramifications of collective action.

The forms of protest involving active resistance, except in cases provoked by extraordinary circumstances, required some conspiracy in illegal assemblies to decide on a course of action. Therefore, except for riots of a spontaneous nature, any active resistance within the rural community[7]—whether in the form of a boycott of liquor sales or the destruction of taverns, or armed resistance to police detachments sent to support the landowners' claims and arrest peasants, or armed resistance to military units sent to pacify the villages—required previous consultation and organization of the participants. Well aware of the legal consequences of such conspiracies, the peasants nevertheless engaged in them. This raises the interesting organization and social problem of leadership of peasant protests.

I am not certain just how typical or unique the Russian experience is, but the types of social protest discussed above were headed mostly by leaders elevated from among the peasant population. To the extent that the records allow a judgment, we can say that the leaders in most cases were ordinary peasants, perhaps of above-average intelligence and education, sometimes with broader experience gained from work outside the native village. That these were not "agitators from outside," to use a modern phrase, is certain. As in other countries and other social movements, a notable role in providing leadership was played by the lower clergy, whose income status and cultural level did not greatly exceed that of the peasants. In truly exceptional cases, active protests on the part of the peasants were led by members of other estates. That such cases were rare can be explained not only by the social fragmentation of Russian society and the difficulties of intergroup mobility and even communication, but also by the Russian peasants' deep distrust of anyone higher up the social ladder and of their motives in identifying themselves with the peasants' cause. In any event, the problem of leadership deserves further study to reveal many other aspects of the problem, but in general terms it is clear that the peasants provided the leaders as well as the followers.

While active resistance primarily involved a defensive attitude, a determination to preserve the status quo against the actions of adversaries, whether landlords or state authorities, other categories of protest involved more aggressive attitudes.

It is interesting to note that most of the actions which involved violations of property rights were justified by the participants as either a recovery of property which belonged to them, in terms of their sense of justice or their somewhat free interpretation of the law, or retribution for an equivalent loss of their own property.

The objects of such violations of property rights ranged from harvested crops and livestock to agricultural land, meadows, and forest. This form of peasant protest became prevalent following the emancipation of the serfs. For years the courts and administrative offices were busy handing down decisions in cases of conflict between the estates and the village communes concerning the transfer and ownership of land.[8] The peasants, impatient and disappointed in the terms of their emancipation, actively resisted the decisions of the authorities by illegal seizure of what they considered to be taken away from them. Such forms of protest were not limited to the period closely following the emancipation, but continued for decades. Where seizure was impossible, arson was used. The use of arson (the "red rooster" of the estates, in the parlance of the West European peasants) was also conspicuous in the most violent category of peasant protest, the conspiracies against the life of the landlord.

It is unnecessary to list the various forms and circumstances under which hated landlords met their death at the hands of the peasants. In cases other than arson, entrance to the house would often be gained with the assistance of some of the domestic servants. Assault and murder were the ultimate weapons of desperate peasants.

All of the forms of peasant protest discussed above lacked a clearly spelled out program and ideology.[9] It is only through a painstaking analysis of the peasants' demands that some notion of their social ideals can be gained. Therefore it is imperative to review some aspects of the more recent, twentieth-century experience of peasant movements in Eastern Europe, which were marked by a much stronger infusion of ideology. Being neither a student of intellectual history nor a political scientist, I shall walk a dangerous path in trying to provide a political analysis of some features of the more modern peasant movements.

Peasant ideology in Eastern Europe included a number of the following elements:

1. Group solidarity of the peasants as a precondition to the improvement of their social status and economic position;
2. Political action as necessary to effect an agrarian reform;
3. Political alliances, desirable if they preserve the independence of peasant policies from other interests; and
4. The peasantry as the backbone and mainstay of the nation and any national policy to be in harmony with this principle.

The acceptance of the principle of social solidarity and self-help led to the development of economic, educational, and political institutions which embodied this principle. The most significant of the economic institutions adopted by the peasants were the rural cooperatives; as consumer organizations and producers' associations, they became an economically powerful force all over Eastern Europe, providing evidence of tangible economic benefits for their members and contributing to the modernization of agricultural production. In addition, the cooperatives served as a training ground, teaching the peasants the intricacies of modern business, management, and even politics. The educational institutions created in the rural areas not only contributed to the spread of literacy, culture, hygiene, and improved nutritional and health habits, but also, perhaps for the first time, broke the monopoly of the church in education in the peasant milieu.[10] The political activity which resulted from the peasants' notion of group solidarity ranged from sporadic endorsement of and voting for peasant candidates at local elections to the organization of nationwide political parties.

It was through the generalization of long experience and relatively short political activity that the belief in the necessity of political action to bring about agrarian reform took hold among the peasants. In fact, the objective of an agrarian reform became the rallying point and the most general common goal of all sectors of the peasant movement. Although the specifics differed from country to country, the goals of agrarian reform were fairly

uniform throughout Eastern Europe—land distribution and the establishment of viable family farms as the prevailing form of agricultural organization. It was after the agrarian reforms were legislated and the practical
implementation started that the inevitable conflicts of interest within the
peasantry revealed themselves and contributed to splits and schisms of the
movements into less radical and more radical wings.

Thus, peasants came into politics on a major scale in all countries of
Eastern Europe, from Yugoslavia and Bulgaria, through Czechoslovakia
and Rumania, to Poland, the Baltic countries, and Finland.[11] To rule dem-
ocratically in Eastern Europe either against or without the participation (or
at least consent) of the peasant parties during the interwar period was impossible. Thus, the peasant parties were faced with the problem of political alliances.

The peasant parties recognized the desirability of cooperation with other
political parties under the conditions of independence of the peasants' interests which they represented. The trouble with such a political position
was that national policies which in the long run might have been beneficial
for the whole country, including the peasants, were often in conflict with
the short-run interests of the peasants. Even where the agrarian reforms
were carried out in the manner desired by the peasant parties, many major
problems of agriculture remained unsolved, particularly in the worldwide
agricultural crisis of the 1920s. The peasant parties could not rise intellec-
tually to embrace policies of economic development and industrialization
as being helpful in solving some of the economic ills of the situation.
Instead, the peasant parties advocated policies of agricultural supports,
tariff barriers for agricultural products, and free trade policies for industrial
goods, which could not always be accepted by their political allies of the
center or the right. As a result, with few exceptions, governments based
on a peasant alliance with another major political party turned out to be
unstable. There is no doubt that one of the characteristics of most of the
peasant parties or the peasant movements (perhaps with the notable exception of Czechoslovakia) was parochialism, reflecting both the narrow
views of the constituents as well as the relatively short tradition of peasant
political leadership on a national scale. But perhaps one of the major
sources of political instability on the part of the peasant movement itself
was the economic condition of the Eastern European peasant—capital
scarcity, high labor-land ratios, and the frustrations resulting from the land
reforms as insufficient solutions of the agrarian problems. Thus the vacil-
lation between the right and the left, which not only affected the peasant
movement itself but also the national policies of the particular countries.

In its heyday the peasant movement believed that the peasants represented the backbone of the nation; that they were "the salt of the earth"

was widely accepted, and not only among rural dwellers.[12] That this belief was particularly strong in Eastern Europe can be explained by some historical circumstances. Most of the countries of Eastern Europe achieved or restored their nationhood as a result of the collapse of two multinational empires, the Hapsburg and the Romanov. In both empires, the upper social groups of the previous national minorities not only collaborated with the regime, but often identified themselves with the dominant culture. The indigenous, urban middle-class was insufficiently developed, both economically and culturally weak. The intelligentsia, the true guardians of the national tradition (since the peasants followed the tradition more out of a lack of opportunities to assimilate in another culture than by rational choice), often accepted peasant symbols of that tradition in the exhibition of their allegiance.

As a result of all the phenomena described above, the resurgence of nationalism in Eastern Europe in the twentieth century was tied to the awakening of the social and political activity of the peasants. Although the actual participation of the peasant masses in the task of nation building was much less than their numerical strength (after all, tilling the soil is an almost full-time job for peasants), the combination of nationalism and peasant political activity was probably one of the most significant political events of the twentieth century in this region. There is no doubt that by tying their interests to the surge of nationalism, although perhaps in a more mystical than political way, the peasant movement overcame the worst of its localistic and parochial tendencies (although many remained) and was able to build and maintain a national following and to provide peasants with a feeling of self-respect and social importance which they were previously deprived of. That this provided a great deal of social and political momentum was realized perhaps more by the ideological adversaries of the genuine peasant movement than by the leadership of the movement proper.

If one would concentrate on the efforts by some of the adversaries to emulate this combination of peasants awakening to political action and nationalism, one would find a whole array of attempts (with varying degrees of success) to win the sympathy and political support of the peasants. Without necessarily going back to the example of Louis Bonaparte, one could study the political history of *Krestintern* with some benefit.[13] What is proposed is not a study of communist political diversion with regard to the peasant movement, but an inquiry into what attracted their adversaries to some of the basic tenets of the peasant movements. In our own political reality, the extremely condensed version of *Krestintern* preachings, if not motives, survived in the political theses of Mao Tsetung.

A great deal of the strategy of "wars of national liberation," not perhaps in the minds of the strategists but certainly in the minds of the participants, is based on the combination of peasant awakening and nationalism as a stage in the process of the active incorporation of peasants into modern nationhood.

SIX

Social Structure, Public Policy, and the Development of Education

Research on the economic aspects of education and training in pre-revolutionary Russia is terra incognita to most western students of economics. To deal exhaustively with the subject would require more time and other resources than the space given to it would warrant. Here, I will turn, first to a brief consideration of Russian social structure and public policy as they conditioned both opportunities and demands for schooling, then to an examination of the pace at which literacy and schooling diffused through the society as a whole before and after the Crimean War and the emancipation of the serfs. At the end I hazard a few remarks concerning the contrast between the actual as against the "optimal" pace of educational developments in Russia in relation to economic growth.

Despite the remarkable progressiveness of the Petrine period and the policies for development and recruitment of high-level manpower at that time, the progress of education over the following century was slow in relation to what was happening in the West. Indeed, far from catching up, Russia lagged further behind. Educational facilities and access to educational opportunities were extremely limited and socially selective. It must be borne in mind that until 1861 serfdom existed over most of Russia, and that social and even territorial mobility were strictly regulated for the bulk of the population. Even after 1861 mobility of the peasants was impeded by the terms of emancipation. It is against such a background that both educational statistics and the history of government policy with respect to education must be understood.

Throughout this period, the Russian government saw education almost exclusively as a pragmatic means to achieve certain utilitarian (from its own point of view, mostly political) ends.[1] Schools were established primarily to train officers for the army and navy or specialists for the mining and armament industries.[2] Special schools and instruction for the children of the gentry and the top echelon of the bureaucracy furthered the "westernization" of Russian society.[3] But elementary education for the lower classes made little progress.[4]

Government action outside the areas of its immediate interest could be influenced by public opinion, but during the pre-emancipation period this was equivalent to the vocal opinion of the gentry, perhaps including also the upper strata of the merchants. Such opinion was not in favor of providing educational outlets for the lower classes; and the lower classes themselves, when faced with barriers to future advancement, obviously considered this type of investment almost useless. Serf-peasant agriculture did not provide any opportunities for getting a return even from elementary education. Crafts and manufactures relied primarily on on-the-job training; internal trade required only rudiments of education, and even the lowest ranks of bureaucracy required bare literacy. Because of the impediments to intergroup mobility and the income restraint, the demand for education was not vigorous. Although there were quite interesting cases of interclass mobility in which education played a dominant role in the eighteenth century, the economic advantages of education had not yet been discovered or become attractive to the mass of the population.[5]

Thus, given the nature of the Russian state and economy in the eighteenth century, the achievements of government policies in the field of education could be expected to be very modest indeed. The data in table 6.1 summarize the state of education in Russia by the end of the eighteenth century.

Eighteenth-century governmental policies and social attitudes had produced education services for only 0.33 per cent of the total male population of the Russian Empire. In addition, an approximate distribution of the total number of students between elementary education, on the one hand, and secondary, specialized, and higher education, on the other, would indicate that about 53,000 received an elementary education only, while about 9,000 received more advanced education.[6]

The pace of providing educational facilities for various groups of the population quickened during the first third of the nineteenth century, although the total students relative to the population remained insignificant. The available data for 1834 illustrate this contention. The total number of students receiving instruction in all types of schools at all levels was 245,448, or 0.49 per cent of the total population; most students received only an elementary education.[7] In the schools under the supervision of the Ministry of Education, only 1,880 of 77,600 students were peasants, or about 2.4 per cent. The establishment of elementary schools for state peasants in 1842 increased the opportunities for a part of the peasantry and raised the total school attendance in the country as a whole.[8] Nevertheless, by 1856 only 450,000, or 0.7 per cent of the total population were enrolled

Table 6.1 Educational Institutions and Their Enrollment at the End of the Eighteenth Century

Type of Institution	No. of Institutions	No. of Students
Universities and gymnasiums	3	1,338
Cadet Corps	5	11,980
Gentry boarding schools	8	1,360
Private boarding schools	48	1,125
Art Academy	1	348
Medical schools	3	270
Mining schools	2	167
Church seminaries and schools	66	20,393
Schools for soldiers' children	116	12,000
Elementary schools (4-year)	49	7,011
Elementary schools (2-year)	239	15,209
Other Schools	9	765
Total	549	71,966

Source: *Vestnik Moskovskogo universiteta*, no. 2 (1959), pp. 110–19.

in schools. In 1856 more than 300,000 of these students were in urban schools (or 5.8 per cent of the urban population), so it would follow that the rural population had a much smaller school attendance than the average for the country. In addition, 38 per cent of all students attending schools were concentrated in a tenth of the administrative districts, thus manifesting a very uneven territorial distribution of schooling.

Literacy among the youth of 1850–60 may be inferred from data for the age group 60 and over in the 1897 census, shown along with younger age categories in table 6.2. Rates among urban males approximated 50 per cent, but they were lower for urban females; among the vast rural population which made up the bulk of the total, only 17 per cent of the male youth were literate around mid-century. This low proportion is evidenced in the army recruitment figures for the 1870s as well (table 6.3). It was not until the last quarter of the century that literacy showed a significant improvement.

In order to provide some indication of what happened between 1897 and 1917 with respect to literacy of the total population, the data of a census taken in 1920 for European Russia may be compared with the 1897 data for European Russia and for all of Russia (table 6.4). Literacy rates increased for the total population by about 50 per cent, with the largest gain made by women.

Such a rise could certainly not exclude the industrial labor force. In fact, the 1918 RSFSR (Russian Socialist Federated Soviet Republic) census of factory workers provided data for the total manufacturing labor force and for a number of particular industries; these data are helpful in an appraisal of the change that took place from one age group to the next (table 6.5).

Table 6.2 Percentage of Literacy for the Total Population of Russia in 1897

	Age Group							
	10–19	20–29	30–39	40–49	50–59	60 & over	10–60	Total
Total Population								
Males	45	45	40	33	27	20		29
Females	22	20	16	13	11	10		13
Total	34	32	28	23	19	15		21
Urban Population								
Males	72	69	64	59	54	47	66	54
Females	56	49	40	32	32	26	44	36
Total	64	59	52	47	42	35	56	45
Rural Population								
Males	41	39	35	28	23	17		25
Females	17	15	12	9	8	7		10
Total	29	26	23	19	15	12		17

Source: Obshchyi svod po Imperii rezul'tatov razrabotki dannykh pervoi v seobshchtioi perepisi naselenia, proizvedennoi 28 yanvaria 1897 g. (St. Petersburg, 1905).

Table 6.3 Percentage of Literacy among Males Taken into Military Service in the Russian Empire, 1880–1913

Year	% literate	Year	% literate	Year	% literate
1880	22	1891	32	1902	(52)
1881	23	1892	35	1903	53
1882	24	1893	36	1904	56
1883	25	1894	38	1905	56
1884	26	1895	(39)*	1906	58
1885	27	1896	40	1907	62
1886	28	1897	(42)	1908	64
1887	29	1898	45	1909	63
1888	30	1899	(47)	1910	65
1889	31	1900	49	1911	67
1890	32	1901	(50)	1912	68
				1913	68

*Figures in parentheses are estimated.
Source: A. G. Rashin, Formirovanie rubochego klassa Rossii (Moscow, 1958), p. 582.

Table 6.4 Literacy Rates for the Total Population of Russia and for European Russia (1897 and 1920)

	Males	Females	Total
Russia, 1897	29.3	13.1	21.1
European Russia, 1897	32.6	13.6	22.9
European Russia, 1920	42.2	25.5	33.0

This carries us back to the cohort born in the 1860s and schooled around 1875–80.

A comparison between the factory labor force in Vladimir district in 1897 and that of the cotton industry in the census of 1918 is pertinent because the Vladimir district labor force was largely employed in the cotton textile industry (last column of table 6.5); in the Vladimir factory labor force, however, a higher percentage of males is represented than in the cotton industry. Among the workers in manufacturing industries, as in the total population, the evidence points to a continuing increase of literacy from the mid-nineteenth century, when the 60-year-olds of 1897 were young, to the youth of 1918. Male literacy of the factory work force tended to run 30 to 40 per cent ahead of the female rates. Thus, among the cotton mill workers for European Russia in 1897, male literacy was 54 per cent and female 20 per cent; for the RSFSR in 1918 the figures were respectively 77 and 37 per cent.

Two factors were instrumental in accelerating the growth of educational facilities: 1) the emancipation of the serfs, and 2) the growth of modern industry. The emancipation of the serfs, although followed by institutional arrangements that impeded the peasant's mobility, not only provided more freedom of choice to the peasants, but made it imperative to raise the productivity of the agricultural labor force on both the peasant farms and the estates. This need met with the approval of the spokesmen for the gentry in the countryside and found its expression in the accelerated rate

Table 6.5 Percentage Literacy of the Labor Force by Age:
RSFSR, All Manufacturing and Selected Industries, 1918,*
and Vladimir District, Factory Labor, 1897

Age Group (years)	RSFSR, 1918			Vladimir, 1897
	Total	Metal Industry	Cotton Industry	
Under 14	80.6	95.6	80.3	62.8
15–17	}77.1	}92.1	}71.7	55.7
17–19				48.0
20–24	69.2	88.6	59.3	46.5
25–29	66.2	87.2	53.0	40.3
30–34	64.8	86.7	49.8	}36.7
35–39	59.2	81.1	43.8	
40–44	58.2	79.7	43.3	}33.8
45–49	51.9	72.6	47.6	
50–59	}42.7	}62.8	}30.2	31.3
60 and over				29.2
All age groups	64.0	82.6	52.2	41.9

*The 1918 census of factory workers gives the breakdown of literacy and illiteracy for 973,600 workers.
Source: A. G. Rashin, *Formirovanie rabochego klassa Rossii* (Moscow, 1958), pp. 595, 602.

of school construction in rural areas and subsequent increases in enrollment. The demand for literacy among actual or prospective factory workers fostered the improvement of urban educational facilities in general, and in newly developing industrial regions in particular. Thus, students of elementary schools increased from 400,000 in 1856 to about 2,200,000 in 1885, an increase of 450 per cent. The largest part of the increase could, of course, be accounted for by the rural schools. One of the chief characteristics of the rise in enrollment was its uneven distribution by sex; in 1885, 147,300 out of 429,500 students in the urban elementary schools were girls, while girls were only 393,500 out of 1,754,500 in the rural schools. (This explains the literacy rate differential in industry at a later date.) Although much could probably be said about the quality of education in the one- or even two-grade elementary schools of that time, nevertheless, it brought considerable progress in literacy of the population, as can be seen in the data on literacy of the military draft (table 6.3).

While elementary education contributes to advancement on the job, it simultaneously constitutes a widening of opportunity to continue education on a higher level. It should also be considered as a vehicle of social advancement or as a substitute for the accumulation of wealth; in fact, probably more people advanced into a "higher class" with the assistance of education but without wealth than vice versa. Although a modern society probably ought to welcome such a pattern of social advancement as approaching a more rational utilization of human resources, this was not always true in nineteenth-century Russia. The available evidence points to a lagging utilization of education as a vehicle of social advancement, a process that was accelerated considerably in the twentieth century. This is reflected in the data provided in table 6.6. The explanation for this ought to be sought in the zigzags of government policies. During the reign of Alexander II (1855–81) the obstacles to enrollment in institutions of secondary and higher education were the "normal" ones (income, quota systems in various schools, favoritism, etc.), but during the reign of Alexander III (1881–94) a clear directive of governmental policy sought to prevent social advancement through education. This policy probably inflicted losses on the Russian economy at a later point.[9]

The Russian government oscillated between the Scylla of the demand for educated manpower in industry and business and the Charybdis of the preservation of a rigidly stratified society fortified by traditional (or archaic) criteria for stratification. The result was half measures and inconsistency in educational policies. All the government claims of progressiveness in the area of education were outrun during the 1890s by the growing popular demand for educational facilities, a demand that grew with the increasing number of educated persons.[10] The dual nature of the educa-

Table 6.6   Social Selectivity of the Student Body in Secondary and Higher Education

A. Percentage Distribution of Secondary School Students
by Social Origin for Selected Years (1826/27–1914)

Social Group	1826/27	1871	1881	1894	1904	1914
Gentry and officials	72.2	59.5	47.5	56.4	36.5	24.7
Clergy	3.1	4.6	5.2	3.4	4.0	4.7
Urban taxpaying groups	20.8	27.8	37.2	31.6	43.5	41.7
Rural taxpaying groups	3.9	5.7	8.0	6.0	14.1	25.5
Foreigners and others	n.a.	1.1	2.1	2.6	1.9	3.4

B.   Percentage Distribution of University Students
by Social Origin for Selected Years (1864/65–1913)*

Social Group	1864/65	1880	1907	1913
Gentry and officials	67.2	46.7	45.1	36.0
Clergy	9.5	23.4	11.2	10.3
Urban taxpaying groups	8.9	21.5	34.4	35.2
Rural taxpaying groups	14.0	3.2	6.9	13.3
Foreigners and others	0.4	5.2	2.4	5.0

*Serious questions could be raised with regard to the representativeness of the university students; the universities in 1913 contained only about a third of all students enrolled in institutions of higher education. *Source: Istoricheskie zapiski,* no. 37 (Moscow, 1951) pp. 72–75.

tional policies can perhaps be illustrated by citing two positive attempts to meet the demands from various pressure groups. The first was the establishment of the so-called *real schools,* which were secondary schools with less emphasis on humanistic subjects than the *gymnasia* and better preparation in mathematics and business- or industry-oriented subjects. It is clear from both the location of the schools and the social backgrounds of their pupils that this was a less "gentleman-like" education in terms of prestige, but it could more successfully meet the needs of the business community for managerial or technical personnel.[11]

The second measure was even more successful in terms of growth. This was the establishment of *gymnasia* and *pro-gymnasia* for women. Previously, education for women had been available in very few institutions, mostly private boarding schools, and even girls of the gentry had had to rely on private tutoring of questionable quality. In an attempt to raise the level of education of women in the higher classes to assure a particular "cultural atmosphere" in the homes of the well-to-do, a considerable effort went into the development of secondary schools for women. Between 1873 and 1914, or in a period of forty years, the number of students increased more than fourteen times.[12] Perhaps the fact that the expenditures per pupil were lower in the womens' schools facilitated their higher rate of growth.[13]Although the impact of women's education was very significant in terms of long-run growth, the immediate effect in the labor market was probably much less than the proportion of women in the total increase (in years of education) of the educational stock would indicate. Thus we are dealing here primarily with a long-run derived effect rather than with a calculable return to particular educational outlays (considered as investments).[14]

During the period 1860–1913, the number of employed industrial, construction, and railway workers increased about 4.3 times (from 1,960,000 to 8,415,000), while pupils in elementary and secondary schools increased 16 times (600,000 to 9,840,000). In 1860 there were three times as many workers as school attenders; by 1900 the number of students already exceeded the number of workers by about 40 per cent. However, during the years 1900–13 the number of workers increased relatively faster than pupils, and by 1913 students exceeded workers by only 12 per cent.

The average costs of education per student at the various levels of education cannot yet be calculated, since most of the available estimates are given in terms of concepts (not always identical) of current net costs. It may, however, be useful just to present the data on relative costs per pupil at the different levels for comparison with costs in other countries. Strumilin's calculations yield 21 rubles per student in elementary schools in 1913, 116 rubles in secondary schools, and 261 rubles at the university. The elementary-to-secondary cost ratio was approximately 1:5, and the secondary-to-university ratio was 5:12.4. The striking feature of this relationship is the differential between the costs of elementary and secondary education. On the assumption that both items were computed using identical conventions, they might reflect two important characteristics: first, the low salaries in elementary schools (particularly in the rural areas) against the relatively higher salaries in secondary and higher education;[15] second, costs of buildings and equipment probably were vastly different, even more so per student, and account for a part of the differential.

Apart from cost factors, one could probably question the economic rationale behind a policy that admitted so few into secondary schools and institutions of higher education. The distribution of enrollments among the three levels in the school year 1914–15 was 92 per cent for elementary (grades 1–4); 7 per cent for secondary (5–10); and 1.3 per cent for higher education.

Perhaps the scope of the educational effort in pre-revolutionary Russia on the eve of World War I and a reflection of the growth of school enrollment in the twentieth century could best be shown by the data in table 6.7. These figures are cited to present the state of education at the end of the period of our primary interest. The productivity effects of the rapid growth

Table 6.7   School Enrollment in Russia,* 1914–15 (in 1,000s)

General education, grades 1–4		9,030.7
General education, grades 5–10		679.3
Formal education	625.0⎫	
Technical education	54.3⎭	
Higher education		127.4
Total		9,837.4

*Russia in the present political boundaries of the USSR.

**Table 6.8   Number of Students Enrolled in 55 Institutions
of Higher Learning and Specialized Secondary Education**

Type of Institution	Higher Education		Secondary Specialized	
	Jan. 1, 1907	Jan. 1, 1914	Jan. 1, 1907	Jan. 1, 1914
Liberal education	28,672	41,161	—	—
Technical, engineering	8,162	12,947	42,975	53,665
Business	410	4,874	28,406	58,365
Medical	1,792	3,955	6,313	9,863
Teacher training	1,016	2,241	16,271	32,252
Law	852	854	—	—

Source: L. K. Erman, *"Sostav intelligentsii v Rossii v kontse XIX i nachale XX u,"* *Istoriia SSSR,* no. 1 (1963), p. 172.

of education in Russia during the decade preceding World War I could be realized only as the new youth became part of the labor force in the 1920s.

A problem often faced by economists studying the role of education in economic development is how to determine or rationalize the "optimal" proportion of various levels of education of particular cohorts, or the distribution of various skill levels in the labor force. The problems of returns to investment in education at various skill levels (or various "amounts"), as well as the question of the social contributions of various skills or occupations to the process of economic growth, are diligently studied. I will not attempt to provide answers to these fascinating problems in the Russian experience at various stages of its economic development. I would like only to indicate the scope of the problem of the rise of higher education in Russia and its relation to the economy (see table 6.8).

Until the middle of the nineteenth century, the government bureaucracy was the source of the chief demand for educated and more highly skilled manpower. For obvious reasons this demand increased very modestly over time, and, more important, it did not provide for much upward social mobility. This situation changed during the second half of the nineteenth century. Approximate data (based on the 1897 population census) point to the fact that, by the end of the century, the total employment of salaried white-collar workers in the nonagricultural sector of the economy exceeded the total employment in the government apparatus, and that employment in the educational system exceeded the government civil service. The tentative data in table 6.9 provide some idea of the numbers of educated white-collar workers in the few selected areas.

The significance of this development lies in the fact that a new element of dynamics was injected in the demand for secondary and higher education and for training in higher specialized skills. This development brought about a broadening of the market for educational services and led to much more competitive market behavior. It also brought about an acceleration of the process of growth of educated, skilled, professional manpower.

In the absence of detailed data on the growth of most of the separate categories of professional manpower, these demands in the growing branches of the economy and in the educational system itself can be indicated by the supply response of students at the levels of higher and secondary specialized education.

The data in table 6.8[16] indicate the general trend, which, given the typical laggardness of Russian educational authorities, must have been even stronger in reality. Obviously, the impact on the economy of training an increasing number of highly skilled specialists was uneven, depending on the nature of the profession. Since in 1897 there was a total of 4,010 engineers employed in Russia, and by 1913 the yearly number of graduates of engineering schools was about 1,500,[17] the impact on technology and the performance of Russian industry must have been visible and marked. On the other hand, an increase of the number of physicians in Russia (the present territory of the Soviet Union) from 13,344 in 1905 to 21,944 in 1913 could have had a long-run effect on the volume and quality of medical services and health of the population, but the short-run effect was probably minimal.

Turning back to the nineteenth-century data on the literacy and schooling of the Russian labor force, one might ask the question: Was this much or little for the particular stage of industrial development? My answer

Table 6.9 **Number of Employed White-Collar Workers Based on the 1897 Population Census (in 1,000s)**

Branch		Employment
Government bureaucracy: armed forces	52,471 }	203,816
Civilian bureaucracy	151,345 }	
Education		172,842
Industry, railways, trade, and banking		298,623
Medicine, law, and other free professions		52,825

would be that it was too little; schooling dragged back on development. I suggest that there is a range within which the level of formal education is related to industrial performance in a particular historical context. In other words, a particular phase of industrial development presupposes (that is, requires), within a range, a particular average level of formal education. It is basically an empirical problem to find out what the relationship has been in various countries that start on the road of industrialization. Russian experience seems to indicate that the type and level of the technology borrowed might provide a clue to this rule of thumb.

One of the features of industrialization in the second half of the nineteenth century and in the twentieth century is the presence of certain discontinuities, particularly involving the borrowing of foreign technology; the discontinuities are not only technological but organizational. A program of rapid adaptation of foreign technology ought to set the requirements of particular types of labor, which implicitly involves a specific level of education. The level of borrowed technology therefore determines an "optimal" level of education higher than the one that was developed to satisfy the needs of the previously existing and less advanced level of techniques. Perhaps the level of formal education of the labor force in a country entering the stage of industrialization ought to be set, as a maximum, at the level of the country (countries) from which the basic technology was borrowed.[18] Since Russia's pre-revolutionary industrialization used a borrowed basic technology from Germany, a more nearly "optimal" level of education of the labor force would then have been one that corresponded to that prevailing in Germany during this period, rather than to that which prevailed in England during the early stages of industrialization.

SEVEN

"Hereditary Workers" Hypothesis and the Development of a Factory Labor Force in Eighteenth- and Nineteenth-Century Russia

Eighteenth-century Russia lacked a developed system of apprenticeship within either the craft or factory system; literacy was low and there was no extensive network of either general or trade schools. Nevertheless, that century saw the beginnings of a modern factory labor force. This entailed not merely the learning of skills. Indeed, under the conditions of early industrialization or pre-industrialization, the development of work discipline, cooperation within the manufacturing establishment, and other habits that we usually associate with industrial employment (or take for granted in a developed industrial society) is as important and poses at least as great a problem as the formation of skills. The acquisition of the requisite work habits can be painful, costly, and slow.[1]

One of the means by which the acquisition of industrial "habits" and the facilitation of skill transfer from one group of industrial workers to another could be achieved assured continuity of industrial employment within a particular occupational or social group—in other words, the formation of an expanding nucleus of an "hereditary" labor force. It is therefore of interest to trace the development of the hereditary component in the total labor force. The concept "hereditary workers" as used here includes employed second-generation factory workers in general, regardless of whether or not they followed their parents' specific occupations. This may be a crude application of Torsten Hägerstrand's concept of "information fields" in nongeographic as well as geographic dimensions.[2] For lack of a measure of "inheritance," I am fundamentally hypothesizing patterns of exposure ("tellings"). Economic choices, given such exposure, are the other half of the story.

Needless to say, the mere percentage of hereditary workers in the total labor force will vary with the pace of industrial change (probably declining relatively in a period of rapidly increasing demand for wage labor) and could therefore not be considered an accurate measure of industrial progress. But over a long period this indicator coupled with some others (urban origin, degree of literacy) might together imply the progressive spread of industrial arts. To investigate this problem, I began with data for the earliest period of the development of manufacturers in Russia; these eighteenth-century data reflect the situation prior to the general enserfment of the skilled labor force. Data for the period 1897–1913 were then used to provide evidence concerning the period of early Russian industrialization based on modern technology. The first even halfway reliable and indicative data on the social origin and literacy of the labor force in Russian manufactures are those for the second quarter of the eighteenth century. Perhaps their presentation is more of an historical curiosity than an enlightening contribution on this subject. They may be of interest, however, for the similarities or contrasts they present with the formation of an industrial labor force in other countries (see tables 7.1 and 7.2).

A larger sample, covering a broader variety of manufactures during 1737–40, and therefore more representative than the figures in tables 7.1 and 7.2, provides information with regard to the same general questions (see table 7.3).

The majority of the manufacturing labor force sampled for the data in table 7.3 was of urban origin; for obvious reasons (the newness of the manufactures and the low mobility of the craftsmen), nonindustrial groups supplied the majority of employees. Further, descendants of workers were given preference in the hiring policies of the entrepreneurs; this can be inferred from the age distribution of the various groups of employees at

Table 7.1   Urban Origin, Descent, and Literacy Rate among Employees in Linen and Cotton Cloth Manufactures, 1732 and 1737–38*
(in percentages)

	Urban Origin		Worker Descent		Craftsman Descent		Literacy Rate	
	1732	1737–38	1732	1737–38	1732	1737–38	1732	1737–38
Total								
Workers	42.4	42.8	9.1	13.3	9.7	9.7	6.2	8.6
Males	36.5	39.0	9.2	15.0	7.7	7.7	6.2	8.6
Females	68.3	55.1	8.2	8.2	2.9	2.6	—	—

*The total number of workers in the sample for the two respective years was 1,535 and 1,954, of which males were 1,116 and 1,367 and females 419 and 587, respectively.

Source: The availability of documents that enable us to look into these problems is explained by the orders of January 7 and March 2, 1736, to report the state of the labor force in manufactures following the enserfment of the skilled and semi-skilled workers by the decree of January 7, 1736 (PSZ No. 6858). The data were published in Akademia Nauk SSSR, *Sotsial'nyisostav rabochikh pervoi poloviny XVIII Veka* (Moscow-Leningrad, 1934).

Table 7.2   **Social Origin of the Skilled Labor Force in State-Owned Iron and Copper Works, Ural and Siberia (1726, 1745)***

	1726		1745	
	Number	Percent	Number	Percent
Peasant serfs	456	34.5	2,780	78.5
Workers	336	25.5	586	16.5
Raznochintsy[†]	500	37.7	170	4.8
Foreigners	30	2.3	9	.2
Total Identified	1,322	100.0	3,545	100.0
Unidentified	215	16.3	34	.95

*S. G. Strumilin, *Istoriia chernoi metallurgii v SSSR* (Moscow, 1954), pp. 286, 321.
[†]*Raznochintsy* was a description for free members of various service classes.

Table 7.3   **Urban Origin, Descent, and Literacy Rate among Employees in Manufactures, 1737–40***
(in percentages)

	Urban Origin[†]	Worker Descent	Craftsman Descent	Literacy Rate[‡]
Total				
Workers	60.6	10.8	1.1	9.9
Males	64.2	10.9	1.1	9.9
Females	27.6	8.2	.6	(n.a.)

*Number of employees in the sample 6,992, of which 6,405 males and 587 females.
[†]Percentage of the 6,063 employees who responded.
[‡]Percentage of the 5,116 employees who responded.
Source: Akademia Nauk SSSR, *Sotsial'nyi sostav rabochikh pervoi poloviny XVIII Veka* (Moscow-Leningrad, 1934).

the start of their employment (see table 7.4). In favor of such a policy the argument might be advanced that in numerous cases the skill training for the young workers was provided directly by their employed fathers. In addition, as table 7.5 shows, early entrance into manufacturing employment may have spared a number of workers the cruel experience of "vagrancy" and other perhaps similar alternative opportunities open to the early urban laboring class. The impression of relative stability of the worker descendant group when compared with the other groups suggests that formation of a stable work force for manufacturing had begun.

Early entrance into the labor force was more frequent among descendants of factory workers in subsequent periods. Increasing degrees of attitude "commitment" aside, the economic rationality of such behavior has often been observed; the demand for income by workers' households in which a child was primarily a consumer, not automatically an income earner (as in agriculture), could explain the data almost perfectly. One could probably add that, given the short life expectancy during this period,

**Table 7.4 Percentage Distribution of Employees by Age at the
Start of Employment in Manufactures, 1737–40**

Age	Descendants of Employees	Total Labor Force
Less than 11 years	48.6	32.2
12–14	25.3	22.2
15–19	17.0	22.8
20–24	6.1	9.5
25–29	1.3	5.3
30 and over	<u>1.7</u>	<u>8.0</u>
	100.0	100.0

Source: Same as table 7.3.

**Table 7.5 Percentage Distribution of Total Manufacturing Employees
and of Manufacturing Employees of Worker Descent according to
Their Prior Means of Earning a Living**

	Total Employees	Employees of Worker Descent
Stayed with relatives	31.7	67.6
Vagrancy	21.6	9.7
Other wage employment	22.6	8.8
Employment in other manufactures	13.9	8.8
Trade	2.2	1.2
Crafts	1.8	.9
Other odd jobs	6.2	3.0

Source: Same as table 7.3.

it was advantageous to begin training as early as possible in order to be able, after the completion of training, to compensate the household for previous outlays.

As long as the income position of workers' households required the early earnings of the rising generation, and as long as technology was more or less stable and general education a prerequisite for few industrial skills, the manufacturers resisted attempts to place on them the responsibility for educating their young workers. It was plausible for both household and factory to accept a decrease in child labor only after the government had assumed the direct costs of elementary education. Meanwhile, developing technology was coming to require general education as a prerequisite for some kinds of skill training and as a partial substitute for others.

In the eighteenth century, however, early entrance into the labor force provided a visible advantage in skill acquisition in absolute terms (one became a skilled worker at an early age). There is also indirect indication that the early entrants (and the descendants of employees) had the advantage of being able to train for the more highly skilled occupations.

Although skill training was probably the obvious road toward advancement in manufactures, it appears that it was both competing and complementary with more general education (as expressed by literacy). The distribution of literacy among the labor force could almost serve as a proxy for its distribution within the social groups that supplied labor to the manufactures (table 7.6). The more detailed data on literacy rates for the sample used in table 7.6 indicate that in a substantial number of manufacturing occupations there was a close relation between literacy level and level of skill.[3] Literacy among the more highly skilled workers was substantially above that among the less skilled ones. The data are too fragmentary to argue that literacy was a precondition of higher skills or that the income differential in the past made it profitable to invest in education (although table 7.6 might provide a hint in this direction). The relationship between skill level and literacy, however, is present.

A jump of 150 years, prohibited to historians, can perhaps be pardoned an economist. Thus, a factory census of 1897, covering 116,798 workers in the Vladimir district of central Russia, provides us with information on the literacy of hereditary workers. The sample in table 7.6 is biased to the extent that it heavily represents the textile industry, which had a very high proportion of women employees.

The information on hereditary workers by age groups points to the fact that the supply of hereditary workers exceeded the rate of increase of the total labor force during the approximately fifty years preceding the census date, and that the last decade witnessed an accelerated growth of the share of hereditary workers within the labor force. That this tendency continued can be discerned from the data in table 7.8, which were derived from a much later factory worker sample, covering six industries.

Table 7.6 Percentage of Literacy by Social Origin of Employees in Manufactures, 1737–40

Social Group of Parents	Per cent Literate
Clergy	31.7
Government officials	18.3
Postal employees	15.0
Nonmercantile urban inhabitants	14.1
Merchants and traders	13.1
Inhabitants of craft and mercantile settlements	10.6
Soldiers	7.4
Workers	6.8
Peasants	6.8

**Table 7.7 Percentage of Hereditary Workers and Literacy Rate of
Various Age Groups of the Factory Labor Force
(Vladimir District, 1897)**

Age Group	Percentage of Hereditary Workers*			Literacy Rate of Total Labor Force		
	Males	Females	Total	Total	Males	Females
12–15	62.2	80.6	68.0	62.8	72.3	43.7
15–17	54.1	50.1	52.3	55.7	76.8	29.8
17–20	44.0	41.4	42.7	48.0	69.8	22.8
20–25	42.6	39.0	41.0	46.5	57.4	18.5
25–30	37.8	34.4	36.5	40.3	59.3	11.1
30–40	32.9	29.1	31.5	36.7	53.3	6.6
40–50	28.5	24.3	27.3	33.8	45.6	4.0
50–60	25.9	18.4	24.3	31.3	39.8	2.1
Over 60	24.9	15.2	23.7	29.2	33.5	1.4
Average	37.7	36.7	37.2	41.9	59.6	15.5

*That is, their fathers worked in factories. Incidentally, this was a district of preponderant out-migration.
Source: I. M. Kozminikh-Lanin, *Fabrichno-zavodskoi rabochii Vladimirskoi Gubernii* (1897 g.)
(Vladimir, 1912).

**Table 7.8 Percentage of Hereditary Workers by Duration of Work
Experience,* according to the 1929 Factory Worker Sample**

Branch of Industry	Duration of Work Experience	
	More than 24 Years	16–24 Years
Cotton	48.9	52.8
Metalworking	52.0	57.4
Metallurgy	60.0	56.8
Coal mining	35.6	38.6
Oil	30.8	32.5
Total	48.7	51.7

Source: A. G. Rashin, *Sostav fabrichno-zavodskogo proletariata SSSR* (Moscow,
1930).
*The first category embraced 54,500 workers, and the second category 43,701. The
first category represents workers who entered employment prior to 1905, the second category entrants in employment during 1906–13. Further information, unfortunately un-
available, concerning the attrition rates for both categories would make the data more
conclusive and valuable. Metallurgy had shifted during the previous generation from the
Urals to this district. Coal and oil were young industries. Inheritance in this table refers
to factory-work types of occupations in general.

My original hypothesis asserted that the "hereditary workers" phenomenon was important during both the preindustrialization phase and the
early phases of industrialization, when both rudimentary technical skills
and "industrial habits" were rare. The continuation of the industrialization
process, accompanied by urbanization, some mechanization of agriculture, increasing levels of education, and the provision of facilities for tech-

nical training outside the industrial plants, all tended to decrease the importance of the "hereditary workers" for the development of industry. It would be my guess that if the process of industrialization in Russia had continued uninterrupted after 1913, "hereditary workers" would have lost their economic and social significance during the next decades. If this phenomenon did in fact persist, the causes ought to be sought primarily outside the economic sphere.

EIGHT

Determinants of the Incidence of Literacy in Rural Nineteenth-Century Russia

In rural Russia in the middle of the nineteenth century, one out of every six boys and one in fourteen girls, at the most, acquired literacy to a level that enabled them to retain it. This is judging from data concerning literacy rates among men and women over 60 years of age in the 1890s. By the last decade of the century, two-fifths of the rural male and one-sixth of the rural female youth between the ages of 10 and 19 were literate.[1] Male literacy rates among army recruits, which reflected predominantly rural rates, rose from one-fifth in 1874 to two-fifths in the mid–1890s and to two-thirds in 1913.[2] Among those recruits, the rates of literacy at the low extreme (Ufa district) and the high extreme (Lifland district) were: 7 per cent and 95 per cent for 1874–83; 13 per cent and 97 per cent for 1894; and 27 per cent and 99 per cent for 1904. Evidently rural literacy was rising rapidly during the second half of the nineteenth century but in a pattern of great diversity. The incidence of literacy both among and within geographic areas varied with the characteristics of subpopulations and with the extent of contacts with markets (rural and urban) and with urban life.

About 1900 the relationship between the various degrees of literacy within the rural population and the levels of income or nature of employment of different groups within that population became the subject of study by economists and statisticians in Russia, giving rise to prolonged controversies. The most widely accepted hypotheses concerning the relationship between literacy and income levels or occupational structures of the rural population were those advanced by Vorobiov and Lositskii and tested and substantiated by Vikhliaev and others.[3]

In essence Vorobiov and the others attempted to prove the following propositions: 1) literacy is positively related to income within the broad income and occupational groups of the rural population; 2) rural residents engaged in nonagricultural activities have a higher literacy rate, regardless of their income position relative to the agricultural population; 3) the relatively higher literacy rate of the nonagricultural rural population varies with the degree of their contact with the market, particularly with urban markets. One should therefore differentiate, within the nonagricultural rural population, among activities connected with the rural markets, activities performed in the rural areas for the urban market, and employment (seasonal and semipermanent) in urban areas. Literacy increased to the degree that the rural population was exposed to contact with urban areas.

In order to prove his first proposition—that literacy is positively related to income within particular groups of the population—Vorobiov cited a number of surveys. Table 8.1 is illustrative; taking size of farm as a proxy for income, it indicates a quite systematic association between income and literacy in the farm population. In table 8.2 (from the 1920 census in the Russian Socialist Federated Soviet Republic) this relationship is not nearly so neat; literacy actually declined with size of landholding to about the 5 hectare level, stabilized through a middle size range, and then rose again only for farms above 8 or 10 hectares. However, the explanation is clear enough and supports Vorobiov's second proposition—that individuals engaged at least part-time in nonagricultural activities have on the average a higher literacy rate than the agricultural population, regardless of the income they may derive from agriculture. An even more striking relationship between the degree of literacy within a particular area and the development of nonagricultural activities is suggested by comparing the percentage of workers in nonagricultural seasonal employment with the literacy rate of draftees into military service from the same locality (table 8.3).

Having established the relationship between literacy rates and nonagricultural activities, it was logical to expect that extent of contact with the market would be a determining factor in the degree of literacy. The study of Vorobiov on literacy of peasants engaged in nonagricultural activities points both to the relation between income and the literacy level and to the

Table 8.1 Percentage of Males in Farm Households,
Literate or in School*

Size of Landholding (in desiatin)	Heads of Livestock			
	Less than one	1–2	2–4	4 and over
Below 3	42	50	55	52
3–4.9	49	53	54	59
5–6.9	50	55	56	58
7–9.9	48	54	57	59
10–14.9	55	57	61	62
15 and over	—	—	69	64

*Farm households that possess livestock. These data are derived from an 1897 survey of a typical county (*uyezd*) in Iaroslavl district in which land and livestock are used as a proxy for income.

Table 8.2   Percentage of Literacy in Peasant Farms according to the
Agricultural Census of 51 Districts of RSFSR, 1920

Size of Landholding (in (Hectares)	% of Literacy		% Farms with Nonagricultural Incomes
	Males	Females	
0.1– 1	48.1	24.5	25.0
1.1– 2	46.2	21.4	16.0 ·
2.1– 3	42.8	18.6	12.5
3.1– 4	40.7	16.6	10.5
4.1– 5	39.7	15.5	9.6
5.1– 6	39.1	15.1	9.0
6.1– 8	39.1	14.9	8.8
8.1–10	39.6	15.0	8.7
10.1–13	39.7	16.1	7.9
13.1–16	41.2	17.1	7.2
16.1–19	42.1	18.1	7.5
19.1–22	42.9	19.4	7.5
22.1–25	43.4	20.2	7.7
25.1 and over	46.6	23.6	7.6

Table 8.3   Comparison between the Percentage of Literacy of Draftees
during 1887–89 and the Percentage of Passports* Obtained by
Peasants in 1887 (some counties of Kostroma district)

Rank by % of Passports	Counties	% of Passports per 100 Males in 1887	% of Literacy among Draftees
1.	Chukhlomskii	29.1	84.0
2.	Soligalichskii	22.4	69.8
3.	Galichskii	20.8	64.3
4.	Kologrivskii	9.2	53.0
5.	Buiskii	8.9	49.2
.			
.			
.			
12.	Vetluzhskii	.4	33.3

*Passports were documents indicating the permission of the village authorities for the peasant's absence of more than a few weeks.
Source: Materialy dlia statistiki Kostromskoi gubernii (1891), Vypusk 8, pp. 208, 332–33.

difference in literacy rates between occupations which can be identified in terms of degree of contact with rural or urban consumers, middlemen, or employers (table 8.4).

The distinction between village crafts and urban crafts as being important in determining the literacy rate is supported by the evidence from a study of craftsmen. This study, using a sample of 43,575 rural and urban craftsmen in 1890, gave the results shown in table 8.5. Clearly the village trades are at the lower end of the literacy scale, while urban crafts are

**Table 8.4 Percentage of Literacy among Peasants Employed in
Various Nonagricultural Activities (Vorobiov's Sample)**

Potters	36	Distillery workers	90
Herdsmen	46	Restaurant service	91
Stevedores	54	Restaurant cooks	94
Tailors, Carpenters	57	Meat merchants	96
Day laborers	59	Pastry makers	97
Local coachmen	60	Retail merchants	98
Urban coachmen	84	Dairy merchants	98
Sausage makers	85	Fruit merchants	99
Bakers	86	Textile merchants	100

Source: K. Ia Vorobiov, *Gramotnost' sel'skogo naseleniia v sviazi s glavneishymi faktorami krest'ian-skogo khoziaistva* (St. Petersburg, 1902).

Table 8.5 Percentage of Literacy among Rural and Urban Craftsmen, 1890

Toymakers	100	Coopers	33.8
Artist-painters	100	Agricultural implement makers	32.4
Artist-stonecutters	80	Shoemakers	31.4
Carders and reeders	75.4	Weavers and embroiderers	31.2
Leather workers and tanners	72.8	Bristle brushmakers	17.4
Turners	63.3	Carpenters	16.0
Nailmakers	44.0	Sieve weavers	15.4
Blacksmiths and Locksmiths	42.3	Cart and sledgemakers	5.0
Cabinetmakers	40.2	Wheelwrights	2.4
Basketweavers	39.0	Total sample	39.5

Source: F. A. Danilov, "O vlianii gramotnosti, shkol'nogo obucheniia i professional'nogo obrazivaniia na razvitie kustarnykh promyslov," in *Ekonomicheskaia otsenka narodnogo obrazovaniia* (St. Petersburg, 1896).

marked by a higher degree of literacy. To the extent that literacy represents education, the relationship between education and higher skills becomes established. The influence of urban areas, as centers of industry and trade, in the spread of education on their peripheries was steadily increasing. Given the slow pace of commercialization of Russian peasant agriculture in the nineteenth century, contact with the urban community through the commodity market or employment triggered the process of discovering the value of education for the rural population.

Numerous studies and surveys in Russia established the dependency of the literacy rate on the distance from cities as well as the dependency of the frequency of school attendance on the development of rural trades and home industries.

The data assembled in the various surveys seem to suggest that, at intermediate levels of income, the labor demands of the farm household hindered school attendance. However, even in cases when the increase from small to middle size landholdings had a detrimental effect on school attendance of males, this was in part compensated by increased education of females. The process of social and economic differentiation, which weakened subsistence farming and accompanied the commercialization of agriculture, increased the amount of education at both ends of the income scale and thereby contributed to the rise of the average level of literacy.

The rise in the level of literacy among both the higher income groups of the peasant population and the agricultural laborers becomes the precondition for the introduction of machinery and more modern farming methods.[4] The decline of subsistence farming, a type of farming which had not offered visible incentives for education, made it easier to overcome the long-lasting inertia and maintenance of the status quo and to inject an additional impetus to mobility and change in the economy and society.

Against this background one should not overlook the dynamics of the process underway. Two figures might be sufficient to illustrate the relative rapidity of the spread of education despite the various obstacles and shortcomings cited above.

The number of pupils in rural elementary schools increased from 1,754,000 in 1885 to over 7,000,000 in 1914. The number of teachers in rural schools increased from 24,389 in 1880 to 109,370 in 1911. What is significant, however, is that during the same period the number of teachers of peasant descent in those schools increased from 7,369 to 44,607. Thus an indigenous group fostering education in this milieu was growing rapidly, a group committed to the task of progress.

NINE

Russian Scholars and Statesmen on Education as an Investment

Awareness of the role of education in national economic progress can be traced in Russia at least back to the eighteenth century. The efforts of Peter the Great to train and educate the Russians, so that commerce and industry would contribute to the military and political strength of the nation, are well known. It may be interesting to note that the main clause in all the contracts with "imported" foreign specialists during the Petrine period was the obligation to train a certain number of Russian nationals in their particular skill or occupation.[1] In addition, education and skill became important criteria in the formation of, and admittance into, the ruling elite. Thus general criteria of usefulness and personal merit moderated the considerations of ancestry and class, encouraging increased upward social mobility through education and skill acquisition.

Members of the Petrine administration also tried, in the post-Petrine period, to exert pressure on the government and private entrepreneurs to continue the policies of skill training and education in a more organized and systematic manner.[2] However, while merchants and industrialists understood that special skill training was beneficial, in the first half of the eighteenth century they still refused to accept formal education as a component of an economic development program.[3]

In the second half of the eighteenth century the importance of education as highly useful for successful business for the individual as well as for the state, was recognized. During the 1760s merchants started to petition the government for the establishment of elementary and secondary schools to provide education that would meet the needs of the business community. Although this clamor for education by the merchant class could conceivably be attributed in part to the demonstration effect of "westernization" among the gentry, the arguments used were phrased primarily in terms of economic needs for and advantages from education in the area of commerce.[4]

But the progress of education and skill training was slow during the next hundred years. The country not only failed to catch up with the West industrially, but, in fact, fell considerably behind the countries that first went through the various phases of the industrial revolution. It was only after the resounding defeat in the Crimean War and the liberation of the serfs that the government embarked on an active program to provide the overhead capital for subsequent industrialization. It then began to regard industrial development as a high priority among the national goals. It is no wonder that the spokesman for the government's industrialization policy, Finance Minister I. A. Vyshnegradskii, became concerned in the 1880s with the level of skill and education of the industrial labor force. He felt that the low levels of skill and education were the chief shortcomings of Russian industry and called for remedial action:

At the present, the large majority of workers in our industrial establishments do not receive a general education. The on-the-job training is of the most narrow, practical type. They are specifically trained in the industrial plant exclusively for the work to be performed at the particular plant. The lack of general education prevents the workers in most cases from elevating themselves to the level of a conscious and clear understanding of the operations that they perform in their work and thereby downgrades the dignity of the work performed. A barrier to the necessary improvement of industry is therefore erected. . . . Our industry, regardless of all protective tariffs, is involved in a bitter struggle against foreign production in which our competitors can rely upon an element of workers with a relatively high general education and special training. Those workers considerably exceed, both in terms of the quality of their products and speed of production, the performance of the uneducated people who constitute the majority of the work force in our industrial plants, so that our industry has to conduct its struggle against foreign competition equipped with inferior weapons, and this of course leads to economic defeats. Because of all these circumstances, both the areas of general education and of special training of Russian workers call for the most energetic and urgent measures on the part of the government.[5]

Finance Minister Vyshnegradskii's concern with the level of skill and education of the Russian industrial labor force in the 1880s both expressed and stimulated a concern with education as an economic investment of the society. His pronouncement was soon reflected in a large number of studies, both empirical and normative, and policy oriented.

An early and probably representative example of the latter is an interesting collection of essays published in 1896 under the general title of *Economic Evaluation of Popular Education*. It contains contributions by I. I. Yanzhul', A. I. Chuprov, and I. N. Yanzhul'.[6] That by I. I. Yanzhul' (which is still of considerable historical interest) is based on the assumption that various "external" stimuli of economic growth (tariffs, subsidies, government regulations) are less effective than education and training. He invokes the authority of J. S. Mill, Thomas Brassey, and Alfred Marshall and provides empirical data from American experience to argue that the level of productivity of labor in various countries is positively correlated with per capita expenditures on education and with rates of literacy.[7] The general conclusion of the essays is summarized by the authors as follows: "There are, of course, many factors impeding the development of the Russian economy, but the foremost among them is the general illiteracy which distinguishes our country from all other civilized countries. . . . An increase of labor productivity is the only means to erase poverty in Russia and the best policy to achieve it is through the spread of education and knowledge."

It was now left for the statisticians and economists to provide the empirical proof for the "normative" judgment, expressed in various pamphlets, books, and articles, that the phenomenon observed in the United States and other countries was also valid for Russia.

The first study, by L. L. Gavrishchev, dealt with two sample groups of 1,506 and 1,934 workers in Nikolaev during 1895 and 1896 under the title "On the Impact of General Education of Workers on the Productivity of Their Labor."[8] Gavrishchev established two facts. First, the average literacy rate among the skilled workers was 75 per cent, while among the unskilled it was only 49 per cent. Second, he also concluded that for all age groups the literacy rate of employed skilled workers was above that of their social environment.[9] From his data, by ranking the main occupations according to the rate of literacy and average daily wage, we get the relationship shown in table 9.1.

A rank correlation is evident, though we cannot assume that literacy is the major determinant of the wage level. The correlation would have been improved had yearly instead of daily wages been used, since both carpenters and boilermakers were most subject to seasonal unemployment. Of

Table 9.1   **Ranking of Selected Occupations by Rate of Literacy and Average Daily Wage, 1895–96**

Occupation	Rate of Literacy	Average Daily Wage
Locksmiths and metal workers	1	2
Carpenters	2	1
Battleship construction workers	3	3
Boilermakers	4	5
Blacksmiths	5	4

**Table 9.2 Level of Average Daily Wage by Occupation
and Years of Education, 1895–96
(Illiterate = 100)**

Occupation	Years of Education								
	1	2	Home*	3	4	5	6	7	8
Locksmiths	104	101	106	112	116	118	117	119	114
Carpenters	104	107	108	108	109	125	119	103	95
Battleship construction workers	99	105	106	121	123	—	—	—	—
Boilermakers	94	109	106	106	116	103	—	—	—
Blacksmiths	106	108	116	114	113	128	—	—	—
Total, first sample	102	105	107	114	116	119	120	112	110
Total, second sample	102	105	107	114	116	118	120	—	—

*Literacy acquired outside of school. The original ratios were rounded.

even greater interest is the relationship between the level of education and the average daily wage within the major occupations represented in Gavrishchev's sample. Table 9.2 provides the information in terms of the ratio of wages of workers with successively more schooling to the average wage of illiterate workers within each occupation.

The usefulness of the data would be considerably increased if the sample could be standardized by age or years of job experience within the broad occupations. Nevertheless, they are suggestive as they stand. Gavrishchev himself concluded on the basis of his studies that the interest of industry demands from workers an average formal education of about five or six years. He claimed that industrialists prefer expensive (educated) workers over cheap (illiterate) ones because the increment in labor productivity exceeds the increment in wages.

The example given by Gavrishchev's study was followed in two directions: first, the trend to test the wage differential between literate and illiterate workers continued, with standardization for age and sex; second, scholars started to compare the economic effects of education with the effects of job experience and also attempted to calculate the private and social returns to education. Exemplifying the first category of research, S. S. Kolokol'tsov's study of 2,912 weavers in the Tver' district yielded wage differentials between literate and illiterate workers within particular age groups, as shown in table 9.3.[10]

The data and evidence of Gavrishchev and Kolokol'tsov, who both used small samples, were reinforced in a survey by K. M. Kozminikh-Lanin of 69,000 textile workers in the Moscow district in 1912 (table 9.4). The data in this survey also showed the change in wage rates between successive age groups for both literate and illiterate workers (table 9.5). While for the age group 15–20 wages were approximately equal for literate and

Table 9.3 Yearly Wages and Percentage of Literacy of Weavers, Tver' District, 1902

Age (years)	Wages of Literates as % of Wages of Illiterates		% of Literacy	
	Male Weavers	Female Weavers	Males	Females
18–22	108	107	87	33
23–27	114	121	80	16
28–32	106	106	79	14
33–37	110	—	72	—
38–42	114	—	70	—
43–47	114	—	54	—
48–52	107	—	46	—

Table 9.4 Wages of Literate Textile Workers as Percentage of Wages of Illiterate, Moscow district, 1912

Age Group (years)	Wage (%)	Age Group	Wage (%)
20–25	115	41–45	132
26–30	122	46–50	135
31–35	129	50 and over	135
36–40	126		

Source: K. M. Kozminikh-Lanin, *Gramotmost' i zarabotki fabrichno-zavodskikh rabochikh Moskovskoi gubernii* (Moscow, 1912).

illiterate workers (the literate ones received a lower wage in the age group below 15), the rise in wages until the age of 35 was much more rapid for the literate workers, indicating the impact of literacy (or education). The rise in wages for the illiterates virtually ceased at the age of 40, while for the literate workers it continued until the age of 50. The somewhat smaller decrease in wages for the illiterate group after the age of 50 was insufficient to offset the relative "losses" suffered earlier. Although this survey supported some of the general conclusions reached by other authors, the data suffered not only from limitations in the use to which they could be put but also from the concentration in a few industries, determined by their location in the Moscow district.

The relationship between the duration of formal education and the level of skill as measured by wage rates is confounded by associated on the job learning of skills. It is therefore necessary to distinguish the impact of formal education separately from skill acquisition on the job. The first attempt in the Russian literature to cope with this problem was made by the economists S. G. Strumilin and B. N. Babynin in the early 1920s.[11] In articles that now are mostly of historical interest, Strumilin attempted to

Table 9.5   Percentage Change of Monthly Wage between Successive
Age Groups for Literate and Illiterate Workers, 1912

Age Group (years)	% Change	
	Literate	Illiterate
Under 15	—	—
15–20	76.3	47.3
20–25	50.9	29.6
25–30	18.3	11.9
30–35	10.7	4.2
35–40	2.1	4.7
40–45	4.8	0.04
45–50	1.6	−0.2
50–55	−1.5	−1.2
55–60	−5.8	−4.8
Over 60	−13.0	−12.3

calculate the total returns to education, private as well as social. His goal was to advocate an investment program in educational facilities—". . . a more profitable 'capital' investment would be difficult to think of, even in a country of such immense possibilities as our Soviet Russia," he argued on the basis of empirical data. He analyzed two samples, one of 2,602 lathe operators (from the year 1919) and the other of 2,307 white-collar workers. Since he was mostly interested in the effect of education, he tried to establish the functional relation between age, job experience, years of formal education, and skills.

For his physical workers sample, Strumilin had the following equation coefficients:

$$K = 2.53648 - 0.002719(t - 37) - 0.0008644\,(t - 37)^2 + 0.1247(e - 2.36) + 0.04937(s - 11.06),$$

where K = skill level, t = age, s = years of job experience, and e = years of education. The increment of skill levels (in assumed units) as a result of education, expressed in per cent to uneducated as a base, is shown in table 9.6. Strumilin also found for his sample of physical laborers the increments of wages related to education shown in table 9.7.

Each year of school attendance contributed, by a large margin, a larger increment to the increase of manual wages than a year of factory job experience.[12] Also, in the existing wage structure, the increment of skill attributable to education in comparison with job experience was relatively

Table 9.6 Years of School and Skill Levels in Strumilin's Samples

Physical Workers		White-Collar Workers	
Years of School	Skill Level	Years of School	Skill Level
1	115	1–2	100
2	126.5	3–4	120
3	134	5–7	148
4	139.5	8–9	180
5	144	10–12	208
6	147.5	13–18	220

Table 9.7 Wage Level of Various Educational Groups, Physical Workers, in Strumilin's Sample (No education = 100)

Years of School	Level of Wages	Years of School	Level of Wages
Under 2	124	4	143
2	129	5	148
3	137	6	152

higher for white-collar workers than for manual workers. This difference tended to increase with the number of school years, which indicates the relatively higher return from advanced education for white-collar workers as compared with manual workers. Another observation by Strumilin concerns "the law of diminishing productivity of formal education analogous to the decreasing productivity of each additional year of job experience for the increment of skills." In other words, he found diminishing returns from education for each segment of the labor force, but setting in at different levels of education.[13] Nevertheless, Strumilin's data pointed to the fact that under the conditions of the pre-revolutionary period there was a clear incentive to invest in education at almost all levels, and that the incentive persisted during the early period after the revolution.

I pass over the interesting way in which Strumilin combined his empirical observations with the labor theory of value to arrive at his claims of social returns to education. It is worth noting, however, that a more successful attempt to use mass data to derive the relative contributions of formal education to increases in skill was made in 1930 by the Soviet economist E. Liustikh.[14] He standardized the data for age and job experience and found education to be the major factor determining wage differentials in his sample, thus basically supporting Strumilin's findings.

The subsequent direction and findings of economic research in Russia and the Soviet Union justified Strumilin's claim: "A long time ago we had already arrived at the conclusion that the expenditures of the state budget to raise the cultural level of the country ought to be considered along with the expenditures on technical reconstruction of production as capital expenditures, and as equal in terms of their importance to our economy." [15]

TEN

Data for the Study of Russian History

Introduction

Anyone superficially acquainted with Russian history would assume the existence of ample data for its study, at least since the beginning of the eighteenth century.[1] A centralized state apparatus controlling the daily lives and destinies of the Russian people must have left vast documentary evidence of its efforts. The normal assumption is that a fiscally motivated, mercantilistically oriented government that taxed everything from beards to coffins (if diapers had been in use, they too would have been taxed) would leave a rich legacy of quantitative data bearing on the relationship between the government and the economy as a whole, or at least the areas affected by government operations.

Indeed, for Russian history before the nineteenth century, most of the surviving documents concern activities in one way or another connected with the government rather than with private contractual relationships or other dealings among the citizens themselves. The public or semipublic nature of the surviving documents tends to slant our understanding of social and economic processes and activities in Russia. To paraphrase a remark by the Russian historian M. N. Pokrovsky, we know much more and in greater detail about Russian cannons than about Russian pots and pans.

There are relatively few private collections of documents that would provide quantitative materials for historical studies. The surviving documents pertain mostly to large landed estates and, for the nineteenth century, to business firms. There is a conspicuous scarcity of documentation left by social groups, by the urban merchants and artisans, and by the peasants who "wrote only with the plough on the soil." Peasant petitions, litigation, and government investigations involving peasants have been documented. But the quantitative data for the study of Russian history may still be compared to an iceberg, with the published items constituting the

199

visible tip. Most of the data are available only in unpublished sources in the archives of the Soviet Union and abroad.

A few factors will help explain this phenomenon. First, since much of the data were collected and accumulated by various government agencies, the publication of data was selective, depending upon various turns of government policies and in particular upon what the ruling elite or the not-very-enlightened bureaucracy considered, at each time, to be in the national interest. Second, the publication of documents involved expenditures which particular branches of the administration had to justify to those holding the purse strings. Third, the majority of Russian historians prior to the revolution were interested less in social and economic history than in intellectual and general political history. Even those who were concerned with social and economic history did not consider it necessary to find or provide empirical proof for their hypotheses. Thus there was little demand on the part of historians for extensive publication of quantitative data.

During the early Soviet period, a massive effort was started to publish documents of social and economic history. During the Stalinist period, however, the secret police administered the state archives, and the publication of documents was highly selective. As a result, the output decreased drastically in quality as well as in quantity. It was only during the 1960s that both the use and publication of quantitative data pertaining to Russian history started to grow and constitute an integral part of the revival of published historical scholarship in the USSR.

Extensive bibliographies and descriptions of available archival collections, published recently, provide the historian with an insight into the wealth of untouched primary sources. The state of the primary sources is such that in all probability in the near future we may expect a whole series of "finds" of significant sources, as yet unknown or hardly utilized, for the quantitative study of various periods in the history of Russia.

Valuable materials containing quantitative data concerning Russia are available in the major archives and libraries of Europe and the United States. Many of the diplomatic papers and much of the correspondence concerning Russia were published either abroad or by the Russian Historical Society (RIO) prior to the revolution. But consular reports, economic intelligence reports, and travel reports dealing with nonpolitical matters such as population problems, agriculture, commerce, and industry are still dispersed in the British Museum, Public Record Office (London), Bodleian (Oxford), and in the archives of Paris, Amsterdam, The Hague, Stockholm, Istanbul, and even the United States. And these archives have not been sufficiently tapped for Russian data.

Population Data

Prior to the eighteenth century, population data for Russia were available indirectly through household counts, which were carried out occasionally for the purposes of military service (in the case of the nobility and service population) or fiscal policies. Although the data of the household counts for various regions provide a basis of comparisons, they suffer from a lack of the precision that would be needed to assess population changes reflected in the size of households rather than their sheer number. A major change took place early in the eighteenth century at the time of Peter the Great, when the head count of the male population, which became the new unit for the poll tax, replaced the previous unit of the household as a basis for both taxation and population estimates.

From the first quarter of the eighteenth century until the revolution, Russia had ten census-like counts of the male population (*revizii*)[2] and one modern population census. The revizii had the following shortcomings from the point of view of population statistics:

1. Irregularity. The revizii were not conducted at regular intervals; their dates depended upon fiscal considerations (levying of taxes) or military and political considerations (assessment of the aftermath of the Napoleonic War or the Crimean War).
2. Lack of uniformity of territorial coverage. Due to the territorial expansion of Russia, on the one hand, and to territorial changes of the administrative units, on the other, it is difficult to establish the changes either in total population or in the population of particular regions.
3. Insufficient coverage and exemption of some population groups. This is probably the major shortcoming of the revizii, since they were counts of the male population and not of the total population. Moreover, they were for all practical purposes counts of the taxable male population rather than of the total male population. A relatively large portion of the population, including whole groups and large geographical areas, was exempt from the reviziia. These categories included the members of the nobility and gentry, the clergy, those employed in state service, some groups in military service (e.g., the Cossacks), people having academic degrees, teachers, the Bashkirs, the Kirgiz, the inhabitants of the Caucasus, the autochthons of Siberia, the inhabitants of the Polish Kingdom and Finland, and a number of other categories embracing smaller population groups.
4. The notorious underestimation of even the taxable population groups. This can be attributed to the largely fiscal and military service goals of

the reviziia, which gave people an incentive to underreport their numbers. The additional counts following each reviziia could only partially remedy this shortcoming. Still another cause of underreporting was confusion resulting from the complexity of primary documents and the low level of literacy of both local officials and officials sent from the center to conduct the reviziia or to check on its accuracy.

In spite of all the shortcomings of the revizii, when viewed either as substitutes for population censuses or as near-substitutes for current vital statistics, they are useful sources for historians. The few available publications based upon the revizii data, starting with those of the statisticians of the early nineteenth century, provide us with a wealth of indispensable information. Modern historians will deplore most, not the qualitative shortcomings of the data, but the relative paucity of studies providing the information that could be extracted from the revizii by skillful historical demographers.

During the first half of the nineteenth century, three vital statistics systems were established:

1. Civil records (*Spiski po sostoianiiam*), separate for the gentry, the clergy, and the urban estates;
2. Fiscal records, separate for homeowners, urban taxpayers, and rural taxpayers; and
3. Police records, exclusively for urban areas, with differing coverage and scope.

On the basis of these three types of records, the district (*guberniia*) statistical authorities were obliged, beginning in 1857, to record and submit the population estimates for their districts, including the counties (*uezdy*) and cities, to the Central Statistical Committee. Given the imperfection of the primary data, confidence in the district or total estimates was not very great. Nevertheless, it signified progress and improvement over the system of irregular revizii.

A major change was introduced by the first general population census of the Russian Empire. A number of foreign censuses were used as models for this, which was conducted on 28 January 1897 of the Julian calendar (9 February). The questionnaire included the following information:

(1) last and first name, including patronymic, as well as information on physical handicaps (blindness, deafness, muteness, and mental illness);
(2) family status (single, married, widow, etc.);

(3) relationship to head of household;

(4) sex;

(5) age;

(6) membership in an estate, rank, and (for foreigners) nationality;

(7) religion;

(8) birthplace;

(9) permanent address; (10) place of registered habitat; (11) remarks about temporary presence and temporary absence; (12) mother tongue; (13) literacy; and (14) employment, craft, or profession.

For a while the census, despite its inadequacies, provided a much more solid base for population estimates than had previously been available. In fact, it helped to revise previous population estimates and was used to refine subsequent ones. However, since the machinery for generating current population data was not changed—the parishes continued to act as offices of vital statistics, supplying their registrations of marriages, deaths, births, and baptisms to the district statistical committees—the discrepancies between the estimates of the Central Statistical Committee and other estimates grew, particularly in the absence of further population censuses between 1897 and 1913.

The significance of the 1897 census was that for the first time the whole population of the empire was covered (although the count in some regions on its fringes was probably not exact), and a number of interesting demographic data were made available for the first time.

Land and Agricultural Data

Data reflecting landholdings by institutions and individuals were collected and recorded in Russia as early as the period of Mongol supremacy. During the centuries of Moscow's rise to a position of dominating power in Russia, land redistributions and grants of various kinds were recorded. The rivalry between the service gentry and the old nobility, which was as much a rivalry for land and peasants as for political power within the state, produced more land data.

The late sixteenth and the seventeenth centuries provide us with landholding estimates for institutions (churches and monasteries) as well as for the members of the nobility. Although the descriptions occasionally provide a breakdown of arable land or plowland, it was not until the middle and second half of the eighteenth century that land titles were established based upon a primitive version of a cadastre.[3] But even this cadastre did not always draw a distinction between meadows, pasture, forests, and wasteland, so that an accurate distribution of the different kinds of land by use is not so far available. We still operate in this area with various kinds of estimates; the most accurate, or rather the least inaccurate, might be estimates of the area of plowland, but even those are more or less educated guesses rather than accurate measurements.

One of the curious results of the lack of a cadastre was the inability of the Soviet government to supply a reliable figure of the total land confiscated under the terms of its agrarian reform. Since the first agricultural census was conducted during World War I (in 1916) for a smaller territory than the Russian prewar empire, comparisons of the available data of an earlier period have to be treated with caution. Land data first became important around the time of the emancipation in connection with the size of transferred landholdings to be held in communal ownership by the former serfs. For most districts, we know the distribution of landholdings by ownership, since, after the liberation of the serfs in 1861, special studies of land ownership were conducted in 1877–78, 1895–96, and 1905. Nevertheless, the data are not very helpful in the assessment of the value of the landholdings unless they can be adjusted for the differing qualities of land.

Scattered data on grain yields are available for some regions for the eighteenth century, collected either in conjunction with the cadastre or by district governors at the command of the central authorities. Demands for grain-yield reports to be sent to St. Petersburg by the district governors were usually prompted by the frequent droughts and famines in Russia. During the eighteenth century the records of yield estimates—reported in terms of output-seed ratios—were spotty and probably inaccurate. The system of reporting did not improve much during the first half of the nineteenth century. It was only with the establishment of district statistical offices that the Ministry of the Interior started to collect yield data. During the second half of the nineteenth century, at least in the districts of European Russia, yield data were collected and published by two more authorities besides the Central Statistical Committee, namely by the Chief Administrator of Land Settlement and Agriculture (GUZIZ), later superseded by the Department of Rural Economy and Agricultural Statistics of the Ministry of Agriculture, and by the regional authorities of the organs of local self-government known as *zemstvos*.

In addition to the inaccuracy of the land-use data, resulting apparently in a systematic underreporting of the planted area, the following criticisms of the agricultural statistics may be made:

1. The system of collection of agricultural data by the Central Statistical Committee, which relied upon the reports of local administrative officials, was imperfect and did not accurately reflect the level of yields. To the extent that the conflicting tendencies to underreport (on the part

of the producers) and overestimate (on the part of the officials) tended to cancel each other out, and in the absence of a prevailing bias in one direction, the data covering a large territory (e.g., a district) were more accurate than the county data, and the long-term averages reflected the long-term trend quite accurately (although at a level of estimated yields lower than the reality).

2. The reports by the various departments of the Ministry of Agriculture were the least reliable because of the relatively small, unrepresentative group of correspondents they used.

3. The zemstvo data were the most accurate for yearly levels of yields and for yield differentials between regions; however, they were inferior in reflecting the changes of yields over time.[4] Thus the current yield (and output) statistics suffered from a number of fallacious methods of data collecting and aggregating, and the service of providing prognoses of yield levels (to the trade or transportation sectors of the economy) was poorly organized.

4. A major shortcoming was the exclusion of the fringes of the empire—Siberia, the Caucasus and Central Asia, whose share of agricultural output was growing—from the total crop output statistics until the beginning of the twentieth century.

In spite of these and other shortcomings, the crop yield and output data can be used (since we know their bias) much more readily than the data pertaining to the livestock and workstock herds and to livestock output. Since the veterinary service was subordinated to the military authorities, who were also interested in horse breeding and the acquisition of horses for the army, livestock estimates were provided primarily by the military; from the 1880s on, a survey of livestock known as the Military-Horse Count was conducted. The agricultural census of 1916 revealed the inadequacy of the previous estimates.

Price data were generated by some of the same authorities who produced the agricultural estimates. The first stimulus came from the state, which demanded information on the prices prevailing during famines and grain shortages in order to decide whether to prohibit grain exports, to impose price controls, or to provide famine relief in various other forms. The data were spotty and did not lend themselves to the construction of price indexes. More consistent were the price data reported by the army quartermaster of payments for food and forage and the wholesale food prices collected after the 1830s by the Trade and Manufacturing Department of the Ministry of Finance. The most reliable wholesale price data for agricultural products started to appear after the 1890s in the form of information given to the government by the commodity exchanges. The lack of continuity and reliable documentation by public or private institutions (hospitals, schools, etc.) deprives us of some price-data collections of types available for earlier periods in Western European countries. As in other areas of social and economic activity, data were reported primarily by central government authorities, even in agriculture. The major exception are the zemstvo statistics.

The Zemstvo Statistics

Among the most useful sources of data for the social history of Russia are the various works published by the zemstvos. The zemstvos had the authority to collect taxes, primarily on land, for local needs. Hence, determining the ability to pay was of major concern to them. Out of fiscal considerations arose the need to collect data pertaining to the economic and social situation of the largest social stratum, the peasantry.

This led to a spontaneous process of collecting data by the late 1860s and to the establishment of statistical offices at the district level by the early 1870s.[5] Subsequently the results of these studies began to appear in print. The basic forms of study were both the one-time census-like questionnaire and the continuing observation of selected households. The unit chosen was invariably the peasant household. These studies expanded constantly both in territorial coverage and in scope of the questionnaire, which included an increasing number of questions pertaining to different aspects of production, income, consumption, and education. The censuslike household studies varied in coverage from a general census of households of a particular district to a more-or-less representative sample of households or farm groups. The continuing, usually annual, observations involved selected households or correspondents and were used as a sample for the study of the changes in peasant agriculture over time rather than cross-sectionally.

The zemstvo statisticians constantly introduced changes and improvements in the techniques of data collection and analysis. One curious check upon the accuracy of the primary data was introduced very early in the data-collecting process by conducting the interviews during the meetings of the village assembly, thus having the potential or actual reaction of knowledgeable neighbors to the data supplied. However, in spite of their best intentions, the statisticians never eliminated some basic deficiencies. The major one, from the point of view of an aggregate analysis of peasant agriculture, was the lack of uniformity of program, procedure, and techniques among the various districts and provinces. Thus, even had the zemstvo statistics covered all Russia, the aggregation of the data would not have produced a full picture. In addition, changes in procedure, scope, and emphasis prevent us from building continuous series even for the particular localities.[6]

These criticisms of the zemstvo statistics, however pertinent to economic analysis, ought not to deter the historian interested in cross-sectional data. Particularly for the period 1880–1913, the zemstvo statistics represent a wealth of materials on a number of subjects. Among the pioneering efforts of the zemstvo statisticians are the attempts to study peasant budgets, which provided interesting insights not only into the role of peasant households as farm producers, but also into the behavior of households as consumer units. The peasant budgets, published for various localities beginning in the 1880s, reflect the adjustment of agriculture and the agricultural population to changes in prices, supply of factors of production, technology, and so forth. Before the revolution, about 11,500 peasant household budgets were studied for purposes of research and publication.[7]

Another area of broad interest was the work of the zemstvo statisticians on educational levels of the rural population. This included data on schools and schooling in the various provinces and, in some cases, library facilities and adult education. This area of the zemstvo statistics was moving toward a uniform program of classification, which was recommended by the all-zemstvo conference on school statistics in 1913, when the war upset all such plans.

The zemstvo statistics pioneered in other fields as well, notably health. They constitute an indispensable source for the social history of Russia of the postemancipation period.

Industry

One of the basic problems of industrial statistics in Russia was that of defining an industrial enterprise. For better or worse, the definitions did not change much from the beginning of the eighteenth to nearly the end of the nineteenth century. Even the definition of an industrial establishment provided by the Statute of Industry of 1893[8] did not deviate substantially from the earlier statutes of 1723 and 1820. But matters were complicated by ambiguities in the definition, particularly pertaining to size—distinction between large and small industry and handicrafts.

The two major problems affecting the quality of the data on the industrial sector of the economy were the divisions between the various government departments that collected and processed the data and the reporting of the data by the enterprises themselves. The data pertaining to industry were collected, by and large, by three government agencies, all under the Ministry of Finance: data for the mining and ferrous metal industries were collected by the Mining Department; those for industries subject to the excise tax, by the Revenue Department; and those for all other industries, by the Trade and Industry Department (later the Ministry of Trade and Industry). Although these agencies were all under the same ministry (except for the period when state-owned enterprises reported to the Ministry of State Estates), each agency collected and reported on its own basis, using a different methodology and internal classification of output, labor force, and description of technology. This made it very difficult to assemble data for the whole industrial sector.

The reporting during the eighteenth century was largely sporadic, except for a few attempts to conduct a quasi-censuslike review of mining and manufacturing. The first official attempts to regulate reporting to the government agencies were made by a decree of 30 June 1804. Additional rules for reporting were published in 1830, 1834, 1835, 1862, 1867, and 1893. The decrees, however, did not assure coverage, promptness, or accuracy of the reports. Furthermore, the district administrations had no incentive, except in the cases where revenue was involved, to check upon the accuracy of the reported data. Thus the yearly reports of the performance of the industrial sector, including the published reports, were inadequate.

The best sources for the industrial sector during the period 1900–1913 are the publications of the censuslike studies for 1900, 1908, and 1910–12. Conducted by the statistician V. E. Varzar for the government, these studies utilized some of the experience of the zemstvo statistics. Although the data were reported by the owners of the enterprises, there were some built-in checks of consistency that gave the factory inspectors a greater measure of control over the primary data than was possible for the district administrations.

Of the three census-like studies, that of 1900 was least inclusive in terms of geographic coverage, and it excluded state enterprises as well as mines and ferrous metallurgy. But it was most comprehensive in its scope of information. The studies provided information on quantity of output, use of inputs (raw materials, labor, and machinery), energy supply, capital stock, number of days worked and length of working day. Although the study of 1910–12 was conducted on an abbreviated questionnaire, its reporting of three consecutive years nevertheless provided continuous data for the same enterprises, thus revealing some of the dynamics of industrial development in Russia which could not be obtained from sporadic studies.

The information collected for the periods between the censuslike studies was inferior. Checks for consistency are necessary if that information is to be used at all. For the specific problems of industrial output, the most widely used estimates pertaining to large-scale industry were worked out during the 1920s by the Russian economist Kondratiev. The Kondratiev index has a number of shortcomings that were pointed out by Raymond Goldsmith in *Economic Development and Cultural Change* (1961), who also suggested some corrections.

Transportation and Communication

The availability of transportation and communication data varied with the historical period, but in general it improved over time. The following types of data are available:

1. Among the oldest records are those related to maritime shipping of the different ports. Such data for the eighteenth century can be checked against foreign records and, although incomplete for certain years, are generally reliable. The nineteenth-century data are quite adequate.
2. The documents related to shipping over the internal waterways (particularly the various canal systems) were not completely preserved until the nineteenth century. They provide information about ships, tonnage of freight (mostly in terms of type and tonnage of the ship itself), and in some cases the commodity composition of freight. From the 1830s on, data on internal waterway transportation were published annually. Special emphasis was given to the transportation of food grains, and during the navigation season such data were collected on a monthly basis.
3. Railroad transportation statistics originated and were processed in two ministries, those of finance and communications (*Putei soobshcheniia*). The railway department of the Ministry of Finance was interested both in railway construction and in freight rates. The statistics department of the Ministry of Communications was interested chiefly in the technical and financial aspects of railroad operation. As a result of these divergent interests, two parallel sets of data were produced in the form of monthly and annual reports by the two ministries.
4. In addition to data on railways and railroad transportation, the Ministry of Communications published data on roads of different kinds under its jurisdiction, specifying their length and classification and also the amounts of tolls collected on the roads and bridges. These reports provide some information on goods traffic.
5. Both the Ministry of Finance and the Ministry of the Interior, in their respective yearbooks, published data on the performance of the post office, telephone, and telegraph systems. Most of the data were provided by the respective administrative departments themselves.

Within this general classification, the best data are those for the railroads in terms of both coverage and methodology. The data of the Ministry of Finance on railroad freight cover up to 400 commodities and indicate their points of loading and destination, thus providing information on inter-regional movements of goods and lengths of haul. The data of the Ministry of Communications are very helpful in assessing the costs of transportation and fuel consumption by the railroads. The statistical yearbooks of the two ministries provide the final data, with lags of up to three years. But for historical research this is now no drawback, and the yearbooks tend to be more accurate than the preliminary current transportation statistics used for operations control by the government departments of transportation and communication.

Labor Force, Wages, and the Standard of Living

Quantitative data pertaining to the labor force as a whole were not collected in Russia. Given the deficiencies of population statistics, the estimates of the agricultural labor force can be treated only as guesses. But even for the nonagricultural labor force, the estimates are based upon incomplete primary data collected by various institutions and by different methods. Within the nonagricultural sector, the best data are those of railroad employment. The data on government employment are very incomplete for the simple reason that they were never collected or classified as a single category and are therefore difficult to arrange. For the industrial labor force, the data are mostly scattered. During the existence of serfdom, the industrial labor force data, collected by the government as a by-product of industry surveys conducted among employers in the various districts, did not make a sufficiently clear distinction between free and serf labor. In addition, serf labor was often counted not in numbers but in service equivalent units. The uneven coverage caused by unsystematic reporting renders the data for the period of serfdom almost useless for measuring short-term changes in industrial employment.

Some improvement in data collection occurred after 1861. But even then no uniform methods were employed, and data were collected primarily for European Russia. The labor force data were collected separately for mining and metallurgy, for enterprises paying the excise tax (e.g., alcohol, tobacco, salt, petroleum), and for enterprises not paying the excise tax. Depending upon the degree of government control, enterprises often reported their labor force without distinguishing between full-time and part-time workers and in most cases chose an arbitrary date for reporting.

A valuable source of data on labor and wages was the collection of reports by the factory inspectors, published regularly from the 1890s. Located in the districts, the factory inspectors provided data for the industrial firms subject to factory inspection. Exempt from the inspection were small-size and cottage industry, metallurgy, and industry upon which the excise tax was levied.

Ancillary data pertaining to the labor force can be found in the reports of municipal governments and of employer associations and similar institutions, but they all suffer from a lack of uniformity and continuity. Two collections of data on factory employees, for the years 1900 and 1908, were published by the Ministry of Trade and Industry under V. E. Varzar's editorship. Those collections, together with the 1897 population census, provide the best data that we have for the composition of the industrial labor force. The works by A. G. Rashin and K. A. Pazhitnov published during the Soviet period provide some useful estimates for particular industry branches.

Wage data were, naturally, collected even less frequently. For the agricultural sector they comprise, by district, averages of payments to field hands. Distinctions are made between the sexes; among permanent, seasonal, and day laborers; and often between money wages and wages inclusive of food and shelter. Such data were published in the yearbooks of the Ministry of Agriculture and occasionally in the publications of the Ministry of Finance. Studies of agricultural wages can also be found in the zemstvo statistics. For urban industrial wages, one has to rely upon the data of the factory inspectors and the yearbooks of the Ministry of Transportation. The studies by Varzar provide an additional useful source for wage data for the two years they cover, 1900 and 1908. The archives of some large industrial firms contain wage data that could be used for the construction of wage indexes. Few of the archives, however, have been utilized; of those that have been consulted for writing the history of firms, the wage data have not been published.

To study the changes in the standard of living of various groups, income data have to be developed from wage and price statistics. The sources for such data can be found in the publications of the Ministry of Finance. Price series for 1890–1913 for different regions are available from data collected from commodity exchanges. The number of commodities represented in the series increased over time, until by 1913 it reached about 150. The price indexes (being arithmetic averages of wholesale prices with a 1890–1900 base) were published periodically by the Ministry of Finance and after 1905 by the Ministry of Trade and Industry.[9] Wholesale prices were published by the *Torgovo-promyshlennaia gazeta,* and local agricultural prices by the Ministry of Agriculture. Retail prices were published for agricultural areas (local rural markets) by the district zemstvos and for urban markets by some municipalities.

The availability of some wage and price data does not solve the problem of standard-of-living changes, since earnings and income statistics as such were not collected. Materials that can be used in the absence of income estimates for Russia, at least for a few years, include the Ministry of Finance publication on incomes of the top income group (over 1,000 rubles per year) for the early part of the twentieth century and the budget studies of industrial workers and peasants in various parts of the country (sponsored by the zemstvos in the case of the peasants and privately in the case of industrial workers). Imperfect as such substitutes are, they nevertheless indicate the general trend in incomes and standards of living in the late nineteenth and early twentieth centuries.

Trade

Foreign trade produced some of the most thorough collections of data. Prior to the eighteenth century the government participated actively in foreign trade, at various periods monopolizing whole branches that appeared advantageous. Not only in the fur trade, but even in the grain and timber trades, the government occasionally monopolized exports. Thus government records concerning certain branches of foreign trade, particularly some of the traditional exports, were relatively abundant. Although the government remained a major exporter of some commodities (iron and timber) during the eighteenth century, the import records became more plentiful and of a higher quality than the export records.

Government records pertaining to foreign trade and particularly to imports were kept more meticulously than other government records. This was perhaps due to the importance of customs revenues in total state revenue, the protective features of the Russian tariff, and the fact that for long periods of the Russian ruble's inconvertibility, import duties were paid in silver.

Given the fiscal motives, the available data for imports were relatively more reliable. The foreign trade data primarily included customs information, largely registering imports and some exports subject to export tax. The major shortcomings of the foreign trade statistics, which were almost entirely supplied by the customs offices, were twofold: the relative inferiority of the export data, particularly for the exports that passed duty free; and the absence of estimates of foreign trade that did not pass through customs. Merchandise that did not pass through customs was considered smuggled goods. Although data for confiscated smuggled goods were published annually from the 1830s, the data are too crude to yield estimates of total smuggling.

In spite of the shortcomings and variations in the degree of accuracy of the customs data, it is possible to reconstruct the patterns of commodity composition and changes in foreign trade, using averages for five-year periods or decades. Year-to-year estimates would be much less reliable. Thus the task of modern research in the area of the relatively abundant Russian foreign trade data is to compare them with available data on Russia's exports found in the trade statistics of her major trading partners. Given the relative concentration of Russian exports within a narrow range of commodities, the trade data could serve (in the absence of violent fluctuations in foreign demand) as indicators of the growth of domestic output of such commodities.

Domestic trade, in the absence of collected data, is terra incognita. For the period before 1753, there were occasional estimates of internal customs receipts that can be used as rough approximations in calculating interregional domestic trade. With the abolition of the internal custom zones and duties in 1753, even this very inaccurate source for estimating the value of domestic trade disappeared, with the exception of the data pertaining to goods whose sale was monopolized at various times by the government (e.g., alcohol, salt, matches). Those data are clearly inadequate for estimating domestic trade as a whole. Two sets of data have occasionally been used as substitutes for direct internal trade data. The first set is that of the trade tax (*promyslovyi nalog*).

For fiscal purposes, trade establishments were classified into five major groups: (1) large wholesale and purchasing firms, banks, credit institutions and insurance companies, grain elevators, hotels; (2) retail firms and medium-size wholesale firms, small hotels, baths; (3) small-size retail shops, bars, saloons, furnished rooming houses; (4) market stalls, teahouses; (5) carrying trade and peddling in rural areas. Within each category, the number of firms and their employees were recorded, and their trade turnover was calculated. The data were reported for counties and districts, separated for rural and urban areas, and finally published by the Ministry of Finance. The last publication covers the year 1912.

The data collected and published in conjunction with the trade tax (which supposedly reflected total trade turnover) had a number of shortcomings that prevent their use as approximations for internal trade estimates. On the one hand, they are not sufficiently comprehensive, since they omit joint stock companies, consumer cooperatives (in other words, the trading firms under the obligation of public accountancy), and government trading. In addition, since the trade tax was not paid in Siberia and Central Asia, the data do not cover these territories. On the other hand, since that data on total turnover of the listed firms also include various financial transactions, credit operations not necessarily of a mercantile nature, insurance, and some other services, the raw data cannot be used in

213

their reported form to reflect trade turnover. An additional adjustment would be required to separate wholesale from retail trade operations.

Nevertheless, given the available data from the trading tax, the sales data of the government monopolies, data on sales of particular raw materials and products manufactured by joint-stock companies and other private corporations, and production data by major industries combined with some export data for the same products, it is possible to arrive at estimates of retail trade for years for which reliable price data are available.[10] Yearly estimates of domestic retail trade thus determined would not be very reliable, and changes reflected by such estimates would not be quite accurate. But estimates arrived at by such methods of utilizing available raw data can be utilized in conjunction with other economic data to reflect long-range trends in the Russian economy. The only serious attempts at estimating the volume and changes in total domestic trade turnover to data have been those of the Soviet economist S. G. Strumilin, who calculated the total domestic trade turnover for the years 1899–1913.[11]

The second set of data for estimating short- and long-term changes in the volume of retail trade, frequently used by economic historians, are the data on the volume of transactions at the Nizhnii-Novgorod (previously Makarievskaia) annual fair. This fair, the most important of the many fairs in Russia, provides estimates on the volume of transactions calculated uniformly since 1817. However, indiscriminate use of the data supplied by a single fair (even the most important one) can lead to serious errors of judgment if generalized for short-term changes in the total of retail sales. But the Nizhnii-Novgorod data can be combined with available data for other fairs and sources of domestic trade to produce more reliable estimates. The scattered data on the domestic trade of Russia require a strenuous effort to provide regional or national estimates.

Bibliography

ABBREVIATIONS

Akad. Nauk	Akademiia Nauk SSSR (Academy of Sciences of the USSR)
CSC	Tsentral'nyi Statisticheskii Komitet (Central Statistical Committee)
GK	Geologicheskii Komitet (Geological Committee)
Gosbank	Gosudarstvennyi Bank (State Central Bank)
Gosplan	Gosudarstvennyi Planovoi Komitet (State Planning Committee)
GUZIZ	Glavnoe Upravlenie Zemleustroistva i Zemledeliia (Chief Administration of Land Settlement and Agriculture)

IRGO	Imperatorskoe Russkoe Geograficheskoe Obshchestvo (Royal Russian Geographical Society)
IVEO	Imperatorskoe Vol'noe Ekonomicheskoe Obshchestvo (Royal Free Economic Society)
KZag	Komitet Zagotovok (Committee of Procurement)
MF	Ministerstvo Finansov (Ministry of Finance)
MGI	Ministerstvo Gosudarstvennykh Imushchestv (Ministry of Government Estates)
Min Zag	Ministerstvo Zagotovok (Ministry of Procurement)
MMF	Ministerstvo Morskogo Flota (Ministry of the Navy, when pertaining to a pre-revolutionary publication)
MNP	Ministerstvo Narodnogo Prosveshcheniia (Ministry of Public Education)
MPS	Ministerstvo Putei Soobshcheniia (Ministry of Ways of Communication)
MRF	Ministerstvo Rechnogo Flota (Ministry of the River Marine)
MS	Ministerstvo Sviazi (Ministry of Communications)
MT	Ministerstvo Torgovli (Ministry of Trade)
MTP	Ministerstvo Torgovli i Promyshlennosti (Ministry of Trade and Industry)
MVD	Ministerstvo Vnutrennikh Del (Ministry of the Interior)
MVT	Ministerstvo Vneshnei Torgovli (Ministry of Foreign Trade)
MYu	Ministerstvo Yustitsii (Ministry of Justice)
MZ	Ministerstvo Zemledeliia (Ministry of Agriculture)
NKFin	Narodnyi Komissariat Finansov (People's Commissariat of Finance)
NKMF	Narodnyi Komissariat Morskogo Flota (People's Commissariat of the Merchant Marine)
NKP	Narodnyi Komissariat po Prodovol'stviiu (People's Commissariat of Food Supply)
NKPS	Narodnyi Komissariat Putei Soobshcheniia (People's Commissariat of Ways of Communication)
NKRF	Barodnyi Komissariat Rechnogo Flota (People's Commissariat of the River Fleet)
NKRKI	Narodnyi Komissariat Raboche-Krestianskoi Inspektsii (People's Commissariat of Workers-Peasant Inspection)
NKS	Narodnyi Komissariat Sviazi (People's Commissariat of Communications)
NK Torg	Narodnyi Komissariat Torgovli (People's Commissariat of Trade)
NK Trud	Narodnyi Komissariat Truda (People's Commissariat of Labor)
NK Vnesh-torg	Narodnyi Komissariat Vneshnei Torgovli (People's Commissariat of Foreign Trade)
NKZ	Narodnyi Komissariat Zemledeliia (People's Commissariat of Agriculture)
NKZdrav	Narodnyi Komissariat Zdravokhraneniia (People's Commissariat of Health)
RIO	Russkoe Istoricheskoe Obshchestvo (Russian Historical Society)

RSFSR   Rossiiskaia Sovetskaia Federativnaia Sotsialisticheskaia Respublika
           (Russian Federative Socialist Republic)
SNK   Sovet Narodnykh Komissarov (Council of People's Commissars)
TsSU   Tsentral'noe Statisticheskoe Upravlenie (Central Statistical Author-
           ity)
TsUNKhU   Tsentral'noe Upravlenie Narodno-Khoziaistvennogo Ucheta (Central
           Authority for National-Economic Accounting)
VSNKh   Vysshii Soviet Narodnogo Khoziaistva (Supreme Council of the Na-
           tional Economy)
VTsSPS   Vsesoiuznyi Tsentral'nyi Sovet Professional'nykh Soiuzov (Central
           Council of Trade Unions)

PERIODICALS

Artilleriiskii zhurnal. 1825–.

Gornyi zhurnal. 1825–1917.

Narodnoe khoziaistvo v . . . godu, MF, 1914–16. Petrograd, 1915–18.

Rossiiskii Morskoi kalendar'. 1804–.

St. Petersburgskii zhurnal. St. Petersburg: MVD, 1805–9.

*Sel'skoe khoziaistvo i lesovodstvo. Zhurnal ministerstva zemledeliia i gosudar-
stvennykh imushchetv.* St. Petersburg, 1865–1905.

Statisticheskii zhurnal. St. Petersburg, 1806–8.

Trudy imperatorskogo vol'nogo ekonomicheskogo obshchestva. St. Petersburg,
1766–1917.

Vestnik finansov, promyshelennosti i torgovli. (weekly) St. Petersburg: MF, 1885–
1915.

Voenno-meditsinskii zhurnal. St. Petersburg, 1882–1914.

*Zapiski imperatorskogo Russkogo geograficheskogo obshchestva po otdeleniu sta-
tistiki.* St. Petersburg, 1886–1916.

Zhurnal glavnogo upravleniia putei soobshcheniia i publichnykh zdanii. St. Petersburg, 1845–65.

Zhurnal manufaktury i torgovli. 1825–.

Zhurnal ministerstva gosudarstvennykh imushchestv. St. Petersburg, 1841–64.

Zhurnal ministerstva narodnogo prosveshcheniia. St. Petersburg, 1803, 1834–
1917.

Zhurnal ministerstva putei soobshcheniia. 1886–1917.

Zhurnal ministerstva vnutrennykh del. St. Petersburg, 1829–61.

Zhurnal putei soobshcheniia. 1826–43.

GENERAL SOURCES

Before 1825

Polnoe sobranie zakonov Rossiiskoi imperii. St. Petersburg, 1830.

Kotoshikhin, G. K. O Rossii, v Tsarstvovanie Alekseia Mikhailovicha. St. Petersburg, 1906.

Kryzhanich, Iu. G. *Russkoe gosudarstvo v polovine XVII veka*. Moscow, 1859–60.

Kirilov, V. I. *Tsvetushchee sostoianie vserossiiskogo gosudarstva*. Moscow, 1831.

Tatishchev, V. N. *Izbrannye trudy po geografii Rossii*. Moscow, 1950.

De Gennin, Vil'lem. *Opisanie Ural'skikh i Sibirskikh zavodov*. Moscow, 1937.

Krasheninnikov, S. *Opisanie zemli kamchatki*. St. Petersburg, 1755. *Orenburg-skaia guberniia* . . . St. Petersburg, 1762.

Rychkov, P. I. *Vvedenie v astrakhanskuiu topografiiiu* . . . Moscow, 1774.

[Schlotzer, A. L.] *Neuveraendertes Russland* . . . Vols. 1–2. Riga, Mitau, Leipzig, 1767, 1772.

Geograficheskii leksikon Rossiiskogo gosudarstva ili Slovar' . . . Moscow, 1773.

Chebotarev, Kh. A. *Geograficheskoe metodicheskoe opisanie Rossiiskoi imperii*. Moscow, 1776.

Georgi, J. G. *Opisanie vsekh, obitaiushchikh v Rossiiskom gosudarstve narodov*. St. Petersburg, 1776.

Shcherbatov, M. M. *Statistika v razsuzhdenii Rossii*. Moscow, 1859.

Maksimovich, L. M. *Putevoditel' k drevnostiam i dostopamiatnostiam Moskovskim*. Moscow, 1782.

Topograficheskoe opisanie kaluzhskogo namestnichestva. St. Petersburg, 1785.

Kraft, M. "Essai sur les Tables des mariages, des naissances, et des morts de la ville de St. Petersbourg . . ." In *Acta academia scientiarum imp. petropolitanea*. St. Petersburg, 1786.

Istoricheskoe i topograficheskoe opisanie gorodov Moskovskoi gubernii. Moscow, 1787.

Novyi i polnyi geograficheskii Slovar' Rossiiskago gosudarstva ili leksikon. Moscow, 1788.

Chulkov, M. D. *Istoricheskoe opisanie Rossiiskoi komertsii, pri vsekh portakh i granitskah*. Vols. 1–7. St. Petersburg, 1781–88.

Chulkov, M. D. *Slovar' uchrezhdennykh v Rossii iarmarok i torgov*. 1788.

Pleshcheev, S. I. *Obozrenie Rossiiskoi imperii v nyneshnem ee novoustroennom sostoianii*. St. Petersburg, 1786.

Herman, B. F. J. *Statistische Schilderung von Russland*. St. Petersburg, 1790.

Topograficheskoe opisanie zavodov lezhashchikh v ufimskom namestnichestve. 1791.

Georgi, J. G. *Opisaniie Rossiisko-imperatorskogo stolichnogo goroda Sankt-Peterburga*. St. Petersburg, 1794.

Recueil sur la Russie du XVIII siecle, Vol. 4, Planches, Cartes, Melanges Statistiques . . . St. Petersburg.

Maksimovich, L. M., and Shchekotov, A. M. *Geograficheskii Slovar' Rossiiskogo gosudarstva sochinennyi v nastoiashchem vide*. Vols. 1–4. Moscow, 1801–9.

Storch, H. *Historisch-Statistisches Gemalde des Russischen Reichs*. Riga-Leipzig, 1797–1803.

Bakhturin, A. N. *Kratkoe opisanie vnutrennego Rossiskoi imperii vodokhodstva*. St. Petersburg, 1802.

Golitsyn, I. A. *Statisticheskie tablitsy vserossiiskoi imperii* Moscow, 1807.

Ziablovskii, E. F. *Noveishee zemleopisanie Rossiiskoi imperii*. 2 vols. St. Petersburg, 1807.

Ziablovskii, E. F. *Statisticheskoe opisanie Rossiikoi imperii v nyneshnem ee sos-toianii.* St. Petersburg, 1808.

Ziablovskii, E. F. *Zemleopisanie Rossiiskoi imperii* St. Petersburg, 1810.

Khvostov, V. *O Tomskoi gubernii i o naselenii Bol'shoi Sibirskoi dorogi do irkust-koi granitsi.* St. Petersburg, 1809.

German, Ivan. *Istoricheskoe nachertanie gornogo proizvodstva v Rossiiskoi im-perii.* Ekaterinburg, 1810.

Vsevolozhskii, N. S. *Dictionnarie geographique et historique de l'empire de Rus-sie.* Moscow, 1813.

Arseniev, K. I. *Nachertanie statistiki Rossiiskogo gosudarstva.* St. Petersburg, 1818–19.

German, K. *Statisticheskoe issledovanie otnositel'no Rossiiskoi imperii.* St. Petersburg, 1819.

1825–1855

Lecointre de Laveau. *Opisanie nizhnego novgoroda i ezhegodno byvaiushchei v nem iarmarki.* Moscow, 1829.

Androssov, V. *Statisticheskaia zapiska o Moskve.* Moscow: S. Selivanskii, 1832.

Pel'chinskii, V. *O Sostoianii promyshlennykh sil Rossii do 1832 g.* St. Petersburg: Akad. Nauk, 1833.

Evetskii, Orest. *Statisticheskoe opisanie zakavkazskogo kraia s prisovokupleniem statii: politicheskoe sostoianie zakavkazskogo kraia v ishode XVII v i sravnenie onogo s nyneshnim.* St. Petersburg, 1835.

Bulgarin, F. *Rossiia v istoricheskom, statisticheskom, geograficheskom, i literatur-nom otnosheniiakh.* 2 vols. St. Petersburg, 1837.

Banki i drugie kreditnye ustanovleniia v Rossii i v innostrannykh zemliakh. St. Petersburg, 1840.

Obozrenie glavnykh vodianykh soobshchenii v Rossii. St. Petersburg, 1841.

Fuks, F. *Kazanskie tatary v statisticheskom i etnograficheskom otnosheniiakh.* 1844.

Obozrenie glavnykh otraslei manufakturnoi promyshlennosti v Rossii. St. Peters-burg, 1845.

Levshin, A. I. *Description des hordes et des steppes des Kirghiz-Kazaks ou Kirghiz-Kaissaks.*

Zhuravskii, D. P. *Ob istochnikakh i upotreblenii statisticheskikh svedenii.* 1846.

Veselovskii, K. L. *Opyty nravstvennoi statistiki Rossii.* St. Petersburg, 1847.

Arseniev, K. I. *Statisticheskie ocherki Rossii.* St. Petersburg, 1848.

1855–1914

Materialy dlia statistiki Rossii sobrannye po vedomstvu ministerstva gosudarstven-nyh imushchestv. St. Petersburg, 1858.

Materialy dlia geografi i statistiki Rossii sobrannye ofitserami general'nogo shtaba. Vols. 1–29. St. Petersburg, 1860.

Geograficheskii Slovar' Rossiiskoi imperii. St. Petersburg, 1863.

Aperçu statistique des forces productives de la Russie. Paris, 1867.

Voenno-statisticheskii sbornik. St. Petersburg, 1871.

Voennyi statisticheskii sbornik Rossii. Atlas. Prilozheniie *k* IV Vypusku. St. Petersburg, 1871.

Livron, V. de. *Statisticheskoe obozrenie Rossiiskoi imperii.* St. Petersburg, 1874.

Vseobshchaia statistika Rossiiskogo gosudarstva. Moscow, 1880.

Sbornik svedenii po Evropeiskoi Rossii za 1882 g. St. Petersburg, 1884.

Sbornik svedenii po Rossii za 1883 g. St. Petersburg: CSC, 1886.

Sbornik svedenii po Rossii za 1884–85 gg. St. Petersburg, 1887.

Ukazatel' izmenenii i raspredelenii administrativnyh edinits i granits imperii s 1860 po 1887 g. St. Petersburg: CSC, 1887.

Supplément á l'annuaire statistique de la Russie, 1884–85. St. Petersburg: CSC, 1888.

Sbornik svedenii po Rossii za 1890 g. St. Petersburg: CSC, 1890.

Relevé général des tableaux de l'annuaire statistique de la Russie, 1896. St. Petersburg: CSC, 1897.

Sbornik svedenii po Rossii za 1896 g. St. Petersburg: CSC, 1897.

Ezegodnik Rossii. St. Petersburg: CSC, 1904–16.

Semenov Tian-Shanskii, Veniamin. *Gorod i derevnia v Evropeiskoi Rossii.* St. Petersburg, 1910.

Statisticheskii ezhegodnik na . . . god. Edited by V. I. Sharyii. St. Petersburg, 1913–14.

Aziatskaia Rossiia. St. Petersburg: GUZIZ, 1914.

POPULATION CENSUSES

Pervaia vseobshchaia perepis' naseleniia Rossiiskoi imperii, 1897. Edited by N. A. Troinitskii. Vol. 120. St. Petersburg: CSC, 1899–1905.

Pervaia vseobshchaia perepis' naseleniia Rossiiskoi imperii, 1897. Raspredeknie naselennyh mest Rossiiskoi imperii po chislennosti v nih naseleniia. St. Petersburg: CSC, 1902.

Pervaia vseobshchaia perepis' naseleniia Rossiiskoi imperii, 1897. Obshchii svod po imperii resultatov razrabotki dannyh pervoi vseobshchei perepisi naseleniia, 28/1/1897. St. Petersburg: CSC, 1905.

Dvizhenie naseleniia v Evropeiskoi Rossii za 1867 g. [–1902 g.], 24 vols. St. Petersburg: MVD, CSC, 1872–1909.

Giliarovskii, F. V. *Issledovanie o tozhdenii i smertnosti detei v novgorodskoi gubernii.* St. Petersburg, 1866.

Prostranstvo i naselenie Evropeiskoi Rossii. St. Petersburg: MVD, CSC, 1871.

Nalichnoe naselenie Rossiiskoi imperii za 1870 g. Edited by L. Karashunskii. St. Petersburg, 1875.

Statisticheskie svedeniia o nasil'stvennyh smertiakh v 1870–1874 gg. St. Petersburg: MVD, CSC, 1882.

Evropeiskoe naselenie i zemlevladenie v iugozapadnyh guberniiakh Evropeiskoi Rossii. Edited by V. Alenitzyn. St. Petersburg: MVD, CSC, 1884.

Nombre d'enfants, 1867–1881. St. Petersburg, 1889.

Statisticheskie dannye o razvodah i nedeistvitel'nyh brakakh za 1867–1886. Edited by P. Bechanov. St. Petersburg, 1893.

Umershie nasil'stvenno i vnezapno v Rossiiskoi imperii v 1875–1887 g. St. Petersburg, 1894.

Umershie nasil'stvenno i vnezapno v Rossiiskoi imperii v 1888–1893 g. St. Petersburg, 1897.

Svod statisticheskih materialov kasaiushchikhsia ekonomicheskogo polozheniia sel'skogo naseleniia Evropeiskoi Rossii. St. Petersburg, 1894.

Statisticheskie dannye po pereselencheskomu delu v Sibiri za 1897 g. St. Petersburg.

Glavneishie dannye po statistike naseleniia krainego vostoka Sibiri, Primorskoi i Amurskoi oblasti i ostrova Sakhalin. Edited by S. Patkanov. St. Petersburg, 1903.

Goroda v Rossii v 1904 g. St. Petersburg: CSC, 1906.

Goroda v Rossii v 1910 g. St. Petersburg: CSC, 1912.

Patkanov, S. K. *Statisticheskie dannye pokazyvaiushchie sostav naseleniia Sibiri.* St. Petersburg, 1911–12.

Novosel'skii, S. A. *Smertnost' i prodolzhitel'nost zhizni v Rossii.* Petrograd, 1916.

Novosel'skii, S. A., and Paevskii, V. V. *Smertnost' i prodolzhitel'nost zhizni naseleniia SSSR.* Moscow, 1930.

Rashin, A. G. *Naselenie Rossii za 100 let.* Moscow, 1959.

Statisticheskii obzor o sosoianii narodnogo zdravia i organizatsii meditsinskoi pomoshchi v Rossii. Edited by S. A. Novosel'skii. St. Petersburg, 1903–14, annually.

AGRICULTURE

Svedeniia o poseve i sbore khlebov i kartofelia v 1870–1872 g. i chislennosti skota v 1870 g. v Evropeiskoi Rossii. Edited by G. Ershov. St. Petersburg, 1875.

Materialy po statistike khlebnoi proizvoditel'nosti v Evropeiskoi Rossii, 1870–1874. St. Petersburg, 1880.

Urozhai v Evropeiskoi Rossii. 1883–85, annually. St. Petersburg: CSC, 1884–86.

Zverinskii, V. *Urozhai v Evropeiskoi Rossii. Obshchie Vyvody.* St. Petersburg: CSC, 1884.

Srednii urozhai v Evropeiskoi Rossii za 1883–1887 gg. St. Petersburg: CSC, 1888.

Glavnye resultaty urozhaia . . . 1889–92, annually. St. Petersburg, 1890–93.

Urozhai khlebov v pudakh s desiatiny po pokazaniiam krestian starozhilov. St. Petersburg, 1893.

Srednii sbor khlebov i kartofelia za desiatiletie 1883–1892 v 60 guberniiakh Evropeiskoi Rossii. St. Petersburg, 1894.

Posevnye ploshchadi po 50 gub. Evropeiskoi Rossii, 1881–1887 i 1893–1899. St. Petersburg, 1901.

Srednii posev i srednii sbor zernovykh khlebov i kartofelia za piatiletie 1896–1900. St. Petersburg, 1902.

Urozhai v . . . godu. 1901–07, annually, excluding 1906. St. Petersburg, 1902–06, 1908.

Urozhai . . . v Evropeiskoi i Aziatskoi Rossii. 1909–12, annually. St. Petersburg, 1910–13.

Sel'skokhoziaistvennye i statisticheskie svedniia po materialam poluchennym ot khoziaev. Vols. 1–11. Ministerstvo zemledeliia, 1884–1903.

. . . god v Sel'skokhoziaistvennom otnoshenii po otvetam, poluchennym ot khoziaev. St. Petersburg, 1894–1916.

Predvaritel'nye dannye o sbore, posevakh i ostatke khlebov v . . . g. St. Petersburg: CSC, 1902–10.

Résultats généraux de la récolte de 1895 céréales d'hiver et d'été comparée aux récoltes de 1890–1894. St. Petersburg: MVD, CSC, 1896.

Résultats généraux de la récolte de 1896 céréales d'hiver et d'été comparée aux récoltes de 1891–1895. St. Petersburg: MVD, CSC, 1897.

Résultats généraux de la récolte de 1897 céréales d'hiver et d'été comparée aux récoltes de 1892–1896. St. Petersburg: MVD, CSC, 1898.

Résultats généraux de la récolte de 1898 céréales d'hiver et d'été comparée aux récoltes de 1893–1896. St. Petersburg: MVD, CSC, 1899.

Résultats généraux de la récolte en Russie—années 1895–1907. 1899–1907, annually. St. Petersburg: MVD, CSC, 1900–1908.

Svod statisticheskikh svedenii po sel'skomu khoziaistvu Rossii k kontsu XIX veka. Vols. 1–2. St. Petersburg, 1902–03.

Sbornik statistichesko-ekonomicheskikh svedenii po sel'skomu khoziaistvu Rossii i inostrannykh gosudarstv. vols. 1–10. Glavnoe upravlenie zemledeliia i zemleustroistva. St. Petersburg, 1906–16.

Chuprov, A. I. *Vliianie urozhaev i khlebnykh tsen na taznye dtorony ekonomicheskoi zhizni.* St. Petersburg, 1897.

Ivanstov, D. N. *K Kritike Russkoi urozhainoi statistiki. Zapiski IRGO po otd. statistiki XIV.* St. Petersburg, 1915.

Ezhegodnik glavnogo upravlenii zemleustroistva i zemledelii. St. Petersburg: GUZIZ, 1907–15.

Itogi ekonomicheskogo issledovaniia Rossii po dannym zemskoi statistiki. Vol. 1. *Obshchii obzor zemskoi statistiki krest'ianskogo khoziaistva.* Edited by A. Fortunatov. Vol. 2. *Krest'ianskie vnenadel'nye arendy.* Edited by N. Karyshev. Moscow, 1892.

Spravochnye svedeniia o deiatel'nosti zemstv po sel'skomu khoziaistvu po dannym na . . . g. 1897–1913. St. Petersburg, 1899–1915.

Veselovskii, B. B. i Frenkel' *Iubileinyi zemskii sbornik, 1864–1914.* St. Petersburg, 1914.

Sbornik materialov dlia izucheniia sel'skoi Pozemel'noi obshchiny. St. Petersburg, 1880.

Pozemel'naia sobstvennost' v Evropeiskoi Rossii v 1877 i 1878 gg. Edited by G. Ershov. St. Petersburg: MVD, CSC, 1886.

Raspredelenie zemel' po ugodiiam i pakhotnykh po raznogo roda posevam v Evropeiskoi Rossii. Edited by P. Struve. St. Petersburg: MVD, CSC, 1884.

Svedeniia o zemlevladenii v privislanskikh guberniiah. Edited by I. I. Kaufman. St. Petersburg: MVD, CSC, 1886.

Glavneiskhie dannye pozemel'noi statistiki po obsledovaniiu 1886 g. (po Guberniiam). Nos. 1–47. St. Petersburg, 1893–1901.

Materialy po statistike dvizheniia zemlevladeniia v Rossii. Vols. 1–24. St. Petersburg: MF, 1896–1915.

Statistika zemlevladeniia v 1905 g. svod dannykh po 50 guberniiam Ev. Rossii. St. Petersburg: CSC, 1907.

Blagoveshchenskii, N. A. *Svodnyi statisticheskii sbornik khoziaistvennykh svedenii po zemskim podvornym perepisiam.* Vol. 1. Moscow, 1893.

Svavitskii, Z. M. *Zemskie povdvornye perepisi 1880–1913. Pouiezdnye itogi.* Moscow: CSU, 1926.

Ovtsevodstvo v Rossii. Edited by S. P. Shepnin. St. Petersburg, 1869.

Issledovanie sovremennogo sostoianiia ovtsevodstva v Rossii. Vols. 1–4, 5–7. 1882–86.

Voenno-konskaia perepis' za . . . 1891–1914. St. Petersburg, 1894–1915.

Opyt rascheta stoimosti pshenitsy, rzhi, ovsa i iachmenia v proizvodstve. St. Petersburg, 1889.

Materialy po voprosu stoimosti obrabotki zemli v Evropeiskoi Rossii. St. Petersburg, 1889.

Stoimost' proizvodstva glavnykh khlebov. Statisticheskie svedeniia po materialam poluchennym ot khoziaev. Petrograd, 1915.

Tseny na zemliu v Evropeiskoi Rossii po prodazham sdelannym v 1882 i 1887 gg. St. Petersburg, 1889.

Tseny na pshenitsu, rozh, oves i iachmen' v Evropeiskoi Rossii v 1881–1887 g. po mestnym svedeniiam. St. Petersburg, 1889.

Tseny na proviant i furazh po svedeniiam intendantskogo vedomstva. St. Petersburg, 1889.

Svod tovarnykh tsen na glavnykh Russkikh i inostrannykh rynkakh za . . . g. materialy dlia togovo-promyshlennoi. Statistiki, 1890–1914. vol. 1, 1890–95; vol. 2, 1890–96; annual 1897–1914. St. Petersburg, 1891–1915.

Sel'sko-khoziaistvennye mashiny i orudiia v Evropeiskoi i Aziatskoi Rossii v 1910 g. St. Petersburg, 1913.

Predvaritel'nye dannye vserossiiskoi sel'skokhoziaistvennoi perepisi 1916 g. osoboye soveshchanie dlia obsuzhdeniia i ob''iedineniia meropriiatii po prodovol'stvennomu delu. Petrograd, 1916.

Schcherbina, F. A. *Krestianskie biudzhety.* Voronezh, 1900.

INDUSTRY

Obzor razlichnykh otraslei manufakturnoi promyshlennosti Rossii. vols. 1–2. St. Petersburg, 1862, 1863.

Materialy dlia statistiki zavodskoi fabrichnoi promyshlennosti v Evropeiskoi Rossii za 1868 g. Edited by I. Bok. St. Petersburg: MVD, CSC, 1872.

Skalkovskii, K. A. *Tableaux statistiques de l'industrie des mines en Russie en 1868–1876.* St. Petersburg, 1878.

————. *Tableaux statistiques de l'industrie des mines en Russie en 1871*. St. Petersburg, 1873.

Orlov, P. A. *Ukazatel' fabrik i zavodov Evropeiskoi Rossii s tsarstvom Pol'skim i vel. kn. Finlandskim (1879)*. St. Petersburg, 1887.

Ukazatel' fabrik i zavodov Evropeiskoi Rossii i tsarstva Pol'skogo (1884). St. Petersburg, 1887.

————.*Ukazatel' fabrik i zavodov Evropeiskoi Rossii*. Edited by P. A. Orlov and I. G. Budagov. 3d ed. St. Petersburg, 1894.

Timiriazev, D. A. *Istoriko-statisticheskii obzor promyshlennosti Rossii*. Vols. 1–2. St. Petersburg, 1883, 1886.

The Industries of Russia. Vols. 1–4. Prepared for the 1893 World's Columbian Exposition at Chicago. St. Petersburg: MF, 1893.

Gornozavodskaia promyshlennost' Rossii. St. Petersburg, 1893.

Fabrichno-zavodskaia promyshlennost' i torgovlia Rossii. St. Petersburg: MF, 1893; 2d ed. 1896.

Russia, Its Industries and Trade. Glasgow: MF, 1901.

Svod dannykh fabrichno-zavodskoi promyshlennosti v Rossii za 1897 g. St. Petersburg, 1900.

Torgovlia i promyshlennost' Evropeiskoi Rossii po raionam. Vols. 1–13. St. Petersburg: MTP, 1902–11.

Nisselovich, L. N. *Istoria zavodsko-fabrichnogo zakonodatel'stva Rossiiskoi imperii*. Vols. 1–2. St. Petersburg, 1883.

Pazhitnov, K. A. *Ocherki istorii tekstil'noi promyshlennosti dorevolutsionnoi Rossii*. 2 vols. Moscow, 1955, 1958.

Fokin, L. F. *Obzor khimicheskoi promyshlennosti v Rossii*. vols. 1–2. Petrograd, 1920.

Lukianov, P. M. *Istoriia khimicheskikh promyslov i khimicheskoi promyshlennosti Rossii*. Vols. 1–5. Moscow, 1954–61.

Strumilin, S. G. *Istoriia chernoi metallurgii SSSR*. Moscow, 1954; 2d ed. 1967.

Sbornik statisticheskikh svedenii o gornozavodskoi promyshlennosti Rossii v . . . zavodskom godu. Gornyi uchenyi komitet 1859–1911. St. Petersburg, 1861–1913.

Varzar, V. E. *Statisticheskie svedeniia po obrabatyvaiushchei fabrichnozavodskoi promyshlennosti Rossiiskoi imperii za 1900 g*. St. Petersburg: MTP, 1902.

Statistika neschastnykh sluchaev s rabochimi v promyshlennykh zavedeniiakh za . . . god. St. Petersburg: MTP, 1912–14.

Svod otchetov fabrichnikh inspektorov za . . . god 1900–1914. St. Petersburg: MTP, 1902–15.

Varzar, V. E. *Statisticheskie svedeniia o stachkakh rabochikh na fabrikakh i zavodakh za desiatiletie 1895–1904*. St. Petersburg, 1905.

————. *Statistika stachek rabochikh na fabrikakh i zavodakh za 1905*. St. Petersburg: MTP, 1908.

Dannye o prodolzhitel'nosti rabochego vremeni za . . . god. St. Petersburg: MTP, 1904–05.

Materialy dlia izucheniia kustarnoi promyshlennosti i ruchnogo truda v Rossii. St. Petersburg: MVD, CSC, 1872.

Sbornik materialov ob arteliakh v Rossii. St. Petersburg, 1874.

Otchet gornogo departmenta za . . . god. 1891–1911 annually. St. Petersburg: MTP, 1892–1913.

Statisticheskie tablitsy po obrabatyvaiushchei fabrichnozavodskoi, dobyvaiushchei gornoi i gornozavodskoi promyshlennosti Rossii 1892–1900. St. Petersburg: MF, 1901.

Materialy dlia statistiki khlopchatobumazhnogo proizvodstva v Rossii. St. Petersburg: MF, 1901.

Statistika bumagopriadil'nogo i tkatskogo proizvodstva za 1900–1910 gg. St. Petersburg: MTP, 1911.

TRANSPORTATION AND COMMUNICATION

Statisticheskii sbornik ministerstva putei soobshcheniia. Vols. 1–144. St. Petersburg: MPS, 1877–1917.

Materialy dlia statistiki rechnogo sudokhodstva v Evropeiskoi Rossii. Edited by V. Zverinskii. St. Petersburg: MVD, CSC, 1872.

Materialy po razrabotke tarifov Rossiiskikh zheleznykh dorog. St. Petersburg: MF, 1889.

Statisticheskii obzor zheleznykh dorog i vnutrennikh vodnykh putei. St. Petersburg, 1893.

Statistika sluzhashchikh na zheleznykh dorogakh, uchastnikov pensionnykh i sberegatel'no-vspomogatel'nykh kass. Vols. 1–4. St. Petersburg, 1896, 1906–08.

Russkoe tekhnicheskoe obshchestvo: Aperçu des chemins de fer Russes depuits l'origine jusqu'ee 1892. Vols. 1–3. Brussels: P. Weissenbruch, 1897.

Aperçu statistique des chemins de fer et des voies navigables de la Russie. Section de la statistique et de la cartographie. St. Petersburg: MPS, 1900.

Volga. Voies navigables du bassin du Volga . . . Moscow: MPS, 1908.

Rossiia v dorozhnom otnoshenii. Edited by V. F. Meien. Vols. 1–3. St. Petersburg: MVD, 1902.

Obshchii obzor pochtovoi deiatel'nosti v imperii za 10 let, 1857–1866. St. Petersburg: MVD, CSC, 1868.

Obshchii obzor telegrafnoi deiatel'nosti, 1860–1866. St. Petersburg: MVD, CSC, 1868.

Pochtovaia statistika, 1875–1914. St. Petersburg: MVD, 1876–1915.

TRADE

Obzor vneshnei torgovli Rossii po Evropeiskoi i Aziatskoi granitsam za . . . g. St. Petersburg: MF, Departament Tamozhennykh Sborov, 1860–1915.

Svedeniia o vneshnei torgovle po Evropeiskoi granitse za . . . mesiats . . . g. 1884–1917, monthly. St. Petersburg: MF, Departament Tamozhennykh Sborov, 1884–1917.

Vneshniaia torgovlia Rossii, predvaritel'nye svedeniia. St. Petersburg: MF, Departament Tamozhennykh Sborov, 1893, 1897.

Kratkie svedeniia o vneshnei torgovle Rossii za . . . g. St. Petersburg: MF, Departament Tamozhennykh Sborov, 1895, 1896.

Tableaux statistiques du commerce extérieur de la Russie. Edited by V. I. Pokrovskii. St. Petersburg, 1896.

Sbornik svedenii po istorii i statistike vneshnei torgovli Rossii. Edited by V. I. Pokrovskii. St. Petersburg: MF, Departament Tamozhennykh Soborov, 1902.

Svod statisticheskikh dannykh o privoze tovarov . . . za 1898–1908 gody. Edited by V. I. Pokrovskii. St. Petersburg: MTP, 1909.

Statisticheskie svedeniia o torgovle Rossii s kitaem. St. Petersburg: MF, 1909.

Vyvoz Rossiiskikh tovarov zagranitsei: svod dannykh Russkoi statistiki vneshnei torgovli za 1900–1911 gg. Materialy k peresmotru torgovogo dogovora s germaniei. St. Petersburg: MF, Departament Tamozhennykh Sborov, 1913.

Eksport zagranitsu produktov gornoi i gornozavodskoi promyshlennosti iuga Rossii. Edited by N. F. von Ditmar. Vols. 1–5. Kharkov, 1911–13.

Vyvoz i privoz glaveneishikh tovarov po vneshnei torgovle Rossii . . . svod dannykh Russkoi statistiki za 1908–1912 g. St. Petersburg: MF, Departament Tamozhennykh Sborov, 1914.

Statistika privoza inostrannykh tovarov . . . v Rossii za 1910–1912 gg. Petrograd, 1916.

Trudy ekspeditsii, snariazhennoi IVEO i IRGO, dlia issledovaniia khlebnoi torgovli i proizvoditel'nosti Rossii. Vols. 1–4. St. Petersburg, 1870–74.

Lodyzhenskii, K. N. *Istoriia Russkogo tamozhennogo tarifa.* St. Petersburg, 1886.

Sobolev, M. N. *Tamozhennaia politika Rossii vo vtoroi polovine XIX veka.* Tomsk, 1911.

Dikhtiar, G. A. *Vnutrenniaia torgovlia v dorevolutsionnoi Rossii.* Moscow, 1960.

MONEY AND BANKING

Gosudarstvennyi Bank. *Gosudarstvennyi Bank. Otchet za . . . god. 1860–1916.* vols. 1–57. St. Petersburg, 1861–1917.

Gosudarstvennye sberegatel'nye kassy. *Otchety gosudarstvennykh sberegatel'-nykh kass po sberegatel'noi operatsii za . . . god, 1907–1915.* St. Petersburg, 1908–16.

Kaufman, I. I. *Statistika Russkikh bankov.* Vols. 1–2. St. Petersburg: CSC, MVD, 1872, 1875.

―――. *Statistika gorodskikh sberegatel'nykh kass.* St. Petersburg: CSC, MVD, 1875.

Reforma donezhnogo obrashcheniia v Rossii. St. Petersburg: IVEO, 1896.

Russkie banki. Spravochnye i statisticheskie svedeniia o vsekh deistvuiushchikh v Rossii gosudarstvennykh, chastnykh i obshchestvennykh kreditnykh uchrezhdeniiakh. Edited by A. K. Golubev. Vols. 1–4. 1896, 1897, 1899, 1908.

Kovanko, A. *Les caisses d'épargne en Russie, 1841–1902.* St. Petersburg: CSC, 1903.

Statistika dolgosrochnogo kredita v Rossii. Edited by A. K. Golubev. St. Petersburg, 1903–12, annually.

Migulin, P. *Nasha bankovaia politika.* Khar'kov, 1904.

Ministerstvo Finansov, *Russkii denezhnyi rynok, 1908–1912.* St. Petersburg: MF, 1908–12.

Katsenellenbaum, S. S. *Kommercheskie banki i ikh torgovo-kommissionnye operatsii.* Moscow, 1912.

Borovoi, S. I. *Kredit i banki v Rossii.* Moscow, 1958.

Gindin, I. F. *Russkie kommercheskie banki.* Moscow, 1948.

———. *Gosudarstvennyi banki ekonomicheskaia politika tsarskogo pravitel'stva.* Moscow, 1960.

GOVERNMENT FINANCE

Ziablovskii-Desiatovskii, A. *Obozrenie gosudarstvennykh dokhodov Rossii.* St. Petersburg, 1868.

Gosudarstvennye dokhody Rossii, ikh klassifikatsiia, nyneshnee sostoianie i dvizhenie 1866–1872. Edited by V. P. Bezobrazov. St. Petersburg: MVD, CSC, 1872.

Kaufman, I. I. *Statistika gosudarstvennykh finansov Rossii v 1862–1884 gg.* St. Petersburg: MVD, CSC, 1886.

Ponizhenie vykupnogo platezha po ukazu 28/12/1881 g. Edited by G. Ershov. St. Petersburg: MVD, CSC, 1885.

Svod dannykh o postuplenii okladnykh sborov po imperii za . . . 1888–1893. Vols. 1–2. St. Petersburg: MF, 1891, 1894.

Svod danykh o postuplenii kazennykh okladnykh sborov po imperii za . . . g. St. Petersburg: MF, 1894–1913.

Postuplenie okladnykh sborov v kaznu s sel'skikh soslovii za 1888–1892. St. Petersburg: MF, 1894.

Svod dannykh o postuplenii kazennykh i zemskikh okladnykh sborov a takzhe otsenochnogo sbora s gorodskikh nedvizhimykh imushchestv va 1888–1892. St. Petersburg, 1895.

Svod svedenii o rezul'tatakh i oborotakh po kazennoi vinnoi operatsii za 1897–1901 gg. St. Petersburg: MF, 1902.

Proekt gosudarstvennoi rospisi dokhodov i raskhodov s obiasnitel'noi zapiskoi ministra finansov. St. Petersburg: MF, 1901–16, annually.

Gosudarstvennye raskhody po glavnym predmetam naznacheniia v 1907–1912 gg. St. Petersburg: MF, 1914.

Statistika dokhodov i raskhodov gorodov Evropeiskoi Rossii s privislanskimi guberniiami s 1870 po 1884 g. St. Petersburg: MVD, CSC, 1887.

Mirskie raskhody i dokhody za 1891 g. v 50 guberniiakh Evropeiskoi Rossii. St. Petersburg, 1895.

Mirskie dokhody i raskhody za 1892–1894 gg. v 50 guberniiakh Evropeiskoi Rossii. St. Petersburg, 1897.

Gminnye dokhody i raskhody za 1892–1894 g. v 10 privislanskikh guberniiakh. St. Petersburg, 1898.

Mirskie dokhody i raskhody 1894 g. v 50 guberniiakh Evropeiskoi Rossii. St. Petersburg, 1909.

Raskhody zemstv 34 gubernii po smetam na 1895 g. St. Petersburg: MF, 1896.

Dokhody zemstv 34 gubernii po smetam na 1896 g. St. Petersburg: MF, 1897.

O Zadolzhennosti zemlevladeniia v sviazi s statisticheskimi dannymi . . . St. Petersburg: CSC, 1888.

Ministerstvo Finansov. *Ministerstvo Finansov, 1802–1902,* St. Petersburg. 1902.

————. *Ministerstvo Finansov.* 1904–1913. St. Petersburg, 1914.

————. *Proekt gosudarstvennoi rospisi dokhodov i raskhodov na* . . . *god.* St. Petersburg, 1862–1916, annually.

————. *Sbornik svedenii i materialov po vedomstvu Ministerstva Finansov.* 1865–68.

————. *Ezhegodnik Ministerstva Finansov.* 1869–1916, annually.

Gosudarstvennaia Kontrol'. *Otchet gosudarstvennogo kontrola po ispolneniiu gosudarstvennoi rospisi i finansovykh smet, 1866–1914.* St. Petersburg, 1867–1915.

Ministerstvo Finansov. *Kassovyi otchet Ministra Finansov 1870–1914.* St. Petersburg, 1870–1914.

Bliokh, I. C. *Finansy Rossii XIX stoletiia.* Vols. 1–4. St. Petersburg, 1882.

Pecherin, Ya. I. *Istoricheskii obzor rospisei gosudarstvennykh dokhodov i raskhodov.* St. Petersburg, 1896, 1898.

Migulin, P. P. *Russkii gosudarstvennyi kredit, 1769–1899.* Vols. 1–3. Khar'kov, 1899–1902.

Petit, P. *La dette publique de la Russie.* Poitiers, 1912.

EDUCATION

Svedeniia po statistike narodnogo obrazovaniia v Evropeiskoi Rossii, 1872–1874. Edited by A. Dubrovskii. St. Petersburg: MVD, CSC, 1872.

Ob''iasnitel'nyi tekst k karte narodnogo obrazovaniia v Rossii 1876 g. St. Petersburg: MNP, 1880.

Statisticheskie svedeniia o sel'skikh uchilishchakh v Evropeiskoi Rossii i privislanskikh guberniiakh . . . *obsledovanie 20/3/1880 g.* Edited by A. Dubrovskii. St. Petersburg: MVD, CSC, 1884.

Universitety i srednie uchebnye zavedeniia v 50ti gub. Evropeiskoi Rossii i 10ti privislanskikh po perepisi 20/3/1880. Edited by A. Dubrovskii. St. Petersburg, 1888.

Spetsial'nye uchebnye zavedeniia muzhskie i zhenskie v 50ti guberniiakh Evropeiskoi Rossii 10ti privislenskikh gub. po perepisi 20/3/1880 g. St. Petersburg, 1890.

Fal'bork i Charnolusskii. *Nachal'noe narodnoe obrazovanie v Rossii po obsledovaniiu IVEO. Ianvar' 1895.* Vols. 1–4. St. Petersburg: IVEO, 1900–1905.

Statisticheskie svedeniia po nachal'nomu obrazovaniiu v Rossiskoi imperii, St. Petersburg: MNP, 1902.

Pokrovskii, V. I. *Odnodnevnaia perepis' nachal'nykh shkol Rossiiskoi imperii, 1911.* St. Petersburg, 1913.

MISCELLANEOUS

Statisticheskie svedeniia o pozharakh v Rossii v 1870–1874 gg. Edited by V. V. Zverinskii. St. Petersburg, 1882.

Pozhary v Rossii, 1875–1882. St. Petersburg: MVD, CSC, 1887.

Pozhary v Rossiiskoi imperii v 1883–1887 gg. i svod za 28 let 1860–1887. St. Petersburg: MVD, CSC, 1889.

Statistika pozharov v Rossiiskoi imperii za 1895–1910 gg. Vol. 1, *63 gub. Evropeiskoi Rossii.* Vol. 2, *Gubernii i oblasti Aziatskoi Rossii.* St. Petersburg, 1912.

Vzaimnoe strakhovanie ot ognia, gubernskoe, zemskoe i gorodskoe, 1889–1892. St. Petersburg, 1893.

Obshchaia stalistika aktsionernykh strakhovykh (ot ognia) obshchestv. izdanie 1906 goda. Vols. 1–2: 1900–1904. St. Petersburg, 1906. *Izdanie 1911 goda.* Vols. 1–2: 1900–1909. St. Petersburg, 1911.

Aktsionernye strakhovye obshchestva (tarifnyi otdel): aktsionernoe strakhovanie ot ognia v Rossii, 1827–1910 gg. St. Petersburg, 1912.

Notes

CHAPTER ONE

1. For January 1914 the estimates of the Russian demographer Zaitsev were accepted instead of the exaggerated figures of the Central Statistical Office that overestimated the growth of Russia's population for the years following the Census of 1897.

2. Except for the famine of 1891 and the cholera epidemics in 1891–92, the impact of such factors was much lessened in comparison with earlier periods in Russian history.

3. The concept of a city in Russia was historically that of an administrative center; it was not related to the size of particular settlements. Thus, we find in Russia many so-called industrial settlements or "villages" with populations in the tens of thousands, on the one hand, and "cities" with populations of less than one thousand, on the other.

4. See S. G. Strumilin, *Promyshlennyi perevorot v Rossii,* (Moscow, 1944), p. 19.

5. P. A. Khromov, *Ocherki ekonomiki tekstil' noi promyshlennosti SSSR,* (Moscow, 1946), p. 49.

6. From June 1884 to May 1887 the tariff rate for imported pig iron was increased in four consecutive steps from 6 kopeks to 25–30 kopeks per pood. S. G. Strumilin, *Istoriia chernoi metallurgii,* 2d ed. (Moscow, 1967), p. 356.

7. The introduction of new technology beginning with the puddling, Bessemer, and Martin processes indicates a gradual shortening of the technical gap between Russia and the West.

8. The data on which the study of the capital in industry is based exhibit a downward bias since they do not include a large part of the value of mines and perhaps also somewhat understate the value of equipment.

9. The size and economic strength of the rural supply cooperative associations that controlled much of the Siberian butter and dairy exports and purchases from suppliers were much larger than that of the consumer cooperatives mentioned here.

10. M. N. Sobolev, *The Tariff Policy of Russia in the Second Half of the Nineteenth Century,* (Tomsk, 1911).

11. These were loans that could be recalled on only seven days notice.

12. See Albert L. Vainshtein, *Oblozhenie i platezhi krest'ianstva v dovoennoe i revolutsionnoe vremia,* (Moscow, 1924).

13. Ibid., table 3, p. 52.

14. The exceptional years are 1861, 1889, 1894, 1903, 1910, 1911, and 1913.

15. A test of this kind has to include the exploration of alternatives available during that period.

16. In the remainder of this chapter all references to Poland will refer to Congress Poland.

17. Wladyslaw Grabski, *Rocznik Statystyczny Krolestwa Polskiego, Rok 1913*, (Warsaw, 1914).

18. If we accept the estimated remittances of Polish seasonal labor in German agriculture for 1904, we would account for a total of 9.4 million rubles in 1904, and 16.4 million rubles in 1908, or 61.4 rubles per seasonal migrant. Ibid., pp. 75, 77, and 81.

19. The changes in the area planted in grains reflect population pressure, exemplified by the growth of the area in rye and oats, and the fluctuations of the market demand for such commercial grains as wheat and barley.

20. See Grabski, pp. 129–30.

21. The source is an article by Zenon Pietkiewicz, "Stan Prezemyslu w Krolestwie Polskiem Wedng danych z r. 1910," in *Przemysl i Handel Krolestwa Polskiego*, vol. 8, 1912. Quoted in Grabski, pp. 151–52.

22. See table 1.53 for the exports of textiles and metal products from Congress Poland to Russia.

CHAPTER TWO

1. The most important economic issue in Russia, the agrarian problem, is omitted from the discussion here for two reasons: first, because its complexity does not permit a short summary; second, everyone interested in this subject will find an admirable analysis in Professor Alexander Gerschenkron's essay in the *Cambridge Economic History of Europe*, vol. 6, H. J. Habakkuk and M. Postan, eds. (Cambridge: Cambridge University Press, 1965).

2. The changes over time in the general trend and some of the year-to-year variations are represented in the following tabulation:

Per Capita Taxes Paid into the State Budget (in Rubles)

Year	Per Capita Taxes	Year	Per Capita Taxes
1881	6.05	1894	7.93
1885	6.41	1895	8.15
1886	6.44	1896	7.95
1887	6.74	1897	8.18
1888	6.99	1898	8.40
1889	7.09	1899	8.87
1890	7.12	1900	8.83
1891	6.53	1905	9.53
1892	6.99	1910	11.79
1893	7.44	1913	11.43

3. About 22 per cent of the national income was accounted for in 1909–10 by about 0.9 per cent of the economically active population, according to the computation of the Ministry of Finance. See Ministerstvo Finansov, *Materialy k proektu polozheniia o gosudarstvennom podokhodnom naloge. Podokhodnyi nalog*, vol. 2 (St. Petersburg, 1910).

4. Theodore H. Von Laue, *Sergei Witte and the Industrialization of Russia* (New York: Columbia University Press, 1963), pp. 100–101.

5. Ministerstvo finansov, *Ministerstvo finansov, 1904–1913* (St. Petersburg, 1914), p. 14.

6. For the last years of the 1890s the presence of foreign investment can clearly be detected, and this biased the results in favor of industrial investment. N. Brzheskii, *Gosudarstvennyi dolg Rossii* (The Public Debt of Russia) (St. Petersburg, 1908).

7. The third group represents, according to the definition used by Brzheskii, the reported

"capital of dividend paying firms" and the "share capital of industrial corporations"; this second component never rose during this period above 9.5 per cent of the total "capital stock" of this third group.

8. That the following estimates are usable approximations can perhaps be surmised from the data for the increase of the capital stock of Russian industry provided by S. G. Strumilin in *Problema promyshlennogo kapitala v SSSR* (The Problem of Industrial Capital in the USSR), (Moscow, 1925), pp. 22–23. Strumilin's estimate of the initial cost of land, buildings, and equipment for 1885–1900 is 1,953 million rubles while the estimate for the same years used below, supposedly exclusive of much foreign investment, is 1,510 million.

9. The fiscal motives for producing revenue were variously estimated as being responsible for from two-thirds to three-fifths of the total customs revenue.

10. In 1890, according to the calculations by the statistician V. E. Varzar for some of the large-scale manufacturing industries, the value of foreign machinery and equipment was 452.3 million rubles versus 270.1 million rubles worth of domestically produced machinery and equipment.

11. A good case could be made for using the arithmetic average of both foreign and domestic prices. The difference in some cases would be substantial. Since I was interested in the utilization of this type of analysis rather than in the precise determination of the costs, the simpler version was employed.

12. Quoted by M. N. Sobolev, *Tamozhennaia politika Rossii vo vtoroi polovine XIX Veka* (Tomsk, 1911), pp. 843–45.

13. Ibid., p. 845.

14. One ought not to exaggerate and attribute the net increase on both accounts solely to the monetary reform. It coincided with greater availability of capital in the international money market, on the one hand, and with the strengthening of the Franco-Russian political alliance, which opened up the Paris money market for Russian government and private securities, on the other. It was also due to the fact that relative to other countries, interest rates in Russia still remained high, and the return on Russian securities and on foreign investment in Russia was still higher than elsewhere.

15. There is a whole host of questions that one could ask pertaining to the regulation of the money supply, which was particularly strongly influenced by government policies, since the State Bank was for all practical purposes controlled by the Ministry of Finance both in the area of note issue and lending operations. Moreover, the government provided the major part of deposits in the State Bank after 1895, and the government's proportion in the total deposits was growing. Although the time is ripe for an analysis of the behavior of the money supply and its impact on cyclical fluctuations as well as on the secular trend of growth of the Russian economy, it will not be attempted here.

16. See V. A. Muskoseev, "Money and Credit," in A. Raffalovich, ed., *Russia: Its Trade and Commerce* (London: P. S. King and Son, 1918), p. 363.

17. The estimates of the gold reserves pertain to the holdings of the State Bank only and do not include the so-called "free cash reserves" (*svobodnaia nalichhost'*) of the Treasury. The data for this type of reserve are very sketchy. (See table on following page.)

**Gold Reserves Held Abroad by the Treasury
(in Millions of Rubles, as of Jan. 1)**

Year	Gold Reserve	Year	Gold Reserve	Year	Gold Reserve
1902	81	1906	47	1910	317.3
1903	138	1907	137	1911	411.6
1904	186	1908	63	1912	451.6
1905	204	1909	166.3	1913	408.0

See Olga Crisp, "Russia, 1860–1914," in Rondo Cameron, ed., *Banking in the Early Stages of Industrialization* (London: Oxford University Press, 1967), p. 231; and A. I. Bukovietskii, "Svobodnoia nalichnost' i zolotoi zapas pravitel'stva v kontse XIX-nachale XX vv.," in M. P. Viatkin, ed., *Monopolii i innostrannyi kapital v Rossii,* (Moscow-Leningrad, 1962), pp. 369–70.

18. (New York and London: Columbia University Press, 1963). Review published in *Slavic Review* 24 (1965): 325–7.

CHAPTER THREE

1. The measure used in the identification of such years is the difference between the yearly observed data for the output-seed ratios and the trend of the output-seed ratios. The raw data for the output-seed ratios were obtained from the report by V. G. Mikhailovskii, "Tezisy doklada V. G. Mikhailovskogo: Urozhai v Rossii, 1801–1914 gg." *Biulleten Tsentral'nogo statisticheskogo upravleniia* (Moscow), no. 50 (July 8, 1921): 2–4. The series adjusted for the long term trend due to technical progress in Russian agriculture was suggested by M. I. Semenov, "K voprosu o zakonomernosti kolebanii urozhaev," in *Vestnik statistiki* 11:63. Semenov's series of output-seed ratios has the form: $Y = 3.69787253 - 0.022223412X + 0.00034512206X^2$. Thus the deviations of the observed output-seed ratio from that interpolated by Semenov can be considered as the deviations from the trend of long term yield levels.

2. The prohibition of exports from the Russian ports, enacted whenever the Moscow price for rye would exceed one ruble per *chetvert'*, was based on the assumption of a stable domestic demand and on the presumption that since the foreign prices for Russian grain were higher than the domestic prices, foreign buyers were driving up the domestic price of grain. An embargo on grain exports would therefore lower the price and increase the quantity available for the consumption of the urban population and the military.

3. One should therefore not be surprised to find government activity in the area of grain supplies in Russia, when government activity under conditions of high risk or high probability of harvest deficiencies can be taken for granted for many periods in human history up to the nineteenth century. Each of the countries in Europe engaged in mercantilist-type policies had either actual or contingency governmental grain policies. In the nineteenth century, due to a number of coincidental economic and political factors, government interference in the area of grain supply became obsolete for most European countries and America. In other words, the agricultural colonization of the North American prairies, the South American pampas, and the Australian wheatlands made it possible to abandon traditional grain policies in the European countries and to rely on market forces for an adequate supply. That this development also coincided with the industrialization of Europe the development of a new economic order as well as new political ideas, was perhaps no accident.

4. During the whole eighteenth century, the grain exports of Russia constituted a smaller share of the commercial output than any of the other components.

5. On some awkward governmental lending operations, see page 122.

6. See N. A. Murzanov, "Khlebnye zapasnye magaziny pri Pavle I-m," in *Arkhiv istorii truda v Rossii,* vol. 3 (Petrograd, 1922), pp. 130–33.

7. See *Zhurnal Ministerstva vnutrennikh del,* no. 12 (1838); no. 6 (1839), and no. 9, (1840).

8. Pitirim Sorokin, *Hunger as a Factor in Human Affairs* (Gainesville: The University Presses of Florida, 1975).

9. The assistance of Eugene Vinogradoff and Leslie Dienes in the compilation of this catalog is very greatly appreciated. The research was carried out under the terms of a grant by the National Science Foundation.

10. It is very difficult, of course, to determine whether the sensitivity to death was the same over a period of centuries, and whether the deaths of a few made a similar impression as the deaths of many. We know very little about the levels of tolerance to human suffering over the ages, and therefore some of the descriptions chosen might strike one not only as imprecise, but also as not entirely convincing.

11. The increased frequency of natural calamities for this period, by comparison with the earlier ones, cannot be explained by superior record keeping alone. The increasing frequency of droughts indicates that other forces and causes were at work.

12. "New Lands" was the designation of the virgin and long fallow lands in Western Siberia, Kazakhstan and the Urals which were plowed up during Khrushchev's campaign to expand the grain area in 1954–56.

13. Thus, for the present decade the coincidence of a drought in Kazakhstan and in parts of the RSFSR will cause a substantial reduction of the grain supply, while a repetition of the drought in Kazakhstan accompanied during the second year by a drought in the Ukraine will create famine-like conditions.

14. *Tsentral'nyi statisticheskii komitet Ministerstva vnutrennikh del. Statistiki Rossiikoi imperii,* vol. 10 (St. Petersburg, 1890), p. 131.

15. For the remaining six years the reduction of grain exports can be explained by wars and other phenomena.

16. Out of twenty-seven years of increases in the volume of grain imports during the nineteenth century, eighteen can be clearly identified as years of low yields or famine. See *Pokrovskii sbornik svedenii,* tables on pp. 63, 121.

17. This was the result, no doubt, of a realistic appraisal of the situation rather than a peasant-favoring policy. When requisition of grain from landlords was officially prohibited by the decree of February 14, 1761, it was recommended (in the same decree) that they maintain a year's supply of food and seed in order to help their serfs in case of emergency.

18. Ministerstvo vnutrennikh del. Departament khoziaistvennyi, *Izlozenie dela po proektu sel'skogo prodovol'stvennogo ustava,* no. 72 (March 12, 1899): 31–33.

19. PSZ 1830, vol. 9, nos. 6569, 6570, 6653, 6682; vol. 13, nos. 9590, 9668, 9709; vol. 14, no. 10299.

20. Perhaps an exception was the introduction of potatoes in Russia by the government as a counter-famine measure, emphasizing the role of potatoes as a grain substitute. PSZ 1830, vol. 17, no. 12406.

21. In 1797 Tsar Paul decreed the accumulation of stocks, 20 poods of rye and 10 poods each of oats and buckwheat per desiatina of plowed land in the Imperial Villages. The stocks had to be replaced every two years. This decree was supplemented in 1799 by another requiring the maintenance of a stock of a yearly consumption size in rural areas. PSZ 1830, vol. 25, no. 19203.

22. The stimulus to organize public works as an anti-famine measure was first given by the drought in Voronez guberniia of 1774. A decree by Catherine II of February 14, 1776 (PSZ 1830, vol. 20, no. 14418), prescribed public works as an effective anti-famine measure. But it was not until 1834 that public works were actually instituted on the scale of the larger administrative units (the *guberniia*). After 1834, public works were set up in 1835–36, 1840, 1844, 1846, 1848, 1851, 1868, 1881, 1891–93, 1899, and 1901. For a detailed discussion on public works as an anti-famine measure, see Maksimov, *Ocherki po istorii obshchestvennykh rabot v Rossii.*

23. The yearly tax assessment was lowered in 1730 by one-third, in 1735 by as much as one-half. For the years 1740 and 1741 it was decreased by one-fourth, and for the years 1757 and 1758 the tax assessment was lowered by one-eighth. See PSZ 1830, vol. 8, nos. 5010, 5844; vol. 11, nos. 8264, 8481.

24. The dates for the natural calamities are from the catalog. The years of low net population increase are selected from Volkov, *Dinamika narodonaseleniia SSSR,* pp. 8, 264–71.

25. The dates for major epidemics in Russia are from Arcadius Kahan, "The Incidence of Epidemics in Russia and Its Impact on Population Growth," unpublished, s. a. The dates of famines are from the catalog.

26. In fact, some of the most severe epidemics recorded in Russia did not coincide or closely follow the famines. This prevents one from arguing even in favor of the low-resistance hypothesis.

CHAPTER FOUR

1. On two occasions I was privileged to discuss the problem of a model of the serf economy with Professor Witold Kula of Warsaw University. In dealing with this problem I have borrowed freely some ideas he expressed. However, he is not responsible for the context in which his ideas are presented here. I have also benefited from discussions with my colleagues Roger Weiss and Donald McCloskey.

2. The work by Peter Struve opened a debate on the profitability of serfdom in Russia at the time of emancipation, in which, unfortunately, his hypothesis was never rigorously tested.

3. Let us also not overlook the fact that what was called "the market" during the Middle Ages did not always coincide with our concept of a free market.

4. I am optimistic with respect to the emergence of economic models of the serf economy from recent contributions. See Witold Kula, *Théorie économique du système féodal: Pour un modèle l'économie polonaise 16e–18e siècles* (Paris: Mouton, 1970); Evsey Domar, "The Causes of Slavery or Serfdom—A Hypothesis," *Journal of Economic History* 30 (March 1970); Sir John Hicks, *A Theory of Economic History* (Oxford: Oxford University Press, 1969); and D. C. North and R. P. Thomas, "An Economic Theory of the Growth of the Western World," *Economic History Review* 23 (April 1970); and idem, "The Rise and Fall of the Manorial System: A Theoretical Model," *Journal of Economic History* 31 (December 1971).

5. In Poland the monopoly of the grain trade held by the nobility retarded urban development and increased the profitability of large estates versus smaller landholdings, the component of transportation services in the total service obligations, the domination of the oligarchy over the smaller gentry, and so forth.

6. "The proprietors of land were anciently the legislators of every part of Europe. The laws relating to land, therefore, were all calculated for what they supposed the interest of the proprietor." Adam Smith, *Wealth of Nations* (New York: Modern Library, 1937), p. 369.

7. Although I share the view that during most of the history of serfdom the central authorities of the state were aligned with the serfowners as a social group, one ought not to ignore conflicts of interest in the relationship between the two.

8. Much confusion has resulted from the nineteenth- and twentieth-century tendency to consider a legal document which spells out mutual obligations (although in fact fixing conditions of dependency) as reflecting a contractual relationship. I believe that Adam Smith was more accurate in evaluating behavior during the Middle Ages when he wrote: "The pride of man makes him love to domineer, and nothing mortifies him so much as to be obliged to condescend to persuade his inferiors. Wherever the law allows it, and the nature of the work can afford it, therefore, he will generally prefer the service of slaves to that of freemen." *Wealth of Nations,* p. 365.

9. Property rights of serfowners in land were neither uniform nor absolute in terms of modern concepts of property. So, for example, a patrimony represented "stronger" property rights than a service allotment. Property rights in land that excluded any and all interference with the exercise of freedom to acquire or dispose of land were rare in the twelfth or thirteenth century in Western Europe and perhaps were more prevalent in the seventeenth or eighteenth century in Eastern Europe.

10. My own inclination, in providing a rough summary of the development from a system of feudal tenure to a fundamentally different system of tenancy in Western Europe, would be to say that the abolition of property in men took place at the price of acquisition of unfettered and unlimited property rights to the land retained by the former serfowning class.

CHAPTER FIVE

1. The volumes were published under the general title of *Krestianskoe dvizhenie v Rossii* (Peasant Movement in Russia) by the Institute of History of the Academy of Sciences in Moscow.

2. Of course, students of intellectual history might like to classify the evidence of such protest in terms of both the social ideals and socio-political objectives which can be found; I am not pursuing the possibilities of exploring its usefulness.

3. In the majority of cases, extra legal forms of protests, regardless of the number of participants, resulted not only in punishment of the participants but in retaliation against the village, group of villages, or region. In most cases, even a moral victory was denied to the peasants. There were only two cases of murder of landowners during the eighteenth century in which the court recognized that the action by the serfs resulted from criminal pathological behavior of the landlords. The serfs were nevertheless severely punished.

4. For example, during the 24-year period 1826–49, out of 1,903 recorded cases of peasant unrest, 25 occurred in 1826 and 201 in 1848. The raw data for this period provide a spread from 1 to 85 cases per administrative district. Of course such regional data have to be adjusted for population size, average size of peasant landholdings, percentage share of peasant land in total arable land, and so forth, to be meaningful. But the availability of such information indicates possibilities of broadening the scope of analysis.

5. The writing of petitions to the tsar by private serfs was not only forbidden but also punishable. Nevertheless, the myth of the charitable tsar, separated from his people by the landlords and officials, was one of the strongest and most persistant myths to which the majority of peasants subscribed almost until the revolution. The petitioning of the tsar continued in spite of the abuse and punishment suffered by the petitioners.

6. The peasants would hide their livestock in the forests to prevent their destruction, and they thereby contributed to the duration and spread of the epidemics and the ineffectiveness of the anti-epidemic measures.

7. This encompasses active resistance to estate owners. There were also cases of active resistance connected with a change in ownership of the estate when the new owners imposed regulations considered by the peasants to be more burdensome than the traditional ones.

8. One is reminded of the conflicts concerning the use of the commons at the time of the enclosures in England.

9. This is the primary reason for excluding from this discussion cases of open mass rebellion, since they had a more specific set of social and political objectives.

10. This is not at all to imply an anti-church or anti-religious attitude of the educational institutions, but to indicate the stress on secular rather than religious elements in the educational goals. The role of the church in peasant movements and protests is a fascinating subject, worthwhile studying, but is outside our primary concern in this review.

11. Russia is not included in this list because of its different pattern of political development in the interwar period. In the only democratic, relatively free election ever held in Russia (in November 1917), the peasant parties received over 50 per cent of the total vote and elected about 63 per cent of all the deputies to the Constitutional Assembly.

12. There is an older tradition, of course, exhibited in the writings of Adolph Wagner, in the claims of the Prussian Junkers, in the Napoleonic myth that a strong, rural population is necessary for the armed forces of a country, and even in the notions of Rousseau about man and nature.

13. The *Krestintern* (Krest'ianskii [Peasants] International) was an organization set up by the Communist International during the 1920s to coordinate Communist activities among the peasantry in various countries.

CHAPTER SIX

1. Examples of such a tradition can be found in the establishment of the Moscow Academy to support the position of the state and church against religious heresies and influences of other denominations; the Petrine school system to supply technicians and military officers; and, in the later period, the schools to train the gentry for the role of a ruling elite.

2. The following schools of the above-mentioned types were established: Navigation School—1701; Artillery School—1701; Engineering School—1709; Naval Academy—1715; mining schools—at state ironworks in Olonetsk—1716, and in Ekaterinburg in the Urals—1721.

3. Among the special schools for the gentry the "Shliakhetskii Korpus" (established 1731) was the best known. The tsar's decree of 1715 required that the children aged 10–15 of the gentry and government officials living in the provinces ought to study arithmetic and geometry. In typical Petrine fashion, the decree provided that without proof that mathematics had been taught in conformance with the decree, no marriages could be concluded. The clergy was instructed to refuse the performance of marriage rites for the ones disobeying the decree. *Polnoe sobranie Zakonov Rossiiskoi imperii* (St. Petersburg, 1830), vol. 5, nos. 2762, 2778.

4. In 1743 the previous *tsifirnye* schools were converted into schools for children of soldiers. It was not until 1786 that an elementary secular school network with two- and four-year curricula was set up.

5. The Baltic gentry of German origin, studying in the political science departments at various German universities, formed the top echelons of the Russian bureaucracy twenty-five years later. They supplied the Russians with a highly influential elite over a period of two hundred years.

6. The estimates are derived by assuming that only 10 per cent of the enrollment in the church schools was in the seminaries, while 90 per cent received an elementary education. The 9,000 students reported in educational institutions above the elementary level might be an overestimate. It would greatly depend on the curriculum in the private boarding schools, for which information was not available.

7. The students in schools under the supervision of the Ministry of Education and the Russian Orthodox Church could be divided in the following categories:

A. Number of Schools and Students under the Supervision
of the Ministry of Education, 1834

Institution	No. of Schools	No. of Students
Universities	6	1.899
Lyceums	6	915
Gimnazium	64	12,561
Boarding schools	209	6,870
Urban county schools	419	25,833
Parish schools	574	23,041
Private schools	172	4,259
Other	12	2,241
Total	1,462	77,619

B. Institutions and Students under the supervision
of the Orthodox Church, 1834

Institution	No. of Schools	No. of Students
Theological academics	3	310
Theological seminaries	41	13,356
Urban county schools	155	} 43,706
Parish schools	186	
Total	385	57,372

Note: In addition, about 19,000 soldiers were receiving elementary education in the schools of the War Ministry.

Source: A. G. Rashin, "Gramotnost' i narodnoe obrazovanie v Rossii v XIX i nachale XX v," *Istoricheskie zapiski,* no. 37 (Moscow, 1951).

8.

**Number of Schools and Pupils in the Villages
of State Peasants, 1842–59**

Years	No. of Schools	No. of Pupils (in 1,000)
1842	226	13.8
1843	1,235	28.5
1845	1,654	49.2
1847	1,819	61.5
1849	1,869	70.2
1851	1,892	75.1
1853	1,744	76.6
1855	1,805	79.4
1857	1,702	74.6
1859	1,799	76.8

Source: Istoricheskie zapiski, no. 37 (Moscow, 1951), p. 55.

9. The "decree about children of cooks" (*kakharkiny deti*) of June 18, 1887, ordered *Gymnasia* and *Pro-gymnasia* to:

prevent the entrance of children of coachmen, manservants, cooks, laundrywomen, small shopkeepers and the like; the children of whom, with the exception perhaps of unusually gifted ones, ought not to be allowed to escape from the environment to which they belong;

because as an experience of many years has proven, it leads them to scorn their parents, to a dissatisfaction with their way of life and instills hatred against the existing, by the nature of things inescapable, inequality of property status.

10. The claim of Russian governments of being more progressive than society itself has deep historical roots, and the view to this effect is subscribed to by many scholars. Usually some government action is compared with some expression of public opinion in order to prove the point. It invariably assumes that the "opinion and attitudes" of the spokesmen for social groups coincided with the groups' interests and real opinions, which would be difficult to prove. But even the apologists and proponents of state benevolence in Russian history would have to concede that in the area of education, whenever the government disregarded the backwardness of society and moved ahead, the means used were not conducive to society's cooperation or to the release of popular initiative.

11. The number of pupils in the *real schools* grew very rapidly, as can be seen from the following figures:

Number of Students in the "Real Schools," Selected Years 1876–1914

Year	No. of Students	Year	No. of Students
1876	8,308	1904	46,425
1882	17,484	1907	55,500
1895	26,002	1914	80,800

According to the data on the students' social origins, the percentage of gentry and clergy was much smaller than in the *gymnasia*, and the share of urban and rural taxpaying classes much larger, thus providing an avenue of social advance through education into business, with the expectation of potential opportunities that business could offer.

12. The number of students for selected years was as follows:

Students in Women's Gymnasiums and Pro-Gymnasiums, Selected Years 1873–1914 (in 1,000's)

Year	No. of Students	Year	No. of Students
1873	23.0	1883	55.1
1880	42.7	1893	65.1

In terms of social origin of the students, the women's *gymnasium* occupied a middle position between the "aristocratic extreme" of the male *gymnasium* and the "democratic extreme" of the *real school*.

13. According to Strumilin, the expenditures per student in 1913 were 75.5 rubles per year in the women's secondary schools and 172.4 rubles in the *gymnasia* and *real schools*. He explains the difference primarily by the relatively less expensive use of female teaching personnel. The explanation might be not entirely convincing, but a cost differential unquestionably existed.

14. The data on women employed in occupations requiring secondary or higher education were not available. To the extent that 1926 census data could serve as a guide for pre-revolutionary patterns, they indicate the concentration of educated women in the teaching profession and to a lesser extent in the lower ranks of the medical profession.

15. The average salary of an elementary school teacher in 1913 is estimated by Strumilin at 420 rubles per year, while the salary of a full professor at the university was 3,000 rubles.

16. The data represent only 55 institutions of higher learning out of 105, and, for the year 1914, approximately 72,000 students out of a total of 127,400. Nevertheless, other evidence supports the contention that the data are representative of all institutions of higher learning.

17. V. E. Komarov, *Ekonomicheskie Osnovy podgotovki spetsialistov dlia narodnogo khoziaistva* (Moscow, 1959), p. 43.

18. Adjustments obviously have to be made for differences between the structure and composition of industry in the model country and the desired composition in the developing country.

CHAPTER SEVEN

1. Factory discipline was instilled in the labor force of the Russian manufacturers of the eighteenth century literally by the whip of overseers, managers, or armed guards. During the nineteenth century, an elaborate system of fines was substituted to enforce discipline and norm fulfillment.

2. See Torsten Hägerstrand, "Quantitative Techniques for Analysis of the Spread of Information and Technology," in C. Arnold Anderson and Mary Jean Bowman, eds., *Education and Economic Development* (Chicago: Aldine Publishing Company, 1965), p. 244.

3. The literacy rate among masters in linen and cloth manufactures was 32 per cent in 1732 and 33 per cent in 1737–38, compared with an average literacy rate for the labor force of 6 and 9 per cent, respectively.

CHAPTER EIGHT

1. See Chapter 6, table 6.2.

2. See Chapter 6, Table 6.3.

3. K. Ia. Vorobiov, *Gramotnost' sel'skogo naseleniia v sviazi s glavneishymi faktorami krest'ianskogo khoziaistva* (St. Petersburg, 1902); A. E. Lositskii, *K. voprosu ob Izucheniiu gramotnosti naseleniia Rossii* (Chernigov, 1900); P. A. Vikhliaev, *Ekonomicheskie usloviia narodnogo obrazovaniia v Moskovskoi gubernii* (Moscow, 1910).

4. In 1895 the Russian Academician Professor Yanzhul' asked the not entirely rhetorical question: "How will the news about an improvement reach our peasant or rural craftsman while the basic means of communication and transfer of ideas—literacy—is lacking?" I. I. Yanzhul', A. I. Chuprov, I. N. Yanzhul', *Ekonomicheskaia otsenka narodnogo obrazovaniia* (St. Petersburg, 1896), pp. 50–51.

CHAPTER NINE

1. In fact, the clause was sufficient to relieve the Russians from their obligations under the terms of the contract, even when the production performance of the foreigner was satisfactory. This would indicate that the government placed the future value of skill acquisition and substitution of domestic production for imports above the value of the current output.

2. An interesting example of such an attempt is furnished by the proposal of Tatishchev (1734) to the owners of ironworks that they should establish and maintain schools for the children of their skilled employees. This proposal was rejected on the grounds of prohibitive costs and the economic advantage of child labor.

3. In effect, in 1721 various urban communities petitioned the tsar to exempt merchant children from the obligation to attend the newly established *tsifirnye* schools, explaining that their training for commerce and their direct assistance in family business would suffer as a

result of their school attendance. The request was granted, although probably on other than the above grounds.

4. The most interesting petition was submitted by the head of the urban community in Arkhangel'sk, Ivan Druzhinin, in 1764. He pointed to the losses suffered by merchants as a result of ignorance: 1) low level of literacy leads to orthographic errors in commercial correspondence which result in incorrect interpretation of orders, directives, etc.; 2) lack of knowledge of arithmetic leads to inability to deal with foreign exchange or foreign weights and measures; 3) lack of knowledge of bookkeeping leads to ignorance about the solvency of the firm or enterprise; 4) lack of knowledge of geography leads to confusion in the area of transportation costs, freight charges, insurance, etc.; 5) the inability to use foreign languages leads to excessive use of Amsterdam firms as middlemen; 6) ignorance of foreign and domestic laws and trade regulations opens many avenues for abuse on the part of government officials to the detriment of the merchants. Only education, the author concluded, could remedy the existing ills. That the establishment of schools would provide for "teaching of attitudes that will produce a good merchant and a good citizen" was maintained by Vasilii Krestinin, another contemporary author. See A. A. Kizewetter, "Shkol'nye voprosy v dokumentakh XVIII v.," *Istoricheskie ocherki* (Moscow), 1915:91ff.

5. "Trudy vserossiiskogo torgovo-promyshlennogo s"ezda 1896 g.," in *Nizhnii Novgorod* (St. Petersburg), vol. 6, vyp. 9 (1897):122–23.

6. I. I. Yanzhul', A. I. Chuprova, I. N. Yanzhul', *Ekonomicheskaia otsenka narodnogo obrazovaniia, ocherki* (St. Petersburg, 1896). I. I. Yanzhul' was a member of the Russian Academy of Sciences; Chuprov was a noted statistician.

7. Circular of Information of the Bureau of Education, no. 3, Washington, D.C., 1879; and "Eighth Annual Report of the Commissioner of Labor, 1892," in *Industrial Education* (Washington, D.C., 1893).

8. L. L. Gavrishchev, "O vliianii obshchego obrazovaniia rabochikh na produktivnost' ikh truda" reported in *Ekonomicheskaia otsenka narodnogo obrazovaniia*, (St Petersburg, 1896), cited in footnote and in *Vtoroi S'ezd russkikh deiatelei po tekhnicheskomu i professional-'nomu obrazovaniiu V Rossii, 1895–96 g.* (Moscow, 1898).

9. The comparison was made by surveying the neighborhoods inhabited by the workers.

10. S. S. Kolokol'tsov, *Sviaz promyslov s gramotnostiu i ekonomicheskimi priznakami, po dannym Tverskoi gubernii* (Chernigov, 1912). Cited from Akademia Nauk SSSR, *Ocherki po istorii statistiki SSSR* (Moscow, 1960).

11. The studies referred to are S. G. Strumilin, "Kvalifikatsia truda i vyuchka rabochikh," in *Materialy po statistike truda*, v. 6 (Petrograd, 1919), and "Khoziaistvennoe znachenie narodnogo obrazovaniia," *Planovoe khoziaistvo*, no. 9–10 (1924). See also B. N. Babynin, "K analizu faktorov kvalifikatsii trudiashchikhsia," *Vestnik statistiki*, vol. 15 (July–December 1923), and vol. 17 (April–June 1924).

12. Strumilin assumed a skill scale consisting of "work-units" (*trudovye edinitsy*) using the existing twelve skill categories (reflecting, in turn, wage differentials) and a conversion coefficient in the equation, $x = 1 + 0.2(n - 1)$, where x = number of "work units"; n = number of skill category in the twelve-category scale.

13. So, for example, a negative return occurs in Strumilin's sample of white-collar workers at the twelfth year of formal education at the existing wage rates of this period.

14. E. Liustikh, "Vlianie obrazovaniia i stazha na effectivnost' truda," *Planovoe khoziaistvo*, no. 7–8 (1930). Liustikh used a survey of 72,596 workers in the metal and machine-building industries from the 1929 factory census. His basic equation is: $X = 327.4 + 11.18e + 4.81s + 37t$, where X = wage, e = years of education, s = job experience, and t = age. From the relationship of the coefficient one can approximately derive the relative contribution of each of the factors.

15. *Planovoe khoziaistvo*, no. 7 (1929).

CHAPTER TEN

1. The section of the chapter dealing with the Soviet period has not been included in this collection.

2. The revizii were conducted in 1718, 1742, 1762, 1781, 1794, 1811, 1815, 1833, 1850, and 1857. The dates are not very meaningful, since in every case the corrections and revisions in the population counts continued almost until the new reviziia.

3. The process of compiling such a cadastre and providing the owners with titles of ownership was known as *generalnoe mezhevanie*.

4. The peasant sector reports to the zemstvos were more accurate than those of the landed estates. Some of the shortcomings in the long-term averages might be due to the changing weights of the landed estate sector in total output.

5. The first data were collected in the Podol'e and Kherson zemstvos in 1869. The first statistical offices were set up in 1871 in Kazan' and Tver'. By the beginning of the 1880s, statistical offices of various sizes and qualities were functioning in all zemstvos.

6. The best treatment of content, methodology, and methodological deficiencies is found in N. A. Svavitskii, *Zemskie podvornye perepisi* (Moscow: Gosstatizdat, 1961).

7. The total includes different numbers for particular districts, collected for different time periods, so they can hardly be compared. Collection started in Voronezh with 230 budgets (1887–96); in Kaluga, with 2,417 (1887–97); Zabaikal'e, 885 (1897); Perm', 666 (1899–1901); and Viatka, 1,987 (1900).

8. *Statute of Industry*, 11:2 (St. Petersburg, 1893).

9. Ministerstvo torgovli i promyshlennosti, *Svod tovarnykh tsen na glavnykh russkikh i inostrannykh rynkakh*.

10. See pp. 206 and 212 above.

11. The Strumilin estimates were calculated and published in the 1920s. A convenient source for the estimates, together with additional information, is G. A. Dikhtiar's *Vnutrenniaia torgovlia v dorevolutsionnoi Rossii* (Moscow: Akademiia Nauk, 1960).

Index